a place called peculiar

Stories About
Unusual American
Place-Names

by Frank K. Gallant

Illustrations by Victoria Roberts

Merriam-Webster, Incorporated
Springfield, Massachusetts

Library of Congress Cataloging-in-Publication Data

Gallant, Frank K., 1948-
    A place called Peculiar : stories about unusual American
place-names / by Frank K. Gallant.
      p.   cm.
    Includes bibliographical references and index.
    ISBN 0-87779-619-X (alk. paper)
    1. Names. Geographical—United States.   2. United
States—History, Local.   I. Title.
    E155.G17   1998
    917.3'003—dc21   97-44615
                                         CIP

Printed and bound in the United States of America

23456QW/K050403

To Karen, Ben, and Nick—my moorings

table of contents

introduction

I've always had a weakness for places with colorful names. Spotting one in an atlas or on a road sign can start my imagination spinning; reading a newspaper, I can be transported halfway around the globe by an exotic dateline. More than once, I have driven an embarrassing number of miles out of my way to visit a town with an unusual name.

I remember trading for Wilmer Mizell's baseball card when I was ten years old, not because the St. Louis Cardinals pitcher struck a killer pose in his photograph or had a good won-lost record. I loved his nickname, "Vinegar Bend," the name of the Alabama town where he was born.

A couple of years later, my big sister Cynthia's boyfriend became an instant hero of mine when I heard he had made up naming stories for all the towns between Boston and Brewster, the town on Cape Cod where we lived. I still remember a few of them: Duxbury—something to do with *burying ducks* and a poor speller; Sandwich—because that is what the first settlers ate at every meal; Barnstable—everyone in town had a *barn* with a *stable*…

Fast-forward to a blistering July day in 1988 (the year I turned 40), and you'd find me in the middle seat of our minivan scanning the narrow columns of the index in our *Rand McNally Road Atlas* for cities and towns with unusual names. It was the fourth day of a cross-country family trip, and my sons and I were making up naming stories to make the miles pass faster.

Now, I've spent the last two and a half years researching and writing this book—this time trying to get the real stories behind the names, which wasn't always easy. It was a journey that took me by telephone and mail down hundreds of winding back roads, into the kitchens of local historians, and to the dusty stacks of public libraries too small to keep regular hours.

There are more than three million place-names in the U.S., the monikers for lakes, streams, swamps, sloughs, gulches, buttes, mountains, hills and valleys, for neighborhoods, villages, towns, cities, and states. I've focused on the places Americans inhabit (or did until recently), right down to the tiniest crossroads with a name that is meaningful locally, leaving the land features to other authors and other books.

A densely populated state like the one where I live, Maryland, can easily have upwards of 1,000 inhabited places with formal names, the locations of which are shown on the official highway map that most states publish. Those maps were my starting point; I pored over them looking for names that were unusual, whimsical, or accidental (a spelling mistake, for example).

And, most importantly, they had to have a good story to tell. Why would someone name a town Toast? Intercourse? Santa Claus? Rough and Ready? Clever? Neversink? What was behind the name Peculiar, a perfectly ordinary Middle American town a short drive from Kansas City?

What I found was a mixture of historical fact and legend—and a no-holds-barred, call-'em-as-you-see-'em, idiosyncratic approach to place naming that is not replicated anywhere else in the world. American cities and towns are named for natural features, for cities and towns in Europe (and every other continent), and for the people who settled them—as you would guess—but they are also named for obscure political parties, slogans, salutations, drunken sentiments, long-forgotten local incidents, songs, slurs, virtues, hopes and aspirations, aromas, freaks of nature, crops, crackers and cereals, card games, radio shows, taverns, brutal translations of lyrical Indian words and phrases, protagonists, and puns.

The U.S. is also the world leader in made-up place-names. This includes names that have been constructed from initials or fragments of words or coined by spelling a surname or a descriptive word backwards. We have, for example, the little community of Seroco, North Dakota, whose name was coined from the first two letters of each word of *Se*ars *Ro*ebuck & *Co*mpany; and *Tesnus*, Texas, *Sunset* spelled backwards. Another type of verbal contrivance is represented by Snowflake, Arizona, which has nothing to do with winter precipitation. The founding fathers of the town were a Mr. *Snow* and a Mr. *Flake.*

For many American towns, it's hard to get to the bottom of the story behind the name. There may be two or more locally believed explanations, but none verified. The authentic story went up in smoke when the town hall burned down, or is buried with a founding citizen under a lichen-stained headstone in the little cemetery behind the church.

People in Arco, Idaho, for example, aren't sure if their town was named for a Count *Arco*, who is said to have visited the area sometime late last century, or for *Arco* Smith, who operated a stagecoach station there. Protection, Kansas, was named for either the People's Grand *Protective* Union, which opposed prohibition in the state, or a *protective* tariff much debated during the 1884 presidential campaign, or for the *pro-*

tection against Indian attack afforded by a fort there. The municipal memory is dim on all three.

Sometimes local people know the real story behind a name but prefer a fictionalized account. Paradise, California, is a good example. Paradise once was a fairly common commendatory name for a new settlement in the frontier, and this one was a veritable Garden of Eden for anyone interested in making a living growing vegetables, apples, or nuts. But people cling to the legend that it was named for the *Pair O' Dice* Saloon, a Gold Rush era watering hole made famous by Bret Harte, the popular 19th-century short story writer. Why tell a tale about a place-name when you know the truth? It just makes a better story, both for the teller and the listener. You'll remember a good place-name anecdote longer than you will the image on the postcard you bought in the town.

Another thing I discovered is that people can live in a place all their lives, or drive through it on the way to work every weekday for 20 years, and not inquire about the origin of its name. "I was born in this community, and I have lived here all my life, and I have no idea," said 66-year-old Robert Holder when I asked about Toast, North Carolina.

Salem, New Hampshire, librarian Debbie Berlin didn't know anything about the origin of the name Cowbell Corners until she looked it up for me in a town history. Telling me what she had found, she interrupted our telephone conversation to share her discovery with some local residents who were waiting at the check-out desk. Up the road in Concord, New Hampshire, reference librarian Robin Bailey was delighted to have someone inquiring about Horse Corner; no one else had asked about its origin in a long, long time.

One of the biggest challenges of this book was to select from all of the available unusual names the 517 to be treated here. And that process was a very subjective one. My taste in place-names runs to the folkloric, homespun, and colloquial—even the pedestrian. I wondered, for instance, why farmers in eastern Kansas named their town Home and how some ranchers living near the New Mexico-Texas border could be so lacking in imagination as to name their post office Highway. For some reason, I had to know what company, Army general, railroad, or religious sect put Headquarters, Idaho, on the map.

It amused me to find out that another tiny Idaho town, May, was named for the month, and that Thursday, West Virginia, was named totally by accident for the day of the week. If May had turned out to be the name of a woman who had lived there, I wouldn't have been as interested in it, because there is nothing unusual about places being named after people. These names predominate.

I also love the patently funny names and the screwball stories told to explain them. Monkeys Eyebrow, Kentucky; Bug Tussle and Smut Eye, Alabama; Tightsqueeze, Virginia; Zap, North Dakota; and Zip City, Alabama; Two Egg, Florida; Toad Suck, Arkansas; Tightwad, Missouri; and Uncertain, Texas, are notable representatives of this category. That these names have lasted through the generations is a tribute to the American sense of personal freedom, including the freedom to choose and perpetuate a humorous place-name, and, if so inclined, to explain it with a shaggy-dog story.

Which brings me to the namers themselves. The thing that separates the U.S. from other countries when it comes to geographic nomenclature is that so many of our towns and villages—particularly west of the 13 original colonies—were named by people with no official authority and not much formal education. They just happened to be there—running a general

store at a muddy crossroads or carving a farm out of the tall prairie grass—when the place needed naming. Some of these pioneers were too busy just trying to stay alive to put a lot of thinking into why one name would stand the test of time better than another. In other cases, they chose a flamboyant name as a way of thumbing their nose at the establishment they left behind back East.

Frequently the impetus for choosing a formal name came from the desire to have a post office; letters couldn't be delivered if the place didn't have a name. So the townspeople met in the school or the church to nominate names. When they had trouble deciding on one, an unusual name like Why Not (North Carolina) could emerge.

Sometimes, the townspeople let the man (and it was almost always a man) who wanted to be postmaster choose the name. Or they took what the U.S. Post Office Department gave them. Both of those forces were at work in 1890 when a Scandinavian community in northern Wisconsin was named. Postmaster wannabe Charles F. Segerstrom sent in the name *Syren*, the Swedish word for the beautiful lilacs blooming outside his home. The government clerk in Washington, D.C., thought it was a misspelling, and commissioned a new post office with the alarming name of *Siren*.

One thing you won't find in this book are many Indian names. They are colorful and frequently poetic, but I've concentrated on names in English. For the same reason, I did not include a chapter on the state of Hawaii, because almost all of its place-names are in the native Hawaiian language. The few Indian names I've included—Neversink, New York, for example—are there to show what naming disasters resulted when our forebears anglicized Native American words and phrases.

I had a lot of fun writing this book. It

fed at least four distinct interests of mine: history, geography, folklore, and travel. I hope it will do the same for you. I think you'll find that you can read it for pleasure, as well as take it with you on driving trips.

People ask me if I visited all 517 places, and the answer is no. Few publishers would bankroll such a project. But I did take side trips to some of the towns in the book when my work as a magazine editor and writer allowed. One that sticks in my mind is a rental-car trip from Mobile, Alabama, to Biloxi, Mississippi, by way of Vinegar Bend, Alabama—an 80-mile detour from a route that was only 60 miles to begin with. It was a blossom-scented Sunday in the Old South, and I didn't need to be in Biloxi until late in the afternoon, so I enjoyed every mile of the drive. And after reaching my destination and knocking on a few doors, I found out why Vinegar Bend is called Vinegar Bend, something that had been rattling around in my brain ever since that day in 1958 when I traded for Wilmer Mizell's baseball card.

My wife calls these little excursions my "long-cuts" (as opposed to short-cuts). I like to think that this book will lead readers on a few pleasurable long-cuts of their own, even if just across the pages of a road atlas. Happy trails!

Frank K. Gallant
Takoma Park, Md.

acknowledgments

I could not have written this book without the generous help of hundreds of librarians, archivists, genealogists, and local historians who spent ten minutes or half an hour—and frequently much more—helping a stranger calling from hundreds of miles away find out how a place like Tenstrike, Minnesota, or Show Low, Arizona, was named. They found the books, the county histories, and the clippings; they made photocopies and mailed them, or stood at the fax machine until the pages cleared. Most of them didn't ask for any credit or compensation, not even for the photocopies. Usually, they were delighted that someone was asking about the places they call home.

The people who were especially helpful are listed here. My apologies if I left out anyone:

Alabama: Lesia Coleman, Linda Floyd. *Arizona:* Andrew Rush, Sharon Seymour. *Arkansas:* Dorothy Partain, Roger Saft. *California:* Evelyn Angier, Elizabeth Kelley, George W. O'Kelley, Mary Robertson, John Walden. *Colorado:* Paul Gilbert, Tania Hajjan, Loline Sammons, Nancy Thaler. *Connecticut:* Barbara Ayrton, Beryl Harrison, Irene Nolan. *Delaware:* Russell McCabe. *Florida:* Karen Conley-Hollis, Hal H. Hubener, Dolly Pollard, Helen Woodward. *Georgia:* Peggy Blackwell. *Idaho:* Larry Almeida. *Illinois:* Connie Heise, Pat McAllister, Yvonne Oliger, Donna Shivers. *Indiana:* Mary Hall, Nancy Poppleton, Mary Seibert, Laurel Wilson. *Iowa:* Beth Draper, Nancy Roe. *Kansas:* Helen Kelley, Yvette Larson. *Kentucky:* Cybil Gibbons, Vicki Hargraves, Elizabeth McKinney.

Louisiana: Sherry Case, Hermione Driskell, Lyle Johnson, Byron Temple, Diana Uzee, Mary Wedgeworth, Susan Williams. *Maine:* Karen Chandler, Susan James. *Maryland:* Lisa Harrison, Gloria Meachem, Cheryl Michael. *Massachusetts:* Rene L. Macomber, Janice Neubauer. *Michigan:* Martha Lavey, Susan Smith-Brudi. *Minnesota:* Irene Koenig, Nora Shepard. *Mississippi:* James Brieger, James T. Dawson, Ruby Rodgers, Marie Shoemake. *Missouri:* Eloise Sletten. *Montana:* Joy Kimsey, Rebecca Sterrett. *Nebraska:* Joan Birney, Lou Anne Eller, Lee Rose. *Nevada:* Gary Aven. *New Hampshire:* Robin Bailey, Debbie Berlin, Marjorie Carr, Sarah Hartwell, Barbara Robarts, Joanne Wasson. *New Jersey:* Edwinna Cahill, Virginia Detrick, Trudy Tianko. *New Mexico:* Liz Garcia. *New York:* Julia Grimsman, Paul Morrell. *North Carolina:* Jean Cross, Cindy Davie, Patricia Strickland. *North Dakota:* Jim Chattin, Cynthia Zahn. *Ohio:* Sandy Day, Naomi Deer, Julia Engle, June Yoder. *Oklahoma:* Reneta Ediger, Catherine Ramsey, Mary Ruhl. *Oregon:* Mary Finney, Martha Pyle, Dawn Troutman. *Pennsylvania:* Jerry Bruce, Vicki Leonelli, Pat Steele, Melinda J. Stevens, Nancy M. Weiss. *Rhode Island:* Greg Chapman, Sue Giguere, Eleanor R. Guy. *South Carolina:* Deborah Nicholson, Debbie Roach, Debbie Roland. *South Dakota:* Bruce Mehlhaff, Judy Witt. *Tennessee:* Marilyn Barber, Ellen Creecy, Claudia Dillehay, Katherine Goodwin, Mary Beth Pruett. *Texas:* Ruth Briggs, Mary Jo Cockrell, Lisa Olson. *Utah:* Jay Haymon, Marian Jacklin, Dorothy Larkin. *Vermont:* Betty Brent, Phyliss Skidmore. *Virginia:* Mary Levine, Ellen G. Parnell, Margaret Reynolds, Carol Vincent. *Washington:* Marie Roper, Marilyn Collins Warner. *West Virginia:* Glenna Queen. *Wisconsin:* Marion Howard, Lucille Jacobson, Margaret Koeller, Ann Perrigo. *Wyoming:* Isabel M. Hoy, Louise Williams.

Others who helped me with my research include: Judi Lech, Larry Frank, Lisa Greaves, Bob Gibson, John Vanvig, and Roger L. Payne, executive secretary of the U.S. Board on Geographic Names.

My thanks also go to Daniel J. Hopkins of Merriam-Webster, who combed the text for errors and made smart suggestions for improving it, and to several other Merriam-Webster editorial staff members who continued where Dan left off: Deanna M. Chiasson, Jennifer N. Cislo, Kathleen M. Doherty, and Michael D. Roundy, who helped with proofreading and corrections; Kara L. Noble and Stephen J. Perrault, who helped put the electronic manuscript in final form; and Thomas F. Pitoniak, who coordinated production. On the design side, my thanks go to Bob Ciano of the Encyclopædia Britannica Art Department, and to Joe Paschke. Finally, thanks to John M. Morse for giving the book the push only a publisher can give, as well as some sharp editing; to Paul Dickson, whose casual but unwavering belief in this project bostered my confidence; and to my wife, Karen, who is always there when I need her.

a place
called peculiar

Stories About
Unusual American
Place-Names

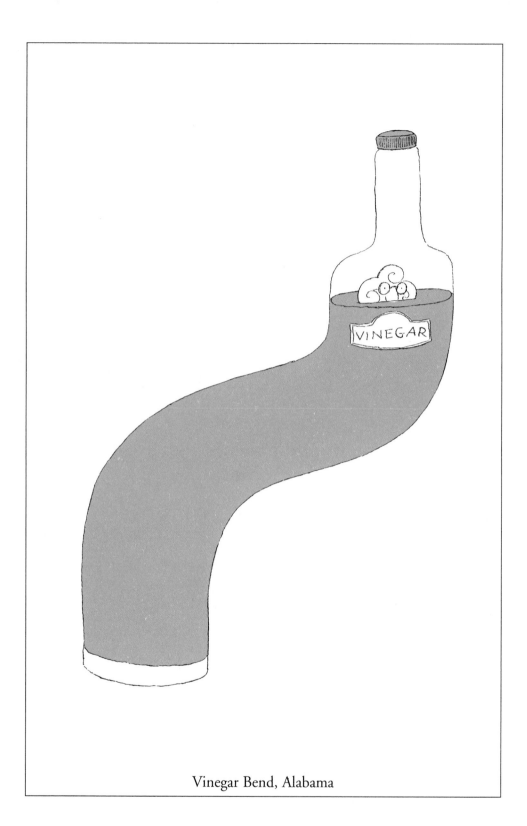

Vinegar Bend, Alabama

alabama

Bug Tussle

On State Route 69 in the north-central part of the state

This little mining and sawmilling community was known only as *Wilburn* until town drunk Charlie Campbell took a walk up the mountain one summer afternoon in 1912, give or take a year. That was the day Charlie observed two tumble*bugs* (beetles) *tussling* with a ball of dung they were trying to roll across a logging road. This display of enterprise and stick-to-itiveness in nature was evidently mesmerizing to him, and he told everyone in town about it.

That's the legend. Others have suggested that *Bug Tussle* is a slur name—that the Charlie Campbell story covers up the embarrassing fact that this was once the kind of place where a traveling salesman might wake up in the middle of the night *tussling* with *bedbugs*.

Bug Tussle made national headlines in 1938 for a much more serious crime: Twenty-eight citizens were indicted for mail fraud for using phony names on orders to Montgomery Ward and Spiegel. They used names they found on gravestones and the names of their dogs and cats. A few used the name of a mentally handicapped neighbor.

Federal agents got into a shoot-out with some of the suspects in nearby Bremen. An eyewitness said there were "people running in and out of the hotel and stores… like a scene in a Western movie."

Here's another good *Bug Tussle* story from *Cullman County Across the Years* by Margaret Jean Jones:

During the Civil War, two Union soldiers came to Dock Boyd's front door and threatened to hang him if he didn't tell them where his son James and another Confederate soldier were hiding. Overhearing the conversation from the kitchen, James's wife sent her 12-year-old son Dan to warn his father. She told the Yankees that it was time for Dan to bring the cows in from their pasture. Dan got the message to his father, and the two Rebels stole back to the house and shot and killed the Union soldiers.

Neighboring Mississippi has a town named *Bug Scuffle*, which folks there swear comes from the swarm of *scuffling bugs* outside a church revival tent on a steamy summer's night many years ago. Mt. Union, Arkansas, has a *Bug Scuffle* Church. A circuit riding preacher with a reputation as a bore was in the pulpit one Sunday morning, so a group of men stayed outside talking. A *scuffle* between two tumble*bugs* over a pellet of chicken manure caught their attention, and they soon were taking bets on which one would win the prize.

These days both the names *Wilburn* and *Bug Tussle* remain in use.

Stretching your legs in Bug Tussle: Ave Maria Grotto, a three-acre hillside on the grounds of Saint Bernard Benedictine Abbey in nearby Cullman, is covered with miniatures of famous churches, shrines, and buildings from around the world. There are approximately 125 of them, all lovingly crafted between 1912 and 1958 by Brother Joseph Zoettl. Address: 1600 Saint Bernard Drive, Cullman. Telephone: (205) 734-4110. Admission charged.

Graball

On U.S. Route 431 about 26 miles north of Dothan in the southern part of the state

before the Civil War, Albert Johnson and George Danzey operated a general store at this location, then called *Hudspeths Cross Roads.* They served ale and whiskey at a bar in the store, which became a casino of sorts with tables for playing cards and other games of chance and a back room where cock fights were staged.

One night during one of these so-called sportsmen's "meetings," the local constabulary burst into the store. People ran for the doors and climbed out the windows. One of the gamblers yelled, "*Grab all* the stakes and run for it!" Someone else lit a match and dropped it in a basket of corn shucks, and the store burned to the ground.

There is no record of anyone having been arrested. But from that day forward, the little community has been called *Graball.*

Nearby is the old *Screamer* section of Henry County, which was named either for the loud *screams* of the Indians when they performed the Corn Dance or, more likely, the *screams* of the boatmen on the Chattahoochee River. *Screamer* referred both to the shouting of directions back and forth between the boats and the landings and to the revelry in the taverns the boatmen patronized when they came ashore.

(See *Graball,* Mississippi, page 129.)

Scratch Ankle

On State Route 41 roughly equidistant from Montgomery to the northeast and Mobile to the southwest

this place no longer appears on maps, but local residents, especially older ones, haven't forgotten where it is, and they're tickled to be asked about it. Twenty years ago, Myron J. Quimby made these same rural folk feel important when he titled his book on American place-names *Scratch Ankle, U.S.A.*

He tells two versions of how the village got its name. The first has to do with the schoolhouse. It was built on the side of a hill, and part of the stone foundation was open on the low side. Cows, goats, mules, sheep, and dogs (probably not all at once) would go under the building for shelter when it was raining, and their fleas and the flies found their way upstairs to the *ankles* of the students. The school, which has been gone many years, was dubbed *Scratch Ankle* School.

Quimby's second story puts the scene of the *scratching* down by the railroad tracks, where horses and cows were kept in pens that attracted thousands of yellow flies on hot summer days. The crews on the log trains remembered the place as the stop where people were always *scratching* their *ankles*.

My vote goes to the first story.

Smut Eye

On State Route 239 about 35 miles from the Georgia border

The librarian in Union Springs, county seat of Bullock County, suggested I call Mrs. Annie Pope, who told me this name had to do with her father-in-law, who ran a blacksmith's shop "up here on the corner." "Uncle" George Pope also pulled teeth, made caskets, served as the horse doctor, and distributed a remedy for ground itch (an itching skin inflammation caused by a parasitic worm). "He got dead before I came in the family," Mrs. Pope explained.

George Pope's smithy was the local gathering place; men played checkers and card games there when there wasn't any work, or if they were too old for it. It was also where you went to vote. The shop was so dirty and smoky that the men went home with *smut* (soot) in their *eyes*.

Storekeeper Walter Caddel (see *Blues Old Stand,* page 4) says he heard it a different way: that the blacksmith's face was always covered with so much *smut* that all you could see of it was the whites of his *eyes*.

Smut Eye was originally called *Welcome*.

Vinegar Bend

Just off State Route 57 in the southwestern part of the state

This tiny town was originally called *Lumbertown* after the sawmill that opened here in 1900. The sawmill company built a railroad to the Gulf Coast (about 30 miles south) to ship logs and lumber out and food and other supplies in.

One day in 1910, as freight was being unloaded near a *bend* in the Escatawpa River, a barrel of *vinegar* burst. From then on, the railroad workers jokingly called the town *Vinegar Bend.* The name soon caught on with the townspeople, and it wasn't too long before the post office adopted the name and the sawmill changed its name to *Vinegar Bend* Lumber Company.

That story comes from retired *Vinegar Bend* postmaster J. T. Davidson. Wilmer *"Vinegar Bend"* Mizell, who pitched for the St. Louis Cardinals in the 1950s and was a North Carolina congressman from 1969 to 1975, tells a slightly different version. He says that his birthplace was named earlier, when the railroad was being built, and some workers had to dump a barrel of sorghum molasses into the river because it had soured and turned into *vinegar.* The workers used sorghum molasses to sweeten their coffee and grits, so this was probably a major blow to morale.

Arkansas has a *Pickle Gap* which some people say got its name from an incident in which a barrel of *pickles* rolled off a wagon and broke open.

Other Unusual Place-Names in Alabama

Awin

At the intersection of State Route 47 and State Route 10 about 45 miles southwest of Montgomery

t he story goes around that the townspeople held a meeting where they voted on each of a number of suggested names. Someone wrote *"a win"* beside the most popular one. The voting results were sent to Washington, D.C., and a few weeks later a post office was approved for *Awin*, Alabama.

Blues Old Stand

At the intersection of County Route 19 and State Route 15 in Bullock County about five miles west-northwest of Smut Eye (see page 3)

W alter Caddel, who keeps the store here, says the name comes from an old man named *Blue* who ran a "shotgun store" out of a wagon. When a permanent store was built (the same building Caddel now owns) by another man, people continued to refer to the locale as *Blue's Stand.* The word *old* crept in between the two words with the passage of time, as it frequently does in the South.

Caddel keeps an old tattered clipping from the Montgomery *Advertiser* behind the counter to show people who ask about the name.

Eclectic

On State Route 63 about 20 miles northeast of Montgomery

d r. M.L. Fielder named the town soon after the Civil War for the *eclectic* medicine he had studied in a northern school. He apparently hoped, too, that it would become an *eclectic* community, because he offered a free acre of land to anyone, black or white, who would build a home here. The town got a post office in 1879 and was incorporated in 1907.

Gallant

On County Route 35 ten miles west of Gadsden

g *allant*, according to *Merriam-Webster's Collegiate Dictionary*, means "spirited" and "brave," "splendid" and "stately," and "chivalrous." That's your author, of course.

The *Gallant* who gave this town its name arrived from Tennessee shortly after the Civil War. Almost all us *Gallants* here in the New World are descendants of Michele Haché-*Gallant*, the first white settler of Prince Edward Island, Canada. French-speaking Catholics, the *Gallants* were among the thousands of Acadians expelled from eastern Canada by the British beginning in 1755. Many migrated to the American South; Henry Wadsworth Longfellow told the story of their exodus to Louisiana in the poem *Evangeline*.

By the way, my given name, *Frank*, appears on the map in the northeast corner of Maryland, near Port Deposit.

Octagon

At the intersection of County Routes 33 and 47 about 40 miles from the Mississippi border

t his tiny hamlet takes its name from the original Bethlehem Baptist Church, which was built in 1868 and was eight-sided.

Opine

On County Route 44 thirty-three miles from the Mississippi border in the northern part of the state

the origin of this strange name has been lost to history, although it has been suggested that it might have started out as *O'Pine* in tribute to the abundant pine forests in the area.

I like to think it had to do with some self-important early settler who was always *opining* about this or that.

Reform

At the intersection of U.S. Route 82 and State Route 17 in the western part of the state

a circuit-riding preacher who had just conducted a series of revival meetings at which many people confessed their sins was asked for advice on what to name the town. *Reform*, he said without a moment's hesitation.

(See *Reform*, Mississippi, page 130.)

Stretching your legs in Reform: If you're heading east on U.S. Route 82, you can get a meal you'll never forget at Dreamland in Tuscaloosa. This storied eatery only serves barbecued ribs, white bread, and beer and soda— that's the complete menu— but draws rib lovers from all over the U.S. But don't go if you're squeamish about dives; this joint is truly funky. Directions: Dreamland is hard to find, so call for directions or ask at any local gas station; the official address is 5535 15th Avenue East, Tuscaloosa. Telephone: (205) 758-8135.

Zip City

On State Route 17 ten miles north of Florence

although this community was settled around 1817, it had no formal name until the Automobile Age, according to Lauderdale County historian Sandra Sockwell. Local resident Alonzo Parker is credited with giving the town its whimsical name after observing cars *zipping* along the Chisholm Road toward the Tennessee line, about three miles north. Liquor could be purchased legally in Wayne County, Tennessee, and at the time (the 1920s) Lauderdale was a dry county.

alaska

Chicken

On the Taylor Highway 58 miles south-southwest of Eagle and about 70 miles west of Dawson, Yukon Territory, Canada

this town was named for the willow ptarmigan, a pheasant-like bird that changes color—from light brown to snow white—as winter comes on. It is the state bird, and *chicken* is its nickname. A mining camp and post office were established here in 1903.

The early Alaskans must have seen these birds every time they turned around. Evidence for this can be found in Donald Orth's *Dictionary of Alaska Place Names* (a principal source of information for Alaskan place-names), which cites 17 geographical features named *chicken*—13 creeks, a cove, a ridge, an island, and a mountain—and more than 30 named *ptarmigan*. Combined, they are the grand champions of Alaska place-names.

Another source says that this place takes its name from the fact that prospectors found nuggets of gold the size of *chicken* feed here. That sounds big to me, but my dictionary says *chicken feed* has been slang for "a paltry sum" (no, not "poultry") since the 1830s.

Nome

On the southern shore of the Seward Peninsula in the western part of the state

this is one of the most notorious examples of accidental place naming in the world, the result of a map-making mistake. Toponymists love it.

About 1850, a navigational chart was made aboard the British ship H.M.S. *Herald* while she lay at anchor in Norton Sound, off the Seward Peninsula. The cartographer wrote *"? Name"* beside a certain cape along the coast and moved on to other locations for which he had names and soundings. Later, when a second cartographer worked on another copy of the map he took the question mark as a "C" and wrote *Cape Name*. The "A" in *Name* apparently looked like an "O" and the location came out *Cape Nome* on the final version of the map.

Nome is the biggest and most well-known town in Eskimo country; it has long been an economic and cultural hub. Gold was found on its beaches in the summer of 1899, and news of the strike brought 30,000 argo-

Sourdough, Alaska

nauts to *Nome* the following summer. Half of them left before winter set in on what some wag dubbed the Golden Sands of *Nome*. Today the population hovers around 3,500.

Nome, Texas, was named at about the same time. In explaining why, people either tell a southern version of the map story or suggest that it was "liquid gold" (oil) that drew people there at the turn of the century.

Sourdough

On the Richardson Highway about 130 miles northeast of Anchorage

this is the only place in the U.S. that I'm aware of that is named after a type of bread. *Sourdough* was a staple of the mining camps during the Gold Rush years in Alaska and the Yukon Territory. It was also the prospectors' term for an old hand—the kind of man who would still be around when the creek froze over and the temperature dropped to forty below.

This community is one of ten localities or geographical features in the state with this name. Gold Rush prospectors, whether they sifted creek sand here or in California, Colorado, or Idaho seemed to have a limited repertoire of place-names that appear over and over again (see *Chicken*, Alaska).

Other Unusual Place-Names in Alaska

Candle

On the northern shore of the Seward Peninsula in the western part of the state

andle was named by gold miners for a shrub that grows along the banks of a creek having the same name. The shrub, like candlewood or greasewood, is easy to light afire.

Circle

At the northern terminus of the Steese Highway 130 miles northeast of Fairbanks

the people who settled here around the time of the Yukon Gold Rush thought the village was on the Arctic *Circle*. They were off by about 43 miles.

Coldfoot

On the Dalton Highway about halfway between Fairbanks and Prudhoe Bay

tens of thousands of gold seekers poured into Alaska in the summer of 1900. One group got to this point on the Koyukuk River before getting *cold feet* and turning around. The story got around and soon the mining camp's original name, *Slate Creek,* was dropped.

Farewell

Along the Iditarod Trail 25 miles west of Denali National Park

alaska toponymist Donald Orth's research suggests that the name comes from *Farewell* Mountain in the Alaska Range, which can be seen from this settlement. Orth says the mountain was so named by two surveyors for the U.S. Geological Survey because "it was the last of the high mountains" they had to cross. They were saying *"farewell"* to them and, perhaps, "good riddance."

North Pole

On the Richardson Highway 14 miles southeast of Fairbanks

this little settlement was called Davis until the Dahl and Gaske Development Company bought it from the original homesteader, Bond V. Davis, after World War II. The developers hoped to attract a toy manufacturing plant with the name. Another of their fantasies was "Santaland," an Alaskan Disneyland.

The real *North Pole* is a good 1,600 miles farther north.

Poorman

At the end of a road that leads south from Ruby (on the Yukon River) in the interior part of the state

besides this settlement, there are five creeks in the interior with this name, and they are all in gold country. Most likely they were named by unlucky prospectors.

Red Devil

Near where the Holitna River flows into the Kuskokwim River in the southwest-central part of the state

this mining camp on the left bank of the Kuskokwim took its name from the nearby *Red Devil* Mercury Mine.

Literary Place-Names

FICTION WRITERS NEED names for their characters and the places they inhabit, and the names on the American landscape often are better than anything they could make up. Bret Harte wrote short stories about **Poker Flat, Fiddletown,** and **Rough and Ready**—all Gold Rush mining camps in northern California (see page 28). Larry McMurtry borrowed the name of a real Texas town, **Lonesome Dove,** for the title and setting of his best-selling Western epic. A musical that was a sideshow at the 1996 Olympics in Atlanta was set in **Frog Level,** North Carolina (a real place in Arkansas). Pulitzer Prize-winning novelist Annie Proulx saw the name Quealy on the map of Wyoming, changed it to **Queasy** and had a great place-name for her novel *Postcards.*

In New York, it worked the other way around: A town changed its name to one made up by a writer, which sounds even more American than the original place-name. In December 1996, **North Tarrytown** became **Sleepy Hollow,** the place where the lovelorn pedagogue Ichabod Crane had a run-in with the Headless Horseman on Halloween. Washington Irving, the author of "The Legend of Sleepy Hollow," is buried in the Sleepy Hollow Cemetery.

Fiction writers seem to love the color, idiosyncrasy—even poetry—in American place-names. "There is no part of the world where nomenclature is so rich, poetical, humorous and picturesque," said Robert Louis Stevenson. Stephen Vincent Benét celebrated our place-names in a poem.

I have fallen in love with American names:
The sharp, gaunt names that never get fat;
The snakeskin titles of mining-claims;
The plumed war-bonnet of *Medicine Hat*,
Tucson and *Deadwood* and *Lost Mule Flat*.

Back to those novelists: One of my favorites, Pete Dexter, who invented a character with the unforgettable name of Paris Trout, lives in **Useless Bay,** Washington.

Bumble Bee, Arizona

arizona

Burnt Ranch

On a dirt road seven miles northeast of Prescott in the central part of the state

In *Arizona's Names: X Marks the Place,* Byrd Granger tells the dramatic story of how Jake Miller lost his ranch. This was shortly after the Civil War, and Miller cared for a small herd of cattle owned by a Prescott judge.

"Once when Miller went to bring in the cattle, he noticed a raven fly up from the brush. It was followed by a second and then a third raven. Looking intently at the brush, Miller observed the head of an Indian," Granger writes.

The rancher hurriedly rounded up the cattle and herded them toward the corral. Halfway there, several Indians broke out of the brush in hot pursuit. Miller wheeled around and shot the lead one with his rifle. His bulldog leapt on the dead Indian and starting thrashing him back and forth. The other Indians stopped to kill the dog, and this gave Miller time to get the cattle into the corral and himself into his cabin.

Miller held the Indians off at first, but was soon down to his last bullet. He knew his only chance of surviving was to use it to kill the chief, because it was customary among Indians to stop fighting when they lost their leader. Cautiously, Miller poked the barrel of his rifle through the chinking in one of the cabin's log walls, only to have it grabbed by an Indian outside. Jumping back, Miller landed on a forgotten horse pistol loaded with buckshot.

A few minutes later he got lucky again, according to Granger. Looking through another hole in the cabin wall, he had a clear view of the chief. He took careful aim, and fired the pistol. The chief staggered backward about twenty feet and fell dead. The attack was over.

When the mail carrier stopped by the *ranch* later that day to water his mules, Miller sent word by him to the judge that he was bringing the cattle into Prescott. That night the Indians returned and *burned* the cabin and the corral to the ground. From then on the place was known as *Burnt Ranch.*

Several states have places named for locally memorable fires. West Virginia, for example, has *Burnt House,* which was named for an incident in which an enraged female slave *burned* down a tavern.

Stretching your legs in Burnt Ranch: Just up the road (Alternate 89) is

Jerome, a small mountain town that was once inhabited by copper miners, but is now peopled by artists, writers, craftspeople, and Sixties dropouts. Its narrow streets are filled with shops, galleries, eateries, bed and breakfast inns, and Old West style saloons.

Christmas

On State Route 77 about 27 miles south of Globe and a few miles northeast of Hayden in southeast-central Arizona

In the late 1880s, three prospectors discovered a thick vein of copper in the dry mountains a few miles north of where the Gila River joins the San Pedro. But they couldn't hold onto their claim because the copper lay within the San Carlos Indian Reservation. Several years later, a politically connected prospector named George B. Chittenden became interested in the claim, and in 1902 he succeeded in getting Congress to pass a bill to move the boundary line of the reservation. Chittenden arranged for a telegraph message to be sent from the nation's capital to Casa Grande when Congress voted, and then relayed to him by mounted messengers.

The news reached Chittenden on *Christmas* Day, his birthday. Chittenden rode immediately to the place where the copper was found and staked his claim, which he named for the day. The copper played out, and *Christmas* is a ghost town now—haunted by a greedy man who stole from the Indians with the help of the U.S. Congress.

Chittenden had a fiery temper, and that's why another Gila County settlement, now gone, was called *Chilito*—Spanish for "little peppers." That's what the Mexicans called Chittenden when he was postmaster there from 1913 to 1918.

Oracle

On State Route 77 forty miles north of Tucson

Albert Weldon had sailed around Cape Horn in his uncle's ship, the *Oracle*, before coming to the Arizona territory to hunt for copper, silver, and gold in the late 1870s. He named his first claim after the ship out of gratitude for having survived a hurricane in the Virgin Islands on a voyage from New York to San Francisco. "Nothing but Providence," he said years later, "saved her from the reefs and cliffs."

Weldon's *Oracle* Mine never produced anything but granite, but the name stuck, despite a strong challenge from Acadia. The Acadia Ranch took its name from the fact that one of its partners, Jack Aldwinkle, came from Nova Scotia. *Oracle's* first post office (1880) was in the lodging house on the ranch.

Built in 1876 for the San Francisco wheat trade, the *Oracle*, a 2,000-ton clipper ship, made ten trips around Cape Horn before sinking near there in a terrifying storm in 1883. Presumably, it was named for the *Oracle* at Delphi in ancient Greece.

Stretching your legs in Oracle: South of town, in the cactus-covered foothills of the Santa Catalina Mountains, is Biosphere 2, a group of otherworldly glass buildings where scientists from Columbia University are studying how the Earth's ecology would be affected by global warming.

Biosphere 2's first incarnation was as a privately funded test site for what life might be like in a space colony with flora and fauna imported from Earth. It turned out to be a nightmare. In 1993, the four men and one woman who had sealed themselves inside in 1991, walked out sick and disillusioned. Their greenhouse Eden had turned into an ecological prison with sour water and foul air. Many of the plant and animal species aboard became extinct; morning glory vines grew everywhere, choking out other plants; food crops wouldn't germinate. The place was overrun with millions of ants, cockroaches, and katydids.

The experiment was called Biosphere 2 because the original Biospherians thought of the Earth as Biosphere 1.

Both the global warming experiments and the old Biospherian residences are open to the public. Location: Visitor Center Road (off Route 77). Telephone: (520) 896-6203. Admission charged.

Show Low

On U.S. Route 60 in southeastern Navajo County in the eastern part of the state

In 1870, cattleman Marion Clark and Corydon E. Cooley, a famous Indian scout, started fencing in the sparse rangeland 40 miles north of Fort Apache. By the time they were done stringing barbed wire they had enclosed 100,000 acres. Several years later, the two ranchers had a disagreement and decided to dissolve their partnership. They would play a card game called seven-up, and the winner would buy out the other.

The game lasted all night. Near sunrise, with Cooley needing just one point to win, Clark, according to legend, challenged him: "You *show low*, and you win." Cooley cut the deck and *showed* the deuce of clubs—and won.

Today, an illustration of the lucky card graces the letterhead of the city of *Show Low*. City hall is on West Cooley and the main street of the small city is named Deuce of Clubs.

Seven-up, according to Hoyle, was the most popular card game among

American gamblers until the rise of poker during the Civil War. It is one of a number of variations on the British game, all fours. In seven-up, the first person to score seven points wins. Points are earned for the high, low, and Jack of trumps and for game.

(See *Midnight*, Mississippi, page 128, for another place that was named for a card game.)

Tombstone

On U.S. Route 80 halfway between Benson and Bisbee in the southeastern part of the state

anyone who knows anything about the Old West has heard of this colorful and violent mining town where at 2:30 p.m. on November 26, 1881, Wyatt Earp and "Doc" Holliday killed three members of the Clanton gang in a gunfight at the entrance to the OK Corral.

The town owes its beginning to prospector Ed Schieffelin, who came here in 1877 and started tramping around the hills with a pickax over his shoulder. Friends warned him that the only thing he'd find was his own *tombstone*. But instead of an Apache bullet, he found ledges of silver that by 1886 had lined miners' pockets with $37 million. Schieffelin named his first claim *Tombstone*.

The shantytown that sprung up overnight on the level ground closest to the mines was known as Goose Creek, but that lasted less than two years. The March 5, 1879 plat of the town bears the name *Tombstone*, a tongue-in-cheek reference to the grim prophecy given to Schieffelin.

The first newspaper published in town (1880) was the *Epitaph*.

Two Guns

On U.S. Route 66 just off I-40 halfway between Flagstaff and Winslow in the eastern part of the state

this ghost town has as bloody a history as any town in the West. Massacres, murders, gunfights, train robberies—it earned its name many times over. But no one knows which *two guns*.

The most significant bloodletting occurred in June 1878 when a band of Apache raiders slaughtered more than fifty Navajos in their hogans. Two Navajo scouts then tracked the killers to a cave in Canyon Diablo (the present site of *Two Guns*). After sending for help, the Navajos surrounded the cave and then gathered wood and built a huge fire. The smoke poured in through the many crevices in the cave. The Apaches killed their horses, butchered them, and used the meat to stuff the crevices. But it didn't work; 42 Apaches choked to death on the smoke.

To this day, the Navajos say the cave is cursed by evil spirits, and anyone who enters it will suffer the consequences.

Other Unusual Place-Names in Arizona

Bumble Bee

On a dirt road off exit 248 of I-17 fifty miles north of Phoenix

the first gold prospectors to pass through this area in 1863 were swarmed by *bumble bees* defending hives in the cliffs above a creek. The name is a permanent reminder of that painful day and a warning to newcomers that the *bees* still congregate here.

Happy Jack, Arizona, a logging town 33 miles southeast of Flagstaff, was called *Yellow Jacket*, for a type of wasp, up until 1947.

Carefree

On a local road on the northeastern edge of Phoenix

two developers, Tom Darlington and K. T. Palmer, bought a 400-acre tract here in 1955 and gave it a name that was sure to attract the retirees that helped make Phoenix the major city it is today.

Double Adobe

On a back road 11 miles east of Bisbee in the southeastern corner of the state

When the West was wild, Arizonans knew this location by a two-room *adobe* building with 18-inch thick walls. It made a good bunker if you were running from angry Apaches or had been seen driving a local rancher's cattle toward the Mexican border.

Adobe Walls, Texas, has a similar history. The nine-foot high *adobe walls* of an abandoned trading post protected traders and buffalo hunters from Indian attack. In 1874, locals survived a five-day siege by Cheyenne, Comanche, and Kiowa attackers.

North Dakota once had a stagecoach stop called *Double Wall Station* in some historical accounts and *Adobe Walls Station* in others.

Flagstaff

Where I-17 meets I-40 in north central Arizona

On July 4, 1876—the nation's 100th birthday— a group of Army scouts camping near a spring along the wagon trail to California stripped a tall pine tree of its branches and lashed the stars and stripes to its top. The naked tree became a beacon for the spring.

Honeymoon

On a dirt road near the northern Graham-Greenlee county line in the eastern part of the state

this town was named by a U.S. Forest Service ranger who took his new bride with him to his wilderness post.

Snowflake

On State Route 77 not quite halfway between Show Low and Holbrook in the eastern part of Arizona

there are about a dozen places in the U.S. named for the cold white stuff. I like this one best, because, if the story is true, the name has nothing to do with weather. It honors the community's two founders, a Mr. *Snow* and a Mr. *Flake.*

Why

At the intersection of State Routes 85 and 86 about 33 miles north of the Mexican border

allan Wolk claims in *The Naming of America* that this desert oasis was named by snowbirds in a trailer park who frequently got a good laugh out of the question *"Why* would anybody want to live in a place like this?"

Stretching your legs in Why: The entrance to Organ Pipe Cactus National Monument is about five miles south on Route 85. The 516-square-mile desert preserve is home to both the organ-pipe cactus, which grows nowhere else in the U.S., and the saguaro cactus, the giant sentinels of the Sonoran Desert, which can stand more than fifty feet high. Location: Park headquarters is about 24 miles south of *Why* on State Route 85. Telephone: (520) 387-6849. Admission charged.

arkansas

Figure Five

On State Route 59 a few miles north of Fort Smith

One of two stories about this place collected by Miss Clara B. Eno in her *History of Crawford County, Arkansas* is that a young man who helped carry the chain in a survey party carved a large *figure five* into a black oak tree. He then wrote to his family, which was looking for a new place to settle down, instructing them to meet him at the tree.

The other story is that the same young man, James Graham Stevenson, and some other men were driving cattle when they stopped for the night and camped under a big oak. The *five* in the bark of the tree was Stevenson's estimate of how many miles the party had traveled that day.

Either way, Miss Eno points out that the Stevenson family did not settle in *Figure Five* but in another place called *Bond Special.*

Hogeye

On State Route 265 ten miles south-southwest of Fayetteville in the northwestern part of the state

Local historian Neva McMurray says there are half a dozen folktales concerning the origin of this name. One says the name is a slurred form of *"Hawk Eye,"* the name of a popular old-time tune (she's also heard the tune was *"Ho, Guy"*). In this tale, an itinerant fiddler offers to entertain the townspeople for a drink of moonshine. He is accommodated several times over, by which time *Hawk Eye* comes out sounding like *Hog Eye.*

McMurray's second favorite folktale about the name is that it comes from the "spit and whittle" club that in pre-Civil War days whiled away the hours on the porch of the general store. Free-range *hogs* snoozed under the porch on hot summer days, and these old geezers would try to spit into their *eyes* through the cracks in the porch floor.

Others say this little crossroads community is "no bigger than a *hog's eye,*" or that the valley it's in is shaped like a *hog's eye.*

Stretching your legs in Hogeye: After you've had a spin around town (it

Ink, Arkansas

won't take long), head up to Fayetteville to James at the Mill, a three-year-old restaurant in a converted 1835 grist mill that has elevated the corn dog to cuisine. Chef Miles James cooked in New York, Paris, London, and Florence, then Washington, Nantucket Island, Massachusetts, and Santa Fe, New Mexico, before coming back to his native Arkansas to cook down-home food in a gourmet way. *The New York Times* praised his homemade andouille sausage corn dog, which stands straight up on the plate and is surrounded by oven-dried tomatoes and mashed potatoes with roasted garlic. A tall, varnished sycamore is the centerpiece of the bi-level dining room, and diners can look out on the old, spring-fed waterwheel. The restaurant is in the 48-room Inn at the Mill. Address: 3906 Greathouse Springs Road, Fayetteville. Telephone: (501) 443-1400.

Ink

Six miles east of Mena in the western part of the state

Vernon Pizer put this tiny hamlet on the map with his book *Ink, Ark. and All That: How American Places Got Their Names.* In it he tells the traditional story of how the townsfolk were instructed by the feds to "write in *ink*" on their application for a post office. They took it literally and wrote in *Ink* as the town's name.

Ernie Deane tells a slightly different story in *Arkansas Place Names* (a principal source of information for Arkansas place-names). According to his version, a lady schoolteacher solicited suggestions for names by sending a note home with her students. She gave the same instructions as the feds and got the same result.

I found a third explanation in a county history. Eighty-eight-year-old Eva Wood told the compilers of the history in 1969 that her father was the first postmaster but her mother did all the correspondence. In 1887, she sent in a list of recommended names, including *Inky*, which she had written on impulse while staring at a bottle of *ink*. A Post Office official wrote back, saying that the name *Ink* had been assigned, because there already was an *Inky* in Arkansas.

Smackover

On State Route 7 ten miles north-northwest of El Dorado in the southern part of the state

a little booklet published by the *Smackover* Chamber of Commerce and paid for by 24 local businesses (mostly oil drilling companies) says that the town, which today has a population of just under 2,300, was settled in 1844 by a band of French trappers and hunters from Louisiana. They named it

Sumac-Couvert, which means "covered with sumac bushes" and sounded like *Smackover* to the English-speaking pioneers who followed them.

An oil boom in the 1920s made *Smackover* famous—there are still more than 2,300 producing wells. A big blowout on the Andrew Blue farm in April 1922 burned for more than a month with a flame that old-timers say looked to be a mile high. This blowout, or one at another well, spawned a popular legend that tells of oil and rock blowing "*smack over* the derrick."

Just a mile or two east of *Smackover* is a village with the curious name of *Standard Umpstead*. It got this appellation that same year when the *Standard* Oil Company struck oil on land owned by Sid *Umpstead*.

Toad Suck

On the big bend in the Arkansas River just west of Conway in the center of the state

first a ferry crossing, *Toad Suck* is now the location of a lock and dam and a bridge. Ernie Deane says that a number of stories are told concerning the name, all having the same theme: that the riverbank here was a weekend gathering place where people would "*suck* up whiskey like *toads*" or "have a regular *toad suck*," as a redneck humorist might put it. One account says the revelers were riverboatmen; another talks of "a wild element" of gamblers, racehorse owners, and bootleggers.

But there may be more than legend and redneck humor at work here: According to the U.S. Board on Geographic Names in Reston, Virginia, *suck* is a descriptive term found from Arkansas east through western Virginia that has at least two meanings when used in place-names. One meaning is similar to the generic *lick*, as in *salt lick*. Arkansas also has a *Panther Suck,* for example. The other meaning has to do with a constricted area in a stream where the water rushes (a rapids or chute). A well-known feature on the Tennessee River is the *Suck.*

Other Unusual Place-Names in Arkansas

Back Gate

On U.S. Route 165 six miles northeast of Dumas and 22 miles west of the Mississippi River

this town was named in the 1930s for a WPA-built community center that was across the road from the *back gate* of a well-known old cotton plantation.

Board Camp

Eight miles southeast of Mena on State Route 8 in the western part of the state

Old-timers say that an extended pioneer family on its way farther west stopped here sometime in the mid to late 1800s because a number of them were sick. They built a *camp* made of *boards* they had hewed and riven, and stayed for many months. This was notable, because at that time all the cabins in these parts were built of whole logs. After the family pushed on, hunters and other travelers who used the camp referred to it as the Place of the *Board Camp*.

Delight

On State Route 26 about 25 miles west-southwest of Arkadelphia in the southwestern part of the state

Simple. Since W. H. Kirkham owned the land on which the town was laid out, he got to choose the name, and he thought the location was just a *delight*.

Dogpatch

On State Route 7 near the Boone-Newton county line 30 miles south of the Missouri border

this town was named in the 1960s for a theme park based on the popular *L'il Abner* cartoon strip by Al Capp.

Nail

On State Route 16 in south-central Newton County in the northwestern part of the state

ernie Deane says that this name probably was the result of a spelling error by postal authorities. The name of the postmaster, *Neal*, was copied down as *Nail* and entered as the name of the community.

Deane also repeats the folktale about a group of men sitting around the stove at a crossroads store discussing what to name the place. Just when they were about to give up on this subject, one of the men spotted a *nail* on the floor beneath his chair.

Sounds a little too simplistic to me.

Old Jenny Lind

On a back road (just east of I-71) about ten miles south of Fort Smith

this town was named for an internationally famous Swedish soprano who was brought to the U.S. in 1850 by showman P. T. Barnum for a nationwide concert tour. It is very likely that she performed in nearby Fort Smith. (*Jenny Lind,* the newer part of the community, is right next door.)

Umpire

At the intersection of State Routes 4 and 84 in northern Howard County about 25 miles from the Oklahoma border

there was a big celebration here the day Quiller Smith opened his new gristmill in the early 1890s. One of the events was a baseball game between this oak-shaded village and another nearby village. The game was the latest chapter in the rivalry between the two villages that had been growing ever since their schoolteachers, Miss Flora Jones and Jimmy Faulkner, had organized a series of spelling bees between their schools.

Nobody in the two villages had ever played baseball, so a visitor named Billy Faulkner (Jimmy's cousin) from Mena, Arkansas, took charge. He told the players where to run when they hit the ball, gave instructions to the fielders and the pitcher, and interrupted the game when things got out of hand. He also served as the *umpire.*

It was a wild game, with balls flying all over the field, bruised knuckles and shins, and probably some bruised feelings. The lead went back and forth, but the home team finally won. Afterward, Miss Flora climbed up on a stump and made a speech. She thanked everyone for coming, and for their sportsmanship, and she proposed that since the new post office needed a name, they should call it *Umpire* in honor of the great job Billy Faulkner had done in refereeing the game. The crowd whooped and hollered their approval.

One of the people who played in that fateful game, "Uncle" Jack Manasco, remembered it for a reporter from the *Memphis Press Scimitar* in 1951. He was 18 the year of the game and a senior in high school. Schooldays, he sat in Miss Flora's classroom, but on Sundays he took her for long romantic strolls around town. Jack was three days older than his teacher.

In the same newspaper article, the manager of the *Umpire* town baseball team complained about the trouble he was having finding an *umpire* for home games. It was embarrassing, given the town's name, he told the reporter.

(See *Bestpitch,* Maryland, page 108.)

"Y" City

With a population of well under a hundred, this place hardly qualifies as a city, but it is a well-known gas stop for motorists traveling between Fort Smith and Hot Springs. The name comes from the fact that the junction of the two highways forms a *"Y"*—albeit one that has fallen on its right, or east, side.

Wye, in Perry County, Arkansas, was named for a *"Y"* junction of railroad tracks.

Fiddletown, California

california

Fiddletown

About 36 miles east-southeast of Sacramento

during the Gold Rush, this place was known for its *fiddlers,* many of whom had come from Missouri to seek their fortunes. It was common for one man to work the claim while his partner entertained him with his instrument.

An upscale explanation of the name is that there were four violinists in the first family to settle here, so they called their new address Violin City. How and why the name was changed is not explained.

Whether you call the instrument a violin or a *fiddle,* or prefer a city or a town, the community's musical tradition is alive and well. Fiddlers from all over flock here in September for the *Fiddletown* Fiddlers Jamboree.

Stretching your legs in Fiddletown: During the Gold Rush, there was a sizable Chinese population in *Fiddletown.* Remaining from those days and recently restored as a museum, is the Chew Kee Store. Its shelves are lined with apothecary bottles once filled with medicines, elixirs, and curative teas. Drawers for cut herbs are identified with Chinese characters, and the walls of the store are covered with newspapers dating back to the 1850s. Location: Main Street, Fiddletown. No phone. Admission free.

Three hundred thousand flowers turn Daffodil Hill (on a ranch a few miles east of town) into a riot of color for a few weeks each spring. Members of the McLaughlin family have been planting bulbs on the hillside since 1887—thousands a year. For directions, inquire locally. Admission free.

Happy Camp

On State Route 96 in Klamath National Forest in the northwestern corner of the state

One starry July night in 1851, fourteen gold prospectors sat around a campfire on the banks of Indian Creek, a tributary of the Klamath River. It was an area of spectacular scenery, with steep forested mountains and narrow valleys, rocky cliffs, and fast, frothy streams.

The miners passed a bottle of whiskey around the circle, and when it was empty, they opened another. Soon all the pains of their rugged work had been temporarily forgotten. Presently, one man proposed that they give their camp a name, and another burst out, "Let's call it *Happy Camp*, for tonight and forever!" This was seconded and voted upon with three hearty cheers, and the bottle was passed again.

Igo, Ono

On County Highway A16 about 12 miles (Igo) and 13 miles (Ono) west-southwest of Redding in the northern part of the state

george Peterson, superintendent of the Hardscrabble Mine, had a toddler named Eugene who worshipped his dad. Every time Peterson left the house for the mine, he begged, "Daddy, *I go? I go?*" When the quartz mine was expanded in 1868 and the work camp had to be moved from Piety Hill to a new location, Charles Hoffmann, the mine's surveyor, who had observed this parting ritual many times, suggested *Igo* as the name for the new camp.

Mining Camp Names

THE FORTY-NINERS CHOSE COLORFUL NAMES for their camps and for geographical features, many of which have either disappeared from the map or were changed when women and other polite company came on the scene.

One of my favorites is **Jackassville**, a mining camp in Siskiyou County, whose first six inhabitants, according to California toponymist Erwin Gude, gave it the grand and dignified name **City of Six**. But miners in neighboring camps just thought of it as a camp inhabited by six *jackass*es.

Here are some other good ones: **Whiskey Flat**, **Helltown**, **Humbug City** (it had a saloon named The Howlin' Wilderness), **Tantrum Glade**, **Delirium Tremens**, **Dirty Sock Hot Springs**, **Poker Flat**, **Quicksilver**, **Git-Up-and-Git**, **Hell-out-for-Noon**, **Knownothing** (because the miners refused to talk about the richness of their claims), **Red Dog**, **Bogus**, **Bullion**, **One Wagontown**, **Last Chance**, **Starvout**, **Sucker Flat**, **Timbuctoo**, **Cut-throat Gulch**, **Portuguese Flat**, **Chinese Camp**, **Afterthought**, **Loafer Flat**, and **Poverty Ridge**.

Near *Igo* and *Ono*, there once was a camp called **Muletown** and another called **One-Horse Town**, which, in fact, it was. This may be the origin of the derisive term for a small town. **Dogtown** was common for a cluster of hovels, particularly of Chinese miners. Magalia, a few miles north of Paradise, is sometimes called **Dogtown**, but for a different reason: Mrs. Bassett, an early settler, bred dogs, which she sold to miners.

By 1888, *Igo* had become an enclave for Chinese miners. When the march of the mine forced another move, their initial response was *"Oh, no!"* And that cry of protest became the new work camp's name. (Another source says this camp was named for Peterson's response to his son—*"Oh, no!"*)

Those are the stories people in *Igo* and *Ono* invented to explain their curious names. The truth is *Igo* is probably an Indian name and *Ono* is a village in the Bible.

Paradise

On State Route 191 about 80 miles north of Sacramento

former Oroville, California, mayor Gene Sylva claims that his great-great-grandfather, William Pierce Leonard, named this popular retirement town on a summer day in 1864, after a hot and dusty ride up from the Sacramento Valley. The crew of his sawmill was outside taking a break when he arrived. Leonard, who was affectionately known as "Uncle Billy," dismounted his horse, took a deep breath of the cool, clean air, and exclaimed, "Boys, this is *paradise.*"

Others have pointed out that the town's location makes the name an obvious choice. It's high enough above the valley floor to stay cool in the summer but low enough at 1,700 feet to escape the heavy winter snows of the Sierra Nevada. And it's a Garden of Eden for anyone growing vegetables, apples, or nuts.

All this may be true, but I still like the often-told story that the town was named during the Gold Rush for the *Pair o' Dice* Saloon. Some say the evidence for this is the fact that the name was spelled *"Paradice"* on an official railroad map printed in 1900. Or, others say, it was the misspelling that gave rise to the saloon story. Gene Sylva, who is a past president of the Butte County Historical Society, asserts that there is not a shred of truth to the saloon story.

Paradise is a fairly common commendatory place-name. *Paradise*, South Dakota, is particularly interesting: American place-name guru George Stewart says it was inevitable that the town would take this name after a homesteader named *Adam* settled near a homesteader named *Eve*, although no union resulted.

Rough and Ready

On a local road in Nevada County 50 miles northeast of Sacramento

a party of Wisconsinites with gold on their minds arrived here on September 9, 1849. They called themselves the *Rough and Ready* Company, because they were led by Captain A. A. Townsend, who had served under General Zachary Taylor—nicknamed Old *Rough and Ready*—during the Mexican Border War. A new federal tax on mines so enraged these anti-government fortune seekers that they organized the Republic of *Rough and Ready*, wrote a constitution for it, and seceded from the Union.

As you can imagine, no one outside the mining camps took this revolutionary outburst very seriously.

The town was immortalized in Bret Harte's short story, "The Millionaire of *Rough and Ready*." He also wrote stories about two other California towns mentioned in this chapter: *Fiddletown* and *Poker Flat*.

Another unforgettable place-name in this part of Nevada County is *You Bet*. The community is gone, but the name lives on in a local road. Folklorists say the name originated in 1857 when Lazarus Beard, the saloon-keeper, brought up the need for a name for the place with two customers. Beard put a bottle of whiskey on the bar and indicated that he wasn't charging for it, so the customers strung him out for a while. Finally, one of them jokingly suggested that *"You bet,"* Beard's signature phrase, would make a good name.

Stretching your legs in Rough and Ready: The time to be in *Rough and Ready* is on Secession Day, the last Sunday in June, when hundreds of Gold Rush patriots and visitors celebrate the town's brief fling with independence (see above) with a breakfast put on by the fire department, crafts, skits, a blacksmithing demonstration, and more.

Usona

On State Route 49 between Mariposa (the town) and Oakhurst and about 50 miles north of Fresno

the residents held a meeting in 1913 and decided to name their rising little community after the United States of North America—*U.S.O.N.A.* They may or may not have known that this name—along with *Columbia* and *Fredonia* (a Latinized version of *freedom* that was later adopted by a town in upstate New York)—was on the table when our founding fathers were debating a name for the new country 140 years earlier.

The story is told that *Azusa*, a location in Los Angeles County, acquired a name only after the townspeople had discussed "every name from *A* to *Z* in the *United States of America*"—*A.Z.U.S.A.* In fact, *azusa* is a Gabrielino Indian word for "skunk."

Weed Patch

On State Route 184 fifteen miles southeast of Bakersfield

This was originally a descriptive name for a 24-square-mile *patch* of ground mostly covered with tall carrot *weeds* that made it distinct from the sagebrush desert and alkali flats surrounding it. By the turn of the century, farmers were growing grapes, figs, alfalfa, wheat, and barley and grazing their cattle in the *weed patch*. They visited with each other when they went there in the evening to gather their cows, and they gave directions based on the compass direction and distance from the *weed patch*.

Throughout the town's history, newcomers—usually Easterners—have tried to rally support to change the name to something that sounded higher class, but they never got much support. Locals are proud of the name. *Weed Patch* has always stood for good land and hard-working people.

In the 1930s, *Weed Patch* was a gathering place for thousands of Oklahomans fleeing the Dust Bowl. John Steinbeck put them and *Weed Patch* on the map in his Pulitzer Prize-winning novel *The Grapes of Wrath*.

Whiskeytown

On State Route 299 eleven miles west of Redding in the northern part of the state

When a barrel of *whiskey* strapped to a mule fell into a creek and cracked open, the miners standing around jawing with the mule driver got out their tin cups and lapped it up. From that day forward the stream, which runs beside the old California-Oregon pack trail, was known as *Whiskey* Creek.

The mining town that grew up on the site was variously called *Whiskey* Creek and *Whiskeytown*, until 1881 when it was changed to *Blair*. Postal authorities had put pressure on the townspeople to clean up their act and give the town a respectable name. *Blair* was later changed to *Stella* and then to *Schilling*, after J. F. Schilling, postmaster and innkeeper. Old-timers never took those names seriously, and on July 2, 1952, the name was officially changed back to *Whiskeytown*.

There's an alternative naming story that only adds to the respectability problem. It says that the town was named by a stage coach driver who claimed that the miners here could drink a barrel of *whiskey* a day.

No doubt *Whiskeytown* was a rowdy place from the day gold was discovered in the creek in 1849. Tellingly, two local histories note that no woman —not one—graced its streets until 1856. One of those histories tells of a barkeep who, fed up with the gibes of a customer, drew his revolver and shot him dead. A crowd then grabbed the barkeep and hung him from "the nearest gibbet tree." (You mean, there was more than one in town!)

Other Unusual Place-Names in California

Eureka

On U.S. Route 101 on the state's northern coast

everyone has heard of the California state motto *Eureka!*, a Greek expression meaning "I have found it." It's what Archimedes exclaimed when he hit upon the theory of displacement while bathing. And it's what forty-niners yelled every time they struck gold.

On May 13, 1850, this became the first American town so named. By 1880, there were 40 of them.

Gas Point

On a local road about 25 miles southwest of Redding (due west of Cottonwood and I-5) in the northern part of the state

Old forty-niners gathered here on Doc Davidson's porch or in the general store to *gas* about gold prices and politics and tell friendly lies about long-expired mining claims.

Likely

On U.S. Route 395 twenty miles south of Alturas in the northeastern part of the state

the following is a *likely* story, never wholly authenticated: When the early settlers applied for a post office in the late 1870s, all three of the names they sent to Washington were rejected, because they duplicated other California names. Some of the settlers were discussing this in the general store when one of them dejectedly remarked that it was not *"likely"* they'd ever get a name and the respectability that went with it. "That's it—let's call it *Likely*," W. H. Nelson piped up. "It's not *likely* there'll be another place in the state with that name."

Modesto

On State Route 99 twenty-five miles southeast of Stockton

One hundred and twenty-five years ago, the railroads were naming new towns for their executives and financial backers as if the towns were swivel chairs in a boardroom. The Central Pacific wanted to name this Central Valley city (which today has a population of more than 160,000) for W. C. Ralston, an influential San Francisco banker whose support the railroad needed to lay more track. But Ralston would have nothing to do with it; he said he wasn't important enough to have his name on the map of California. So the railroad barons, who could hardly believe the banker's *modesty*, gave the town the Spanish word for a *modest* man as its moniker.

Suggestive Names

MOST OF THE PLACE-NAMES in the U.S. with sexual connotations are accidental. Obviously, it's a bad idea to saddle a community with an embarrassing name. Just look at how poor **Lolita**, Texas (page 228), suffered when its name—a lovely girl's name—became associated with a teenage nymphomaniac in a novel.

Here are some suggestive-sounding names I found: **Hookers**, North Carolina; **Climax,** in at least a half dozen states; **Desire,** Pennsylvania; **Skin Tight** (the original name of *Lone Star*), Texas; **Kiss Me Quick Hills** and **Dirty Woman Creek**, South Dakota; **Killpecker Creek**, Wyoming; **Bumpass,** Virginia (page 241); **Ticklenaked Pond**, Vermont (possibly from an Indian word with a totally different meaning), and **Intercourse**, Pennsylvania (page 199). An Alabama town changed its name to *Siloan* after suffering decades of embarrassment from the name **Intercourse**.

Indiana has a place named **French Lick**, and North Carolina has both a **French Lick** and a **French Broad River**. The electric utility that serves the area once put out a newsletter called *The French Broad Electrifier*. Basketball Hall of Famer Larry Bird was born in the Indiana town and was known affectionately as "The Hick from French Lick."

Teton Village, Wyoming, takes its name from the Grand *Tetons*, the mountains that looked like big breasts—*"teton"*—to the love-starved French explorers who named them. This part of the female anatomy appears frequently in the mountainous West. **Two Tits**, California, now more decorously known as *Two Teats*, is a prime example. Colorado has a **Nipple Mountain**, and the nipples of individual ladies—if not the ladies themselves—are remembered in **Mollie's Nipple**, Arizona, and **Nellie's Nipple**, California.

Pizzlewig Creek, California, is said to be named for Sweet *Pizzlewig*, a woman known to give sexual favors to strangers. *Pizzle* is slang for both penis and sexual intercourse. Years ago, four prostitutes put up a tent each spring in **Whorehouse Meadow**, Oregon, to service the Basque shepherds coming down from the mountains with their flocks. The original name of Lewes, Delaware, was **Whorekill**, an anglicization of the Dutch *Hoeren-Kil* —"whores' stream," and most likely took its name from an incident in which Dutch sailors consorted with Indian women.

Wide Awake, Colorado

colorado

Security

An exit off U.S. Route 25 just south of Colorado Springs

With the temperature dropping fast in the Cold War, people yearned for a sense of *security* in the early 1950s, and the *Security* Development Corporation was more than glad to oblige. The planned community that the company started developing in 1953 on a 670-acre tract of farmland filled up fast as new families flooded into the Pikes Peak region at the rate of three a day looking for defense jobs in Colorado Springs. Ten years later, *Security* had 2,500 homes, a library, post office, medical center and fire station, a shopping center, seven churches, a half dozen schools, a community center, a restaurant, and an American Legion post.

Security Development Corporation offered oversized lots at first, so that homeowners could plant vegetable gardens and have the *security* of growing their own food. And with seven deep wells on the tract, there would always be enough water. This was a key selling point—another kind of *security*—because there had been a severe drought in 1954. Sales literature also talked about the "freedom from care" families would enjoy here.

The developers named the main drag *Security* Boulevard, and the main cross street Easy Street.

Tincup

On a gravel road in the mountains northeast of Gunnison in the west-central part of the state

One source says this ghost town was named for the *tin cups* of whiskey served at the first saloon; another says the name had to do with a miner's good luck: In the summer of 1860, Jim Taylor and two other men who were prospecting in the area woke up one morning to find their horses missing. Taylor went looking for them in the next gulch and came upon a dry stream bed where the sand looked promising. He brought a sample back to camp in a *tin cup*, and, sure enough, when he panned it he separated out some flakes of gold.

At the height of the Colorado gold rush, this was a wild town of 6,000 that needed twenty saloons to quench the thirsts of the miners who found the gold and the gamblers and prostitutes who took it away from them. Gunfights were an everyday occurrence, and grizzly bears and mountain lions were frequently seen close to town. A patch of ground in the town cemetery was reserved for those who "died gloriously or otherwise in the thick of smoke from guns," writes Muriel Sibell Wolfe in her fascinating book *The Ghost Towns and Mining Towns of Colorado.*

The gamblers had the upper hand in town politics, and in 1880 they elected a mayor, a town council, and a marshal. The marshal was told he was to "see nothing and hear nothing," and that his first arrest would be his last. His sole purpose was to give *Tincup* the appearance of being orderly so that it would lure the tenderfeet that the gamblers could fleece.

The second marshal was allowed to arrest drunken miners and hold them overnight in the calaboose. The third was shot by a saloonkeeper who pulled a pistol from his pocket as the marshal was marching him to jail. The next marshal went insane, and his successor was killed.

Many people in Colorado know about *Tincup* from listening to Pete Smythe, a popular Denver radio personality who created a fictional East *Tincup* and peopled it with imaginary citizens. He appointed himself mayor.

In the mountains due east of Seattle, Washington, is a short stream called *Tin Cup* Joe Creek, which was named in the 1890s for a roving gold prospector by that name.

Troublesome

On U.S. Route 40 about six miles east of Kremmling and 55 miles west of Boulder

Local historian Paul Gilbert explains that the creek that gives this place its name may be only 20 or 30 feet across, but the thick adobe mud on the creek bottom was always *troublesome* for wagons traveling between Hot Sulphur Springs and the Gore Pass.

Stretching your legs in Troublesome: Historic Hot Sulphur Springs Resort, only 12 miles east on U.S. 40, is surrounded by some of Colorado's most spectacular mountain scenery. The hot mineral water percolates up through the rocks at the rate of 5,000 gallons per minute into various indoor and outdoor swimming pools and soaking tubs. Location: Just off the highway, Hot Sulphur Springs. Telephone: (970) 725-3306.

With a population of less than 500, Hot Sulphur Springs is a tiny county seat, but with a tough—even murderous—past. In 1880, some conniving politicians and businessmen managed to move the county seat of Grand County to Grand Lake. "How did you get it back?" I asked Gilbert.

"We went up there and shot all three county commissioners," he says with a twinkle in his eye.

"Did anybody go to jail?"

"No, they didn't know who did it . . . . It was the Fourth of July, and there were a lot of firecrackers going off when the shots were fired."

Wide Awake

On a dirt road seven miles north of Black Hawk and 25 miles west-northwest of Denver

this ghost town made national news in 1995 when its owners put it up for sale. Verla and Richard Clemens were asking $250,000 for the 46-acre crease in the Rocky Mountains, hoping to take advantage of a real estate boom triggered by the opening of gambling casinos in nearby Central City and Black Hawk.

Wide Awake has been in a deep sleep for much of this century. The town had its heyday around the turn of the century, when dreams of gold pushed the population up over 500. All that is left today is a collapsed post office, the crumbled foundation of a stamping mill, and the wood and tin shack of the town's last resident, Walt Stevens, a jack-of-all-mountain-trades who died in 1964. What were the town's streets are now stands of blue spruce and lodgepole pine that are frequented by deer and black bear.

According to Richard Clemens, a group of miners were discussing what to name the place late one night in the 1860s. A man who was having trouble keeping his eyes open turned to the miner next to him and said, "Let's wait until morning when we're *wide awake.* "

"That's it!" responded one of the miners. "We'll name it *Wide Awake.*"

Other Unusual Place-Names in Colorado

Cripple Creek

On State Route 67 southwest of Pikes Peak

baby boomers know this place-name from the sixties song by The Band. And anyone who knows anything about the Gold Rush knows this was the site of the biggest strike in the West—$300 million big.

The creek and the historic town take their name from a series of accidents suffered by the valley's first family, the Welties, and their cattle. The specific injuries depend on which source you read or who you talk to locally and how much they've had to drink.

Because the gold was found on a cattle ranch, people called *Cripple Creek* "the $300 million cow pasture."

Firstview

On U.S. 40 in Cheyenne County 11 miles west of Cheyenne Wells and 30 miles from the Kansas border

Pioneers stopping here to rest got their *first view* of Pike's Peak, 110 miles west as the crow flies. A plat for the town was filed in September 1911.

Hygiene

Five miles northwest of Longmont in Boulder County

this town was named for the *Hygiene* Home, a sanitarium built by the Church of the Brethren. Popularly known as Dunkards for their baptismal practice of immersing a person three times, the sect settled in the St. Vrain Valley starting in the 1870s.

Ione

Thirty miles north of Denver on U.S. Route 85

W. A. Davis, owner of the original townsite, was asked in 1890 by a Union Pacific official about the deed situation. Davis responded by turning to each of the four directions, extending his arm and saying, *"I own. I own …"* So that's what the railroad man wrote down in his log book of station names, spelling it with a classical twist.

Joes

On U.S. Route 36 about 120 miles east of Denver and 40 miles west of the Kansas border

Originally named Three *Joes* in honor of three early settlers, the name was shortened when the ranchers in the area applied for a post office.
(See *Bill,* Wyoming, page 262.)

Last Chance

On U.S. Route 36 sixty-five miles east of Denver

archie Chapman and Essa Harbert opened a creamery, store, and filling station here in 1926. They called the place *Last Chance* because they wanted motorists to know that this was the *last chance* to buy gasoline before reaching Denver (80 miles west) or Saint Francis, Kansas (104 miles east).

Paradox

Off State Route 90 six miles from the Utah border

the town was named in the early 1880s after *Paradox* Valley, so called because the Dolores River cuts through the canyon walls at right angles, an unusual geological formation.

Early settlers found the valley almost inaccessible, according to George R. Eichler, author of *Colorado Place Names*. The only way into it was to unload all the wagons, dismantle them, and then lower the pieces by rope to the floor of the valley.

Rifle

On I-70 sixty-four miles northeast of Grand Junction

this crossroads town of 4,600 was named after *Rifle* Creek, which was named about 1880 by an army surveying party. The soldiers were busy putting up mileposts along the road between the Colorado River and the White River (north on what is now State Route 13) when one of the soldiers left his *rifle* leaning up against a tree on the bank of a stream. The officer in charge ordered the party to retrace its steps until the *rifle* was found. The officer wrote down "*Rifle* Creek" in the survey log book.

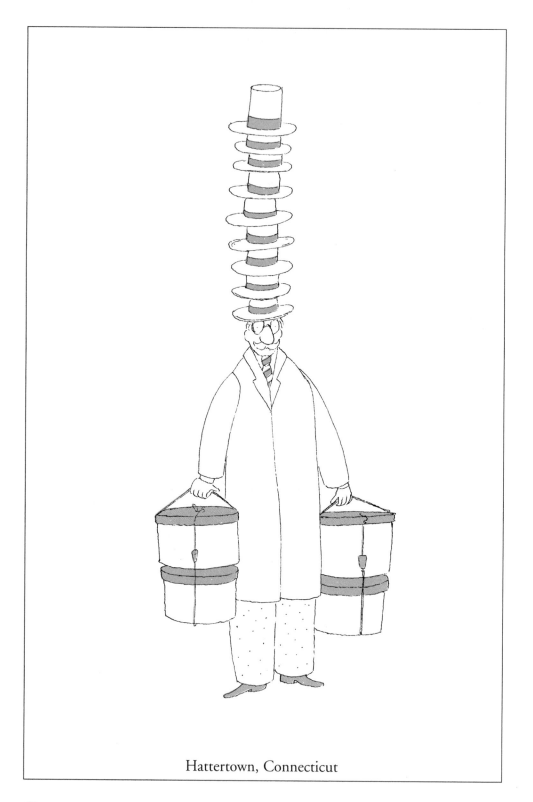

Hattertown, Connecticut

connecticut

Augerville

Just south of downtown Hamden and the Wilbur Cross Parkway

now part of the city of Hamden, the original village took its name from the *auger* factory that Willis Churchill set up beside the Mill River in 1843. The factory also manufactured gimlets and other boring tools, and it lasted into the early part of this century, when it was called W. A. Ives & Company.

Stretching your legs in Augerville: Some of the best ice cream in New England is served at Wentworth Homemade Ice Cream in Hamden, where on summer days the picnic tables under the big oak tree in the backyard are almost always packed with people licking waffle cones piled with Mocha Chocolate Lace, Almond Amaretto (made with real liqueur), fresh peach (Wentworth's trademark flavor), and other flavors in the scrumptious lineup. Wentworth makes all its own ice cream on-site, as well as the waffle cones, which come plain or dipped in chocolate. The ice cream recipes are trade secrets, and one reviewer says Wentworth "beats hands down" any premium ice cream you'll find in the frozen foods aisle at the supermarket—even Ben & Jerry's. Address: 3697 Whitney Avenue (State Route 10), Hamden. Telephone: (203) 281-7429.

Long Society

On State Route 165 two miles east of Norwich center in the eastern part of Connecticut

farmers who had settled in a *long* narrow strip extending nine miles along the eastern border of the town of Norwich petitioned in 1699 to form a separate ecclesiastical *society*, or parish. The petition told of the difficulty the farmers had attending church services in Norwich; the meeting house was a *long* distance from their homes and they had to ferry across the Thames River and then follow a tedious and winding route through the Chelsea Hills.

The petition was granted in 1720, and the *society* hired its first and only minister, the Reverend Jabez Wight, in 1726. When he died in 1786, the church seemed to die with him—even "the meeting house was allowed to decay and fall to pieces," according to a history of Norwich published in 1865.

Tariffville

On State Route 189 twelve miles north-northwest of Hartford

this is a nickname that stuck—for a mill village within the town of Simsbury that owed its economic existence to the *Tariff* Act of 1824, which made the manufacture of woolen cloth and carpets profitable in the U.S. The following year, the Tariff Manufacturing Company built a stone mill and housing for workers and brought in immigrant labor, Scottish weavers.

Stretching your legs in Tariffville: On a short walk around this classic New England village—a district on the National Register of Historic Places—you can see a number of fine examples of 19th-century architecture—Federal, Greek Revival, and Gothic Revival. Along Elm Street and Tunxis Place are eight "double houses" built by the mill, and on Tunxis Road, the mill itself. This long, one-story brick building was erected in 1867 after the original mill burned. It has arched windows set in corbeled panels and an arched tailrace on the Farmington River.

Just a few miles south of Tariffville are two other notable historic districts, *Terry's Plain* and *East Weatogue.* The Gifford Pinchot sycamore—Connecticut's largest tree—stands at the southern end of East Weatogue village.

Voluntown

Four miles from the Rhode Island border on State Route 165

in 1705, a six-square-mile, 160-lot "plantation" named *Volunteer Town* was granted to the Connecticut men who had *volunteered* to fight in King Philip's War. King Philip, less well-known as Metacomet, chief of the Wampanoags, led the Narragansetts, the Nipmucks, and his own tribe against the English colonists in southeastern New England. The two-year war ended on August 12, 1676, when King Philip was killed.

People in *Voluntown* are proud of their tradition of military *volunteerism.* Local men and women answered the call to duty every time it came, right up through the Vietnam War. What they are not proud of, and still a bit confused about, is answering the call to be extras in the silent movies a broken-down New York stage actor named Joseph Byron Totten made here just before World War I.

Totten showed up in town in 1914, and bought a house on State Route 49 that he used as a studio (it's still known by his name for it—Studio Farm). He then proceeded to shoot scads of film of *Voluntownees* running through the woods in costume or riding horses or carrying lanterns in a procession. After the day's shoot he fed them lavishly, and evidently concocted stories about the stars of the movies—Mary Pickford, Douglas Fairbanks, Lillian Gish—who would soon be coming to Studio Farm from their glittering homes in Newport, Rhode Island.

Years later, the local historical society dug into Totten's career and could not turn up any of the movies he is reported to have made here. Some of the titles he claimed as his own were actually movies made by famous Hollywood directors. Lillian Gish, replying to a letter from the researcher, said she had never heard of Totten.

The picture that emerges is this: Short of money and hoping to regain the fame he had enjoyed as a stage actor, Totten used unpaid local people—*volunteers*—to make silent movies that were so bad they never got into theaters, meanwhile charming the people of *Voluntown* into thinking he was turning their little farming community into a film colony.

Whigville

On a town road off State Route 69 six miles north of Bristol and 15 miles west of Hartford

this was a politically derisive nickname that became established in the 1830s when some residents of the village carried a banner and a resolution to keep the name to a big *Whig* Party convention in Hartford.

Whigville started out as *Poverty Hollow* which, according to a historical sketch that was read at a Grange meeting in 1875, had more to do with the character of its inhabitants than their economic standing. One of them, a Mrs. Palmer, was said to be a witch who haunted her house for many years after her death.

Other Unusual Place-Names in Connecticut

Bantam

On U.S. Route 202 sixteen miles northwest of Waterbury

One source says it is a corruption of the variably spelled Indian word *peantum*, a word used for a Christian, or "praying," Indian. Another argues that the name is derived from *Bantam,* the name of a former territory in Java—"a wild region inhabited by a race of barbarians." The name is old, appearing in 1719 in the first deed recorded in the town of Litchfield.

Dodgingtown

On State Route 302 three miles south of Newtown in the southwestern part of the state

befor the Revolutionary War, the taverns and flophouses here were hideaways for swindlers and thieves who were *dodging* the law.

Another folk tale holds that *Dodgingtown* came by its name because of the way its residents took advantage of a long-running boundary dispute between the towns of Danbury and Newtown. When a Danbury tax collec-

Derogatory Names

WHEN WE LIVED IN MAINE, I used to drive through a little place called **Monkey Corner** on my way to work. Intermarriage, people said, had lowered the neighborhood's expectations to the level of apes.

There have always been places with names that derogate either the character of the inhabitants or their cultural isolation. *Podunk,* which comes from an Indian word, came into generic usage before the Civil War as a name for a small, unimportant, and isolated village—a hick town. At one time or another there were villages named **Podunk** in Massachusetts, Connecticut, New York, and Iowa.

A southern version of **Podunk** is **Hogeye** (in Arkansas and other states)—a place no bigger than a *hog's eye.* Even more common is *Pumpkin* as in **Pumpkintown,** South Carolina and Tennessee; and **Pumpkin Center**, Oklahoma, Idaho, South Dakota, and Missouri. Both connote a rural setting and, more than likely, oafish *pumpkin*-headed inhabitants. **Lickskillet,** found in a number of locations in Kentucky and in Georgia, suggests inhabitants so poor they had to literally *lick* their *skillets* to get enough food.

Bug is another bad label. **Bug Tussle**, Alabama (see page 1), **Bug Scuffle**, Mississippi, and **Bug Hollow**, Kentucky, are names that once implied backwardness—of the kind that might make a good habitat for bedbugs. **Fleatown**, Ohio, is even more obvious.

Other derogatory names include: **Ragtown**, Texas and Kentucky; **Shantytown**, Nevada (see page 152); **Dogtown**, California (because the inhabitants lived in hovels fit for *dogs*), and **Monkeys Eyebrow**, Kentucky (see page 89). Alabama once had a locale named **T'aint Much**, and it wasn't.

The generic term *jerkwater town* comes from the early days of railroads, when trains took on *water* by *jerking* a rope attached to a trackside tank. This process was called "*jerking water,*" and it took place in towns too small and unimportant for the train to stop. Another railroad term, *whistle-stop,* was applied to small towns starting in the 1920s, but it never had the sting of *jerkwater.*

tor appeared at his door, a resident would insist that he was a Newtowner; when a Newtown tax collector knocked, he'd say he was a resident of Danbury. This tax *dodging* continued for several years.

Hattertown

On a local road on the west side of State Route 25 twelve miles north-northwest of Bridgeport

In 1821, Elam Benedict moved his wife and 11 children from Danbury to this remote village to go into the *hatting* business with Levi Taylor, up until then a resident of Newtown. The village had at least two things going for it that made it attractive to a *hatter:* Its brooks and ponds were a perfect habitat for muskrat and beaver, and there was no other *hatter* in Newtown. That had changed by 1846, when seven Newtown hat factories turned out 30,400 hats.

Both Benedict and Taylor died in their forties, most likely from mercury poisoning, a mentally debilitating condition that gave rise to the expression "mad as a hatter." Mercury was used to remove fur from animal skins, before being banned in the 1890s.

Upper Merryall, Lower Merryall

On a local road (west of U.S. Route 202) five miles east of the New York border

While surveying the North Purchase, a parcel of land in the town of New Milford obtained from the Indians, a party of surveyors stopped for the night at a spring situated about 20 rods north of the northern boundary of the Purchase, near what is now the Kent town line. After eating, they passed around a bottle (perhaps two), and *all* got *merry*.

This was in either 1726 when the entire tract was surveyed by the county surveyor, or in 1731 when lots were surveyed. The name is one of the few truly accidental—even frivolous—place-names found in New England.

Mermaid, Delaware

delaware

Mermaid

On State Route 7 about nine miles west of Wilmington

betweeen 1811 and 1853, historians surmise, a one-street village started rising around the *Mermaid* Tavern, a local hangout and stagecoach stop on the road between Wilmington and Lancaster, Pennsylvania. Built in 1725, the white stucco and frame building still stands amid condos, tract homes, and a shopping center.

Besides offering food, drink, and lodging to travelers, this roadhouse had a 24-horse stable, a resident blacksmith, and a wheelwright—everything you needed in the event of a run-in with a big pothole. By 1869, the *Mermaid* had lost her tavern license, but she remained an inn until 1880 and was a community focal point well into this century. She housed the post office from 1848 to 1900, served as the Grange hall, and was a polling place from 1830 to 1991, according to the Wilmington *News Journal.* At "The Battle of the Mermaid" in 1862, Democratic party officials tried to stop some AWOL soldiers from voting. They didn't, and a number of people involved in the fracas went to jail briefly.

Stretching your legs in Mermaid: The old tavern, which is on the National Register of Historic Places, is still owned by descendants of its first owner, James Walker. Location: At the intersection of Limestone Road (State Route 7) and Stoney Batter Road, about nine miles west of downtown Wilmington.

Pea Patch Island

In the middle of the Delaware River just above the Chesapeake and Delaware Canal

the story goes that this 70-acre island was "no bigger than a man's hat" until a ship loaded with *pea*s making its way up the Delaware River went aground, spilling its cargo. Before long, the *pea*s began to sprout, and they grew so abundantly that their tangled vines caught any silt and debris floating in the current, and the island expanded rapidly. The story may be exaggerated, but there is something to it, because an 1839 lawsuit over the ownership of the island includes testimony by an old man who said the island was just a speck in 1773 but now was big enough for a fort to be built on it.

Fort Delaware, completed in 1859, was the largest modern fort in the U.S. Pentagon-shaped, it covered six acres and had granite and brick walls that ranged in thickness from seven to 30 feet.

During the Civil War, the fort housed Confederate prisoners of war, including most of the men captured by the Union at the Battle of Gettysburg. At its peak, the prison held 12,500 men—tormented by mosquitoes in the summer, freezing in the winter, drinking brackish water or none at all. Men died every day from scurvy, cholera, and other diseases, sometimes as many as 300 in a 24-hour period. In all, 33,000 were incarcerated and 2,700 died, giving *Pea Patch Island* a reputation for misery on the order of the Confederate military prison in Andersonville, Georgia.

Other Unusual Place-Names in Delaware

Blue Ball

At the intersection of Rockland Road and U.S. Route 202 just north of Wilmington

according to the reference desk at the Wilmington Public Library, this neighborhood takes its name from an 18th-century tavern (like the Pennsylvania town with the same name, page 202). The name was later adopted by the Dupont family for the corporate entity that manages its properties and as the name of Alfred I. Dupont's estate here, now a children's hospital.

Cocked Hat

On State Route 404A twenty-five miles south-southwest of Dover

this town was named for a Colonial-era tavern with a picture of a *cocked hat* on its sign.

Hardscrabble

East of the intersection of U.S. Route 9 and State Route 20 (between Laurel and Georgetown) in the southern part of the state

hardscrabble was once a common term for meager prospects, such as a farm with poor soil. Central Sussex County was one of the last places in Delaware to be settled because it was so swampy.

Pepperbox

Between State Routes 24 and 30 southeast of Trap Pond State Park and three miles from Delaware's southern boundary

ccording to folklore, there once was a store here that was shaped like a *pepper box*. What shape was that? Nobody seems to know. Colonial New Englanders, of course, thought of a *saltbox* when they looked at a house with a pitched roof that was longer, and came down lower, in the rear.

The store may have had a "small cylindrical tower or turret"—one of the definitions of *pepperbox* in *Webster's Third New International Dictionary, Unabridged.*

Shaft Ox Corner

Six miles north of Delaware's southern border

xen were used to haul logs out of the Great Cypress Swamp that 250 years ago covered thousands of acres in the center of the Delmarva Peninsula. The ox on the inside of a two-ox cart going around a corner was known as the *shaft ox*, according to Russell McCabe, spokesman for the Delaware Public Archives, who grew up near the swamp in Sussex County. He says there is a *Shavox Corner* south of *Shaft Ox Corner* (just across the Maryland border), which he assumes has the same origin.

Shortly

Just north of State Route 20 in the central part of southern Delaware

his hamlet is in an area dense with old colloquial place-names: *Hardscrabble, Packing House Corner, Pepperbox, Shaft Ox Corner, Cabbage Corner, Workmans Corner, Bryans Store, Bull Pine Corners, Old Furnace.* Unfortunately, the origins of the names are sketchy at best. *Shortly*, one source suggests, may have had something to do with an expectation—a post office? a railroad station? a package from the city?—and a vague promise of when it would be met. *"Shortly."*

Slaughter Beach

On Delaware Bay at the northern edge of Prime Hook National Wildlife Refuge

different versions of the same legend center around a local Indian tribe that was threatening either colonists or the crew of a ship that had gone aground on a sandbar in Delaware Bay. A cannon from the ship was brought to shore, and the Indians were tricked into lining up in front of it. Many of them were killed or maimed in this *slaughter* on the *beach*.

Slaughter Beach is only a ten-minute drive from the *Murderkill River*, an interesting example of verbal overkill that has appeared on maps since 1654.

Sign Language

HISTORIANS BELIEVE that pictorial tavern signs were popular in the 17th and 18th centuries for the simple reason that many people could not read. So they looked for the sign with the **Mermaid** painted on it, or the **Blue Ball,** or the **Cocked Hat**. Other taverns and inns in Delaware that later became village names were **Rising Sun**, **Red Lion,** and **Cross Keys**. Maryland also has a **Rising Sun**, as well as a **Horsehead**, where John Wilkes Booth once had a drink. Pennsylvania also has a **Blue Ball** and a **Red Lion**, as well as these other tavern towns: **Bird in Hand** (George Washington slept there in 1773), **Broad Axe**, **Compass**, **King of Prussia** (his portrait was on the sign), and **White Horse** (**Blackhorse**, Maryland, may also be derived from a tavern name).

In addition, Pennsylvania has a town named **Yellow House**, which got its name because the tavern was painted *yellow;* a town that could not decide which of *two taverns* should be its namesake, so they called it **Two Taverns**; and a town whose name sounds like the result of a lost weekend in a tavern, **Benderville.**

Virginia, the other mid-Atlantic state where these names are found, weighs in with **Cuckoo**, **Red House**, **Boswells Tavern**, **Georges Tavern**, **Steeles Tavern,** and **Todds Tavern**—all town names now.

florida

Century

On U.S. Route 29 in the northwest corner of the Florida Panhandle

The lumber market was bullish at the turn of the *century*, and on April 26, 1900, timber baron Russell Alger paid $1 million for 250,000 acres of prime yellow pine forest straddling the Alabama-Florida line. Alger, who had already made millions on Michigan white pine, was a general in the Civil War, governor of Michigan, U.S. Senator, and Secretary of War under President McKinley. Like the heroes of the novels of another well-known Alger (Horatio), Russell Alger started out poor—he was orphaned on the frontier at age twelve. He apparently hoped that a new *century* and a new place to focus his capitalistic energy would heal the wound to his pride that opened when he had to resign from McKinley's cabinet under a cloud of controversy.

Century was originally called *Teaspoon*, because, according to one account, it was near a bend in the Escambia River that was shaped like a *teaspoon*. But many more people stand by the story that the town got its name from a black handyman named George Washington who carried a *teaspoon* around with him wherever he worked because, while it was customary for white families to feed itinerant black laborers, they were not allowed to use the family's eating utensils.

Cocoa, Cocoa Beach

On U.S. Route 1 forty to forty-five miles southeast of Orlando

These bedroom communities for the Cape Canaveral space industry were probably named for either the *coco(a)* palm (coconut palm) or for the *coco(a)* plum, both of which are native to the area. But that didn't stop a local woman from concocting the story that the towns were named for the first postmistress's liking for *cocoa*. The postmistress, according to the May 7, 1925, issue of *The Cocoa Tribune*, offered a drink of the beverage to a surveyor, who was much impressed and told her that *Cocoa* might be a good name for the new town, then known as *Scrub City*.

The problem with this story is that the surveyor was hot and tired, and cocoa, hot or cold, isn't especially refreshing. The local woman told the newspaper that it was a "cooling drink" that was new to the surveyor. I wonder if, instead of *cocoa*, it was coconut milk.

Two Egg, Florida

The *coco* plum explanation of the name comes from the same issue of *The Cocoa Tribune*. Another local person told the reporter how an elderly English tourist, apparently diabetic, was told that the fruit of this evergreen tree could supply him with the constant supply of sugar he said he needed.

Frostproof

On State Alternate Route 27 fifty-five miles south-southwest of Orlando in the central Florida Peninsula

When the Post Office Department rejected the name Keystone City because it might be confused with Keystone Heights, another Florida post office, the townspeople submitted the name Lakemont—or at least they thought they did.

No one had taken Joe Carson seriously when he suggested *Frostproof.* It was just what you'd expect from an ambitious young man who had just gotten his real estate license and hoped to make his fortune buying and selling land for citrus groves. Walter Overocker listened to Carson make his case even as he wrote the name Lakemont on a government form and put the form in an envelope.

Before being sent to Washington, D.C., the form had to be signed by the postmaster in Fort Meade, 18 miles west. Carson said he'd be glad to take it there—he could use a good ride—and Overocker could see no reason why not. But a few weeks later he got a letter back from Washington, saying he had been appointed postmaster of the *Frostproof,* Florida, Post Office. Carson had crossed out Lakemont and written *Frostproof* beside it. Overocker was angry, but he didn't want to put off opening the post office any longer so he let it go.

The name did not come with a guarantee. Eight years after it became official (1886), the town had its first recorded *frost*—December 29, 1894, followed closely by its second—February 8, 1895. Orange and grapefruit growers who had put off picking until prices rose, lost a year's pay. Others saw the *frost* kill the buds on what would have been their first commercial crop the next fall.

After another killing *frost* in 1897, the townspeople, embarrassed by the misleading name, successfully petitioned to have it changed to *Lakemont.* But the powerful Carson family never gave up and managed to get it changed back to *Frostproof* in 1906.

Other Unusual Place-Names in Florida

Baseball City

On I-4 twenty-five miles southwest of Orlando

 his is the spring training home of the Kansas City Royals, who play at a theme park/ *baseball* stadium originally called Boardwalk and *Baseball.* Until a few years ago, it was also the home park of the *Baseball City* Royals, a Class A farm team.

Ghost Names

HUNDREDS OF AMERICAN PLACE-NAMES have been abandoned and forgotten since the Civil War—victims of flood, drought, economic downturn, the rerouting of a highway, or the whim of a local business or political leader. Here are some of the more unusual or humorous ones:

Defeated, Dreamer, and **Dumplin** (across the ridge from **Cornbread**), Tennessee; **PO** (for post office), Indiana; **Johnnycake** (more cornbread), Maryland; **Hangtown, Caution,** and **Bedbug,** California; **Frog Level**, South Carolina, now called *Prosperity* (page 212); **Success**, Michigan (it didn't live up to its name); **Nameless** and **Mutt and Jeff** (the two leading merchants in town brought to mind the cartoon characters), Texas; **Removal,** West Virginia, (because the post office had moved so often); **Dogtown,** California (because a woman there bred dogs and sold them to gold prospectors); **Joy, Delight, Success, Tonic, Integrity, Vim,** and **Star**, Nebraska; **Jack Ass Town**, Louisiana (named by a local politician who lost an election); **Bachelor**, North Dakota (because many of the patrons of the post office were single men); **Fearnot, Seek, Drab, Large, Lofty, Brave,** and **Decorum**, Pennsylvania; **Hot Spot**, Kentucky; **Spanktown**, New Jersey (for a doctor who habitually *spanked* his wife); **Henpeck** and the alliterative **Six-Shooter Siding**, New Mexico; **Teapot Dome**, Michigan (it was in the news!); **Seldom Seen** (this hillside neighborhood was always lost in the smoke cloud from the big copper smelter in Butte) and **Hill 57,** Montana (a Heinz Company salesman painted the company's signature number on a boulder in a Great Falls Indian ghetto); **Fleatown**, Maryland and Ohio; and **Monkeytown** and **Varietyville**, Rhode Island.

Another Rhode Island village, **Shun Pike**, was home to some people who had built a short section of road in order to *shun* the turn*pike* and avoid paying a toll. **Peddler's Run**, Maryland, is said to have been named by two travelers who stopped to water their horses at a stream. Suddenly, the stream began to redden. The travelers investigated and found a dead *peddler*—then, hearing a rustle overhead in the branches of a tall tree, his murderer.

Before Boardwalk and *Baseball*, Mattel Incorporated, the big toy company, ran a theme park here called Ringling Brothers, Barnum and Bailey Circus World, which opened in 1974. A Lakeland, Florida, librarian I spoke with said he thinks people called the locale Barnum City then. I think Circus City would have had a better ring to it.

Cantonment

On U.S. Route 29 twelve miles north of Pensacola in the far western part of the Florida Panhandle

a *cantonment* is a temporary quarters for soldiers. This is where General Andrew Jackson's troops camped in 1814 while chasing the British out of Florida, and again a few years later when Spain ceded Florida to the United States. Later, the encampment was known as *Cantonment* Clinch, for General Duncan L. Clinch, who orchestrated the forced exodus of the Seminoles from Florida.

Corkscrew

On the northern edge of Big Cypress Swamp 25 miles east-southeast of Cape Coral

an abandoned village and a vast swamp here take their name from the sharply winding *Corkscrew* River, which doesn't wind much anymore. A development company dug a straight channel for it in the 1950s and renamed it the Imperial River. The 11,000-acre swamp is part of the Everglades.

Stretching your legs in Corkscrew: The National Audubon Society maintains a 2.25-mile boardwalk through the heart of the swamp, which contains the largest undisturbed bald cypress forest in the U.S. Some of these 500-year-old trees are 130 feet high and 25 feet around. Visitors to the *Corkscrew* Swamp Sanctuary also see alligators, otters, owls, and wading birds, including the largest colony of wood storks (an endangered species) in the U.S. Another of the swamp's treasures is the tiny mosquito fish, which eats mosquito larvae—so thoroughly that most visitors don't bother with repellent. Location: Off County Road 846 twenty-five miles northeast of Naples. Telephone: (941) 657-3771. Admission charged.

Intercession City

On U.S. Route 17 twenty-one miles south-southwest of Orlando

he name *Intercession City* was chosen by members of the House of Faith, a Christian sect that settled here in the mid-1930s. *Merriam-Webster's Collegiate Dictionary* defines *intercession* as (1) "the act of interceding" and (2) "prayer, petition, or entreaty in favor of another." Previously, this little place was called *Interocean* because it is about halfway between the Atlantic Ocean and the Gulf of Mexico.

Sawdust

On State Route 65 twenty miles west of Tallahassee

here was a huge pile of *sawdust* outside a sawmill here. Farmers carted it away for bedding for their horse stalls and cowpens; children liked to slide down the pile; it occasionally caught fire.

Locals like to tell the story of the *Tallahassee Democrat* editor who set out to find out if there really was such a place in Gadsden County. Soon after turning south on State Route 65 off I-10, he asked an old man for directions. "Which part, South *Sawdust* or North *Sawdust*?" he replied.

Two Egg

On State Route 69 ten miles south of the point where Florida, Georgia, and Alabama meet

llen Morris, in his 1995 book *Florida Place Names*, retells the story of Walt Williams, a poor black farmer with 16 children. He didn't have enough money to give them an allowance, so as each child became old enough to barter at the general store, he gave the child a chicken. Traveling salesmen (they seem to turn up frequently in small-town naming stories) who overheard one of Williams's brood exchanging *two eggs* for a candybar began calling the community *Two-Egg* Crossing.

Yeehaw Junction

Near where State Route 60 and the Florida Turnpike cross north of Lake Okeechobee

though it sounds like the ultimate hillbilly name, *Yeehaw* comes from "yaha," the Seminole Indian word for wolf.

Experiment, Georgia

georgia

Between

On State Route 10 between Loganville and Monroe 33 miles east of Atlanta

b y the early 1850s, several families had settled near a stream six miles west of Monroe, the Walton County seat. Six miles farther along the east-west road across the county lay Loganville.

Once or twice a week, mail was brought out to the settlement from Monroe in a two-wheel, horse-drawn cart. When the community grew big enough to have its own post office, it needed a name to put on the application to the federal government. One name after another was rejected, as the topic seemingly came up in every conversation between neighbors. At last, the problem was brought to Monroe postmistress Mrs. George Schaeffer, whom everyone called "Miss Puss."

Miss Puss took the issue to heart, so much so that her husband soon wearied of hearing about it. The story goes that when he was completely fed up with the subject he pointed to a map and demanded impatiently, "It's halfway *between* Monroe and Loganville, call it *Between!*"

The name stuck, all the more so because the settlement also was *between* two other villages, Compton, six miles as the crow flies to the northeast, and Walnut Grove, six miles to the southwest.

This story is lovingly told in *Wayfarers in Walton* by Anita Sams.

Social Circle

On State Route 11 forty miles east of Atlanta

t he town had its beginnings in the 1820 Georgia land lottery, according to Sams. Joel Strickland drew Lot Number 96 in the First Land District of Walton County and soon sold the 250-acre tract to three speculators for $118. One of them, John Blackmon, gained complete control of the tract in 1824, having paid only 13 cents an acre when one of the original partners' share was sold at a sheriff's sale.

Blackmon bought and sold several other tracts in the new county, but it was Lot Number 96 that caught his fancy. A pretty stream flowed through it and the ground was fertile. There was an excellent spring, near which the major north-south road through the county intersected the most traveled route to the southwestern corner of the county. It would be a good spot for business, for it already was a place where travelers stopped to rest, where friends ran into each other, and where new acquaintances were made.

Blackmon added his own log cabin to the little patch of pioneer dwellings near the crossroads and donated a nearby parcel for a Methodist church. Soon the cabins, a small storehouse, a shop, and the meetinghouse gave the place the semblance of a village.

One day, according to local legend, a traveler who had stopped for a drink at the spring and was impressed with the pioneers' hospitality, remarked enthusiastically, "This sure is a *social circle.*"

On January 5, 1826, John Blackmon became *Social Circle's* first postmaster.

This may sound like a shaggy-dog story, but it's one local folks stand by.

Stretching your legs in Social Circle: Still a sociable little place, *Social Circle* has a wide main street with diagonal parking on both sides that gives it the feel of a Western town. The street that intersects it at the only stoplight follows the Hightower Trail, which once formed the boundary between the Cherokee and Creek Indian nations. The left wing of Union General William Tecumseh Sherman's army used the trail when it passed through *Social Circle* (November 17 and 18, 1864) on its incendiary march to the sea.

The Claude T. Wiley Company, the old-fashioned general store at the intersection, carries hurricane lamps, bib overalls, and crockery. Straw hats hang from the ceiling, and there's an assortment of locally crafted baskets hanging on one wall. The counters and glass display cases are original.

Social Circle has a number of mansions on the National Register of Historic Places.

Ty Ty

On U.S. Route 82 thirty miles east of Albany

Kenneth Krakow, author of *Georgia Place-Names*, couldn't pin this one down any tighter than these three possibilities: (1) The town, which was incorporated on August 28, 1883, was named by its first postmaster "Daddy" Jelks for the many railroad *ties* cut and sold here in the early days. (2) Like the creek that flows through it, the town was named for the white *titi* (leatherwood trees) and black *titi* (buckwheat trees) that grow along the stream's banks. (3) The name might have come from *tight-eye,* an old coinage for a thicket that is hard to see through.

Krakow notes that locals say there once was a newspaper correspondent in *Ty Ty* named Lulu Bobo.

Other Unusual Place-Names in Georgia

Ball Ground

At the intersection of State Route 372 and Alternate Route 5, roughly halfway between Atlanta and the Tennessee border

The Cherokee Indians loved "*ball*-play," a game similar to lacrosse. *Ball Ground*, according to local legend, was the site of a *ball*-play contest between the Cherokees and the Creeks to decide which tribe would have dominion over what is now Cobb, Paulding, and Polk counties. The Cherokees won.

Another Cherokee ballfield was at *Ballplay* in Etowah County, Alabama, less than a hundred miles west of here. Both Kentucky and Iowa have towns called *Balltown*. Minnesota has a *Ball Club* (see page 124).

(See *Chunky*, Mississippi, page 129, for another town named after a Native American sport.)

Benevolence

On a local road about 40 miles northwest of Albany

Early settler Thomas Coram gave five acres of his land to the town for a church and cemetery. The name was a way of thanking Coram for his *benevolence*.

Coram showed his generosity again a few years later when he volunteered to pick up the mail once a week—and without pay—at the post office in Cuthbert.

Enigma

On U.S. Route 82 ten miles east of Tifton and 50 miles east-southeast of Albany

The townspeople had the darnedest time coming up with a name for this place. So many different names were proposed and then rejected, "it just turned into an *enigma*," according to local historian Theren Griffin.

Experiment

At an exit off of U.S. Route 41 thirty miles south of Atlanta

No, this was not the site of some 19th-century utopian community. It's where the University of Georgia's agricultural *experiment* station is located.

Free Home

At the intersection of State Routes 372 and 20 thirty-five miles north of Atlanta

Captain Delevan Lively, Civil War veteran and the teacher at the one-room school in this crossroads community, offered *free* land to anyone who wanted to build a *home* on his land, with the stipulation that the property would revert back to him if the family moved away.

Gratis

On a local road that links State Route 138 and U.S. Route 78 about 40 miles east-northeast of Atlanta

the story is told that when the residents found out that no money was required to apply for a U.S. post office, they wanted to call their village *Free*. But postal authorities said this Latin synonym would make a better name. This bit of federal arm-twisting took place in 1893.

Another source says that one resident suggested the name *Free,* and another suggested *Free Gratis,* as if to double the effect of the name, and the feds chose *Gratis.*

Jot 'Em Down Store

On a local road three miles northeast of Blackshear (near Waycross) in the southeastern part of the state

the *Lum and Abner* radio show, which aired for 22 years starting in 1935, was centered around two small-town men who owned the *Jot 'Em Down Store* in fictitious Pine Ridge, Arkansas. The man who owned the store here, like millions of people in rural areas, evidently identified with the homespun characters on the 15-minute show that was a Monday night staple.

Texas also has a community named *Jot 'Em Down*. Locals tried to dub the general store with the name in 1936, but the owner resisted, saying it was undignified. Later when a *Jot 'Em Down* Gin Corporation opened nearby, the name stuck, says Texas toponymist Fred Tarpley.

Subligna

On a local road 35 miles south-southeast of Chattanooga, Tennessee

this odd and ugly-sounding name was made up by a Dr. Underwood, who knew Latin and wanted to leave his mark on the map: *sub* means "under" in Latin and *lignum* means "wood."

idaho

Arco

Where U.S. Route 26 joins U.S. Route 93 seventy miles west of Idaho Falls

The Butte County seat was named for:

    A) *Arco*, Italy

    B) A Count *Arco*, who visited the area sometime before 1882

    C) *Arco* Smith, operator of a stagecoach station in the early 1880s

    I don't know the correct answer, but I do know that before 1882 this location was called *Root Hog*, and that another Idaho town was once called *Hog'em*.

    In big letters on the bunker-like stone city hall, *Arco* proclaims itself as the "First City in the World Lit by Atomic Power." That happened on July 17, 1955, when Boiling Water Reactor No. 3 (BORAX-III), 18 miles east of here, generated 2,000 kilowatts of electricity for about two hours. The anniversary of this shocking event is observed annually here during "Atomic Days." (See *Atomic City*, Idaho, page 65.)

    Arco is also famous—although that may be too strong a word—for "the hill with numbers." Every year since 1920, the graduating class of *Arco* High School has painted its class year on the butte above the city.

Headquarters

On State Route 11 about 60 miles east-northeast of Lewiston

Before World War II, this was the bustling logging *headquarters* and company town of the Potlatch Corporation, a big timber company. There were 80 houses for workers' families, a hospital, school, and gymnasium. Now only about 20 people live here; the post office closed in 1994.

    Potlatch, on State Route 6 about 16 miles north of Moscow and 40 miles north-northeast of Lewiston, was also named for the timber company. Both towns are on the edge of the vast national forests that extend 375 miles north from Boise to the Canadian border and cover half of the territory within the state's borders.

    New Mexico also has a *Headquarters*.

Atomic City, Idaho

Stretching your legs in Headquarters: The way to find out what the company town was really like in its heyday is to spend an hour or so at the J. Howard Bradbury Memorial Logging Museum in nearby Pierce. It has a fascinating collection of logging tools and equipment, photographs, and maps, 90 percent of which came from *Headquarters.* Location: Main Street, Pierce. No phone. Admission free.

Other Unusual Place-Names in Idaho

Atomic City

On a county road that leads south from the intersection of U.S. Routes 20 and 26 forty-three miles west of Idaho Falls

t he townspeople dropped the name *Midway* a year after the first peacetime atomic reactor in the U.S. opened here in 1950.
(See *Arco,* Idaho, page 63.)

Stretching your legs in Atomic City: Experimental Breeder Reactor No. 1 (EBR-1) is open to the public from mid-June to mid-September. On view are two nuclear reactors, a control room, remote handling devices for radioactive materials, radiation-detection counters, and many other pieces of equipment that together explain how electricity is produced by splitting atoms. Location: A few minutes south of U.S. Route 20/26, Atomic City. Telephone: (208) 526-0050. Admission free.

The post office in *Atomic City* is worth seeing: It's at one end of an old Texaco station; a neon sign at the other end says "Bar."

Council

Fifty miles up U.S. Route 95 from Weiser and 75 miles as the crow flies north of Boise

t he valley in which this town is situated lies between what were once the hunting grounds of the Shahaptian Indians to the north and the Shoshone Indians to the south. This is where they met for their *councils.*

Culdesac

On State Route 95 twenty miles east of Lewiston

this was the word that came out of the mouth of Charles S. Mellon, president of the Northern Pacific Railroad, when he was shown why a branch line would have to terminate in the town. The Post Office Department would not accept the hyphenated (correct) version of the French word, *cul-de-sac*.

North Dakota briefly had a settlement named *End of the Track* in the early 1880s.

Declo

On State Route 81 forty-five miles east of Twin Falls and eight miles east of Burley

the *De*thles family and the *Clo*ughly family combined their names to come up with a name that sounds like a modern day corporate acronym.

Up in Benewah County, Idaho, the *Easts*, *Millers*, and *Daw*sons squeezed their names into the place-name *Emida*.

Malad City

On I-15 about ten miles north of the Utah border

a party of French-Canadian fur trappers who camped beside a stream here in 1824 became violently ill. One source says it was from drinking the water; another says it was from eating spoiled meat. The trappers identified the location on the map they made as Riviere aux *Malades*—crudely translated as "Sick River." The band of Mormons who settled here in 1864 apparently didn't speak French and unknowingly named their community "Sick City" after the river.

May

Off of U.S. Route 93 about 60 miles south of Salmon in the sparsely populated east-central part of the state

the wife of the first postmaster (1897) chose the name because the government requested a short name, and the application for a postmark was made in *May* of 1897.

Oreana

On a gravel road just south of State Route 78 and 40 miles south-southwest of Boise

this is a cattleman's term for an unbranded but earmarked calf. The community was named in 1884 by Harry Olson, who operated a hotel.

Tensed

On U.S. Route 95 halfway between Moscow and Coeur d'Alene

the town was called DeSmet, after the Jesuit missionary Father Pierre De Smet, when its residents applied for a post office in 1914. But postal authorities rejected the name because there already was a DeSmet in Idaho. So the residents reapplied, submitting the name *Temsed*—DeSmet spelled backwards. A clerical error back in Washington gave the name an emotional twist.

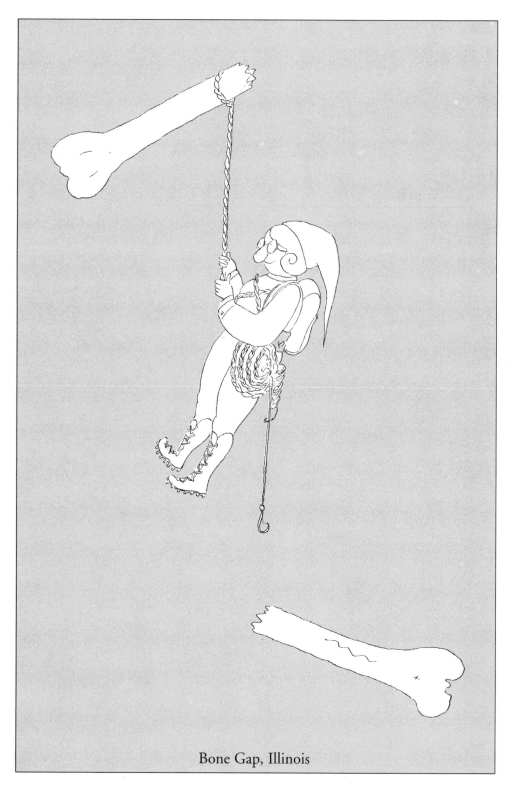

Bone Gap, Illinois

illinois

Preemption

On U.S. Route 67 about 12 miles south of Rock Island

before there was a *preemption* law in the state, pioneers were at risk of losing their land to claim jumpers and moneyed land speculators. Conflicts over claims were a part of frontier life, and they occasionally resulted in violence—even murder.

The early settlers of this prime farmland near the Mississippi River didn't have titles to their land, because the state hadn't offered it for sale yet. When the land did come on the market, the speculators could easily outbid the cash-poor farmers. The claim jumpers preyed upon already-improved but unoccupied land.

The people of *Preemption* and some other nearby townships formed a mutual protection association sometime before 1844. One of the settlers, Hopkins Boone, was chosen recorder, and he set down in writing the size, shape, and location on the prairie of each claim. Claims were limited to what was considered a reasonable amount of land by the members of the association.

When a claim was "jumped," the association dispatched a committee to order the claim jumper to "leave the diggins." This happened twice before the land in *Preemption* township came on the market on October 30, 1844, and both times the claim jumper departed peacefully.

The settlers chose a name for their township that reminded everyone of what they went through to hold on to their land, homes, and barns before there was a *preemption* law to protect them.

Other Unusual Place-Names in Illinois

Bone Gap

On a county road in east central Edwards County 40 miles northwest of Evansville, Indiana

around 1815, a party of woodsmen found a pile of human *bones* and a number of Indian mounds near a *gap* in the forest.

Disco

On a county road six miles from the Mississippi River near the Hancock-Henderson County line

this farming community was named exactly a hundred years before John Travolta's hit 1976 movie *Saturday Night Fever* made *disco* a household word. But the name has absolutely nothing to do with dancing. It probably comes from a description of the town's location, in a flat, *discus*-shaped valley.

Future City

Just north of the Mississippi River city of Cairo at the state's southern tip

no grand plan here, just the local dialect's slurring of Futrell's City, a subdivision of house lots owned by a man named Futrell.

Grand Detour

On State Route 2 between the cities of Oregon and Dixon and 30 miles southwest of Rockford

here, in the town where tractor genius John Deere perfected the steel plow, the Rock River takes a *grand detour* to the northwest before looping back to its southwesterly course to the Mississippi. The name is credited to French traders. English-speaking pioneers called the river feature the Great Bend.

Stretching your legs in Grand Detour: The "self-polishing" steel plow opened the prairies to modern agriculture. Had John Deere not invented it in 1837, many homesteaders would have given up in frustration and returned home. The heavy Midwestern soil clung to the cast-iron plows the farmers had brought with them from back East. They had to stop every few minutes to scrape the soil from the plowshare. Deere took the agony out of their work, and he did something else no American blacksmith had ever attempted; he manufactured his steel plows. Before, each plow was custom-made. Deere's different approach speeded up westward expansion. The agricultural genius's story is told in words, pictures, and artifacts at the John Deere Historic Site, where you can visit a recreation of his blacksmith shop and his home, as well as the archaeological site of his blacksmith shop. And to give you a feel for the land those early Midwestern farmers had to tame, there are two acres of virgin prairie at the Historic Site. Address: 8393 South Main Street, Grand Detour. Telephone: (815) 652-4551. Admission charged.

New Design

On a local road a few miles south of Waterloo and 25 miles south-southwest of St. Louis

i n July 1786, James Lemen, his wife Catherine, and their 11 children arrived by flatboat at Kaskaskia on the Mississippi River. Starting in Wheeling (now in West Virginia), they had floated down the Ohio River before joining the Mississippi at Cairo, Illinois. James soon announced that he had a *new design* (intention) to start a settlement about 25 miles north of Kaskaskia as the crow flies—and he promptly did so. Soon *New Design* was the biggest white settlement in Illinois. It was a very pious place—six of Lemen's seven sons were preachers—and its residents were early opponents of slavery.

Oblong

On State Route 33 eighteen miles west of the Wabash River and the Indiana border

a round 1830, the first settlers looked out on a tract of tallgrass prairie that was *oblong*-shaped, its borders being defined by a number of small streams.

A headline writer once had some fun with this place-name and another in Illinois, *Normal* (named for the teacher-training, or *normal*, school there). The 36-point type head read: "*Oblong* Man Weds *Normal* Woman." In neighboring Iowa, a headline using place-names once read: "*Fertile* Man Weds *Manly* Woman."

Correct, Indiana

indiana

Aroma

On State Route 13 near where Tipton, Hamilton, and Madison Counties converge 20 miles north-northeast of Indianapolis

Something smelled mighty good on that day in 1836 when this little farm center was named. What exactly it was has been lost to history—but there are some hunches. Ronald L. Baker suggests in *From Needmore to Prosperity: Hoosier Place Names in Folklore and History* that the *aroma* might have come from flowering trees or from just-mowed hay.

An article in the Tuesday, February 13, 1973, edition of *The Indianapolis News* says that William Haworth, the owner of the general store, chose the name, and it was the heady *aroma* of flowers in the nearby woods that filled his nostrils that day. That and the smell of fresh-picked corn—in the air around the Citizens Grain elevator—are still the dominant summer *aroma*s in *Aroma*.

Some farmers scoffed at the name in the early days and nicknamed the town *Toadlope* for the loping frogs on Duck Creek. Maybe *Aroma* sounded too prissy, or maybe the real story of the name has nothing to do with William Haworth but with the chicken manure that the farmers spread on their fields or the odor emanating from their hog pens.

There is a town named *Aromas* in Monterey County, California. The name comes from the Spanish word *aromitas*, which means little odors, and probably refers to a hot spring that stinks of sulfur.

Easytown

On a county road 20 miles northwest of Terre Haute and two miles from the Illinois border

Locals say this coal-mining community took its name sometime after 1912 from a resident named *Izzy* Posoco. *Izzytown* was in its prime during Prohibition. It had a "blind tiger" (a speakeasy), and there were a few residents who sold liquor illegally out of their homes.

The biggest business in town was Joe Pizzola's Grocery, which was sometimes called "the big store" to distinguish it from Pete Brazzale's store. Pizzola was murdered while playing cards in the pool hall that was attached to his store. In what sounds like a gangland slaying, two men quietly entered the store, asked the nearest person to point out Pizzola, and then plugged him as he reached for his gun.

Rough town, this *Easytown*!

Gnaw Bone

Five miles east of Nashville and 16 miles east of Bloomington

early one morning in 1874, Jim Schrougham stopped by John Ayers's sawmill on his way to Columbus. When Ayers came to the door, he was *gnawing* on a *bone*.

Seeing that his wagon was empty, Ayers asked Schrougham if he would take a piece of machinery to Columbus with him and have it repaired. That night, when Schrougham returned with the machinery, Ayers again was *gnawing* on a *bone* when he came to the door.

This amused Schrougham so much, he told his friend, "This place ought to be called *Gnaw Bone*." The incident quickly became part of the folklore of the area, and the name stuck.

The Brown County Historical Society stands by that story even though there are a half dozen other explanations for the name. And these same local historians say it is absolutely nonsense that *Gnaw Bone* is a corruption of the French place-name *Narbonne*, as some have said in print. Extensive research shows that French-speaking people never settled in Brown County, they assert.

New York has a place called *Suckabone,* an anglicization of an Algonquian word.

Stretching your legs in Gnaw Bone: A few miles south of *Gnaw Bone* on State Route 135 is a road marker topped with a stern-looking stone head. It was carved in 1851 by Henry Cross, a farmer and a carver of tombstones who gained a considerable reputation for his avocation. Back then, all able-bodied men in Brown County were required to spend six days a year working off their road tax. The road superintendent decided that Cross, instead of hauling gravel and filling chuckholes, should carve three road markers from sandstone. Two of them have been lost, but the one still stands in the village of *Stone Head,* right where the road takes a sharp turn toward *Story.*

Pikes Peak

On a county road in southeastern Brown County seven miles south of Gnaw Bone (see page 74)

unlike the rest of Indiana, Brown County has some big hills, but none you'd call a *peak*. According to the Brown County Historical Society, this dot on the map was named not for a summit but for the folly of the Ward family.

Patriarch James Ward got gold fever a few years before the Civil War and packed his family and all their belongings in a prairie schooner and headed for Colorado. A sign on the side of the covered wagon read "*Pikes Peak* or Bust."

When the Wards reached Madison, Indiana, where they had intended to board a barge for the trip down the Ohio River to Missouri, they were overcome with homesickness and turned back. Soon after they returned to Brown County, James Ward opened a store, which became the brunt of a community joke. Whenever anyone needed to go there for supplies, they said, "I'm going to *Pikes Peak*." The name was then applied to the village that grew up around the store.

Santa Claus

On State Route 245 nine miles south of I-64 and 11 miles north of the Ohio River and the state of Kentucky

according to the Town of *Santa Claus*, which sent me a two-page, single-spaced handout mostly about "the exciting fun-filled center of recreation [*Santa Claus*] is today," *Santa Claus* was named on Christmas Eve, 1852, when a child whose parents had dragged her along with them to a meeting on the naming of the village, heard sleigh bells outside the church and exclaimed, "*Santa!* It's *Santa Claus!*" Right then and there, the people of the community recognized they had the name that eluded them in meetings all that fall.

There were no other Christmas incidents until 1933, when a lawyer named Milton Harris gave up his practice in Vincennes, Indiana, and moved to *Santa Claus* to manufacture decorative sleighs. He also built a souvenir shop and other medieval-style buildings, which attracted several toy manufacturers.

Next, the Curtiss Candy Company of Chicago opened an outlet with a candy castle on the roof. That development was followed by a roadside park with a 40-ton statue of *Santa*. Things kept snowballing after World War II, when Evansville industrialist Louis J. Koch built a full-fledged theme park called *Santa Claus* Land. Today Koch's sons call their sprawling theme and amusement park Holiday World.

Golf courses and vacation homes are the latest developments. Some of the houses are oriented around a string of lakes named Christmas, Noel, and Holly. Street names include Jolly, Chimes, and Three Kings and, for those other holidays, there is New Years Eve Street, Good Friday Boulevard, and Easter Circle. "If present trends continue," the town's promo sheet says, "*Santa Claus* will be bigger and better than ever in the years to come."

Every December, the post office here does a brisk business in envelopes with the *Santa Claus* postmark.

Trevlac

On State Route 45 ten miles northwest of Bloomington

aColonel Calvert came from Cleveland in 1900 to develop a resort on Lake Lemon. By 1905, he had built a hotel and cottages, a bath house, and a clubhouse near the village of Richards. That year, the Illinois Central Railroad was laying track across northern Brown County, and the Colonel recognized the promotional value for his resort if the local station bore his name. He made more than one trip to Indianapolis to lobby railroad officials about naming the local station, and renaming the village Calvert. When the railroad discovered that there already was a town named Calvert in Indiana, the Colonel suggested the name *Trevlac*—Calvert spelled backwards.

Richards officially became *Trevlac* in 1907, but the resort soon failed and Colonel Calvert and his wife moved back to Cleveland. The village lives on, but trains no longer stop at the *Trevlac* station.

Backward Spellings

COLONEL CALVERT wasn't the only person who turned a place-name around to get it on the map. **Retsof** caught my attention as I scanned the map of New York for unusual names; **Nivloc**, Nevada, jumped out as I ran my eyes along the knife-edge Nevada-California border. Others include: **Remlik**, Virginia; **Rolyat, Reclaw, Remlig, Sacul, Tinrag,** and **Maharg**, Texas; **Remlap**, Alabama (the Palmer family is also honored eight miles south of there with *Palmerdale*); **Nagrom**, Washington; **Revloc,** Pennsylvania; **Retrop**, Oklahoma; **Trebloc**, Mississippi, and the unusual instance of a first name, **Lebam**, Washington.

Pekin, Maryland, had to change its name to **Nikep** because it kept getting *Pekin*, Indiana's mail (see page 107). Years ago, *Mount Tabor*, South Carolina, kept getting *Mount Tabor*, North Carolina's mail, so the southern cousin dropped the "Mount" and spelled Tabor backwards to become **Robat.**

Another South Carolina village, **Enola,** originally was named **Alone.** The villagers apparently grew tired of feeling isolated. Mail for a central Missouri hamlet was addressed **None,** for "no name," until a local woman suggested the Biblical name **Enon**.

People in a remote western Colorado locale wanted to name their new town **Range**. When told that name had already been taken, they turned it around to create the gothic sounding **Egnar.** In Brewster County, Texas, **Sunset** seemed like a good name until locals learned there was a *Sunset* in Montague County. So they settled for **Tesnus**.

Adaven, Nevada, may be the only town name in the U.S. which is a state name spelled backwards.

See *Tensed*, Idaho, page 67, for a backwards spelling that was misspelled.

Stretching your legs in Trevlac: Pastoral Brown County has been an artist colony since before World War I. Today most of the galleries and crafts shops are in Nashville, the county seat. One of the leading lights in the early years was renowned Indiana landscape painter T. C. Steele. His home ("House of the Singing Winds") and studio, located eight and a half miles south of Bloomington, are now a state historic site. Steele's paintings are on display, and there are extensive flower gardens based on his wife Selma's original designs. Next door is a 90-acre nature preserve with hiking trails that take you to the scenes Steele painted. Address: 4220 T. C. Steele Road, Belmont. Telephone: (812) 988-2785. Admission free.

Other Unusual Place-Names in Indiana

Advance

On State Route 75 sixteen miles northwest of Indianapolis

this town of 500 within commuting distance of Indianapolis was called Osceola (for the Seminole chief) for its first 52 years, from 1820 to 1872. It was changed to *Advance* on September 24, 1873, because the townspeople desperately wanted a post office and there already was a town and post office named Osceola in Indiana (in St. Joseph County). *Advance* supposedly is a commendatory name chosen to advertise the economic *advancement* the coming of the railroad would bring to the community.

Correct

On U.S. Route 421 four miles south of Versailles in the southeastern part of the state

Correct's name is an error. Sometime in the early 19th century, this hamlet needed a name for its new post office. Halley's Comet was on a lot of people's minds at the time, so William Will, the Versailles postmaster, recommended the name *Comet*. But in Will's handwriting, *Comet* looked like *Correct*, and that was the name postal officials assigned.

Kelp

Within the boundaries of Brown County State Park about 15 miles east of Bloomington

this is a classic case of accidental naming: One day in 1896, Lon Allison, the postmaster in Nashville, the Brown County seat, received a letter from the U.S. Post Office Department in Washington, D.C., asking him to recommend a short name for a post office that would soon open in a place called Hobb's Creek. A boy named Harry *Kelp* walked into the post office while Allison was reading the letter. Allison liked the boy, who had done odd jobs for him, and asked him if he objected to having a nearby post office named after him. He said no and gained a good story to tell about himself for the rest of his life.

Pinhook

On a county road six miles west of Bedford in the south-central part of the state

P*inhook*, in the mid-19th century, was a code name for a town where you could buy illegal whiskey—at least here in Indiana. A store owner came up with the scheme of selling his customers a *pin* at an outrageously inflated price and then giving him a glass (or bottle) of whiskey as a premium. No law was broken, because the whiskey was free. According to a local legend re-told by Ronald L. Baker, the *pin* used was either a common *pin* bent for use as a fish hook or a long ladies hat *pin*, bent and hooked over the edge of the glass.

When someone said, "I'm going to *Pinhook*," you knew he needed a drink. Baker lists three towns that used this code name in his book.

Solitude

On State Route 69 eighteen miles west of Evansville in the extreme southwest corner of the state

n*o one knows for sure how this tight-knit little farming community got its name, so they assume the obvious: because it was a quiet, isolated place. Nothing disturbing ever happened here—no scandals, no crime, no big fire. A veteran Posey County police officer said he'd never heard of an arrest being made in *Solitude* when he was interviewed a few years back by a United Press International reporter.

Probably the last time *Solitude* failed to live up to its name was in 1864, when Andrew Johnson made a campaign stop here. He spoke from a stump beside the covered bridge that spans Big Creek.

iowa

Correctionville

On U.S. Route 20 thirty miles east of Sioux City

When Iowa was being surveyed soon after it became a state in 1846, the plan was for all townships to be six miles square. To account for the curvature of the earth, the surveyors stair-stepped the longitudinal lines every sixty miles. Otherwise, southerly townships would have more real estate than northerly ones. The jogs were known as *correction* lines.

The new town that was platted on the open prairie just east of the big bend in the Little Sioux River in September of 1855 happened to be right on top of one of these lines.

Locals claim *Correctionville* is the longest single-word town name in the United States.

Stretching your legs in Correctionville: You can see for yourself how the main street of the town jogs to follow the *correction* line. Heading north on Central Street in the business district you must turn right on Fifth Street, and then, after only half a block, left on North Main Street to continue crossing the town.

What Cheer

On State Route 21 about 18 miles east of Oskaloosa and 65 miles east-southeast of Des Moines

Locals pronounce it *"Whacheer,"* flatly and with little inflection, as if they've forgotten that the name comes from the old English salutation *"Wot cher,"* meaning "How are you?" in the question form and "I hope you are of good *cheer!*" in the exclamation form. The greeting is found in Act 1, Scene 1 of Shakespeare's *The Tempest.* The master of the ship calls for the boatswain, who responds, "Heere Master, *What Cheere?*" It is still used on London's poorer streets, as in *"Wot cher,* mate!"

According to a town history, the salutation was in common use by the English and Welsh miners who were drawn to the area in the 1850s by the abundance of shallow, easily minable coal. Major Joseph Andrews, the town's leading politician, had heard it in Providence, Rhode Island, where

What Cheer, Iowa

he once lived, and in 1876 pushed for adopting *What Cheer* as the town's name. It was Providence's motto because the Narragansett Indians had greeted the city's founder, religious heretic Roger Williams, with "What cheer, netop" when he arrived here from Boston in 1636. The Indians had picked up the salutation from the English settlers they traded with in the Massachusetts Bay Colony. *Netop* was their word for "friend."

Other Unusual Place-Names in Iowa

Agency

On U.S. Route 34 seven miles east of Ottumwa in the southeastern part of the state

Wherever you see this name on the map you be can be pretty sure it was originally the site of a federal Indian *Agency* office. This was Sac-Fox territory.

Coin

In the southwestern corner of the state about five miles from the Missouri state line and 30 miles from Nebraska

Coin was named by a Wabash Railroad surveyor who found a fifty-cent piece while digging a hole. The *coin* proved to be a charm, because the railroad soon brought prosperity to the town, which was a major junction between Omaha and Kansas City.

Confidence

Just west of the Rathbun Reservoir in Wayne County in the southern part of the state

People were *confident* in the 1850s that the railroad would bring prosperity to their village. But the railroad was instead built through Millerton, a bigger town about 15 miles away. *Confidence* never even got a paved road.

Nearby *Promise City* did a better job of living up to its name. Still, you had to be a patient person to see it that way. Named in 1856, it finally got a railroad, the Keokuk and Western, in 1880, and kept growing until 1913, when its population peaked at 500. Today about a hundred people live there.

Cylinder

On U.S. Route 18 fourteen miles west of Algona in the northwestern part of the state

It is said that when some early settlers attempted to cross a stream at high water on a makeshift barge, the barge sank and the engine (probably steam), or *cylinder*, separated from it and was never found. The settlers named the stream *Cylinder* Creek, and when the railroad came through in 1890, they named the depot after it.

Diagonal

Where State Route 66 meets County Road J23 sixteen miles north of the Missouri border

The town was platted about 1889 at the place where the Chicago Great Western and the Humeston and Shenandoah Railroads intersect—*diagonally*.

Gravity

On State Route 148 in Taylor County in the southwestern part of the state

The topocentric residents of this village felt that with the Washington Center School located here, the village was at the center of *gravity* of Washington Township. That changed in the late 1880s when the village was moved two miles east to be on the railroad line.

Stretching your legs in Gravity: If you're heading north on U.S. Route 71, you might want to make a side trip through Stanton to get a glimpse of "The World's Largest Coffeepot," reputed to hold 640,000 cups. Actually, it's the Stanton water tower, which has a spout and a handle and is painted with brightly colored stenciled designs to resemble a Swedish coffeepot. It honors native daughter Virginia Christine, known to millions of Americans as Mrs. Olson, the kindly Swedish lady who taught newlyweds the secret of making a good cup of coffee on the Folger's Coffee commercials. Location: Stanton is on U.S. Route 34 six miles west of where it crosses U.S. 71.

kansas

Home

On U.S. Route 36 six miles east of Marysville in the northeastern part of the state

When this place grew big enough to warrant a name, a petition was circulated, and then a meeting was held where it was decided to name it Dexter after a leading citizen. But the Post Office Department nixed that because there already was a Dexter in the state. Another meeting was held and other surnames were suggested—Blockerville, Duvertown, Lewisville. But those prominent men—more modest than Thomas Dexter and wise enough to realize that choosing one citizen's name over others would result in jealousies—declined the honor. So it was decided to name the town after the first post office, which was known as the *Home* station, because it was in Gottlieb Messell's *home.*

The mail came into town on the St. Joseph Western Railroad. It was taken "on the fly"—tossed overboard in a pouch from a moving train— because the "fast mail" didn't stop until it reached the next town, Marysville. Messell, who became postmaster on February 19, 1874, put the mail in a wooden box, basket, or even a bureau drawer, which his neighbors had to sort through to find their letters.

Over the next ten to twenty years, *Home* grew rapidly and locals started referring to it as *Home* City, which they still do today. And before the automobile changed the railroad economy, boosters called it "The Biggest Little City in Kansas" (*Protection*, Kansas was known as "The Biggest Little Town in Kansas").

Stretching your legs in Home: U.S. Route 36 follows the old Pony Express route. Six miles west of here in Marysville is the Pony Express Museum, as well as a handsome bronze statue of one of the mail service's riders racing across the plains. The museum is housed in a horse barn used by the riders. Address: 106 South 8th Street, Marysville. Telephone: (913) 562-3825. Admission charged.

Fifteen miles farther west is the Hollenberg Pony Express Station, the only one on the entire route in its original, unaltered state. The station, where riders picked up fresh horses, was built in 1857 at the point where the Pony Express Route met the Oregon Trail. Location: On State Route 243 two miles northeast of Hanover.

Home, Kansas

Liberal

On U.S. Route 54 in the southwestern part of the state near the Oklahoma border

Once upon a time, there was a pioneer in these parts who let travelers take water from his well, free of charge. This was considered highly unusual and generous; the pioneer was described as "a mighty *liberal* man" and the well was known as "the *liberal* well."

For the most part, people in *Liberal* are still pretty generous, but they're hardly *liberal*, according to a *liberal Liberal* librarian. They're all Dole Republicans.

Stretching your legs in Liberal: A few years back some enterprising local business leaders declared *Liberal* the hometown of Dorothy—although no hometown is mentioned in *The Wizard of Oz*— and they fixed up a 1907 farmhouse to look like the one in the movie. Each year about 25,000 Oz fans visit the house. They have to make a special trip, because, as Carolyn Brown, the curator of Dorothy's House, explains, "*Liberal* is not on the way to anywhere." Address: 567 Yellow Brick Road, Liberal. Telephone: (316) 624-7624.

Protection

Just off U.S. Route 160/183 in western Comanche County 50 miles southeast of Dodge City and 12 miles north of the Oklahoma border

There is no question that the town was named in 1884, but just what form of *protection* its citizens found here is the subject of folklore. Two explanations display a faulty historical memory. One has it that during an Indian scare, the early settlers found *protection* in a fort above Bluff Creek. That's true, but the uprising was in 1885, a year after the *Protection* Town Company filed a charter at the state capitol in Topeka, according to the Comanche County Historical Society.

The other legend holds that the name came from the People's Grand *Protective* Union, which opposed prohibition in Kansas. But a prohibition amendment was adopted in 1880, and the group quickly passed out of existence. Also, it was unlikely that the Union's name would have been resurrected four years later by *Protection*'s founders, who, according to the town's newspaper, the *Protection Echo*, made "temperance one of the corner stones on which to build."

More likely the town was named after a *protective* tariff, which was hotly debated during the 1884 presidential election campaign. Republican candidate James Blaine, who favored the tariff, was defeated by Democrat Grover Cleveland, who favored free trade. The town's founders were staunch Republicans.

According to another legend, the pioneers felt that the town could provide *protection* against cattlemen who might try to drive out farmers and homesteaders.

Other explanations were based on the town's location: With creeks on two sides, the town site was said to be *protected* from prairie fires. Indians believed the valley location provided *protection* from tornadoes.

(See *Protection*, New York, page 171.)

Other Unusual Place-Names in Kansas

Agenda

On State Route 148 fifty-five miles northwest of Manhattan and 16 miles south of the Nebraska border

this once-bustling stop on the Chicago, Kansas and Nebraska Railroad (later known as the Rock Island Line) was called Neva until the railroad put pressure on the citizenry to change the name. It was causing confusion with another C, K & N station named *Neva*.

Legend has it that when the townspeople met in 1888 to adopt a new name, *Agenda* was chosen because of an amusing coincidence: Just as the moderator was about to announce the *agenda* item on the name change, someone raised his hand and asked, "What's next on the *agenda?*"

It's a pretty slender story, but it persists.

Others say the town had an Indian Agency office, and back then some people called such an office an *agenda*.

Buttermilk

In southern Comanche County seven miles north of the Oklahoma border

this name was chosen about 1913 for Quincy *"Buttermilk"* Winningham, the local blacksmith. A wheat harvester named Albert Oller had helped set up Winningham in business. He depended on him to keep his threshing rig going. The first winter Winningham lived alone in his shop, and Oller brought *buttermilk* to him as a neighborly gesture. For years afterward, Oller recalled how he had never seen a man drink so much *buttermilk*.

Flush

On a county road 15 miles northeast of Manhattan and 40 miles northwest of Topeka

i thought this might be another place-name having to do with a poker game (see *Midnight*, Mississippi), this time for the hand that won. Or by a homesteader who felt *flush* with the promise of a new life. In fact, it was named for a German settler whose surname was *Floersch*, which turned into mush after the U.S. Post Office Department got hold of it.

Neutral

Five miles north of Baxter Springs in the southeast corner of the state

before Kansas became a state, this part of the territory was known as Indian *Neutral* Lands. The post office and the village had been known as Brush Creek until the name was changed to *Neutral* on July 27, 1883. There was also a *Neutral City* in what was to become Cherokee County; it got its own post office in 1867. *Neutral City* was a stagecoach stop on the road between Fort Scott, Kansas, and Fort Gibson, Oklahoma.

Tribune

On State Route 96 smack in the center of Greeley County and 15 miles from the Colorado border

look at any map of Kansas; bisect it north and south, and then run your eyes all the way out to the Colorado border. There you'll see a nearly empty county with only two towns. All three names—the county's, *Greeley*, and the towns', *Horace* and *Tribune*, celebrate the same man, Horace Greeley, the influential publisher of the *New York Tribune* who was the Democratic candidate for President in 1872, the year Republican Ulysses S. Grant was elected to a second term.

Best-known for his expansionist advice, "Go west, young man, go West," Greeley was an abolitionist, a champion of women's rights, and a union man—and obviously much admired by the farmers and ranchers here on the western High Plains.

Oddville, Kentucky

kentucky

Monkeys Eyebrow

Near Ohio River Lock and Dam Number 53 and the southern tip of Illinois in the far-western part of Kentucky

back before the turn of the century, locals thought the tall grass growing on the ridge of crescent-shaped Beeler Hill resembled the *eyebrows* of a *monkey* (see *Porcupine*, South Dakota). People from Needmore, two miles east and a commercial rival, agreed with that and added that the Ray brothers' general store and house, which were at the base of the hill, were the *monkey's* eyes.

A man who lived near the store once was asked why he patronized the Needmore store. "I ain't buyin' no grub at no place that looks like a *monkey's eyebrow*," he huffed.

These anecdotes are retold in Robert Rennick's *Kentucky Place Names* (a principal source of information about Kentucky place-names). He also says that, according to a WPA researcher, there was a local resident, one Robert Arivett, who was always finding fault with the hamlet and his neighbors, reviling them with remarks about how much they all resembled, or acted like, *monkeys*.

Poor *Monkeys Eyebrow*!

Klondike, a town at the southern tip of Illinois, for years was known as *Monkeys Eyebrow*, because it was long and narrow with all its houses on a strip of land between the main road and the railroad tracks. Klondike is only 20 miles downriver from *Monkeys Eyebrow*, Kentucky, so the description may have been a regionalism.

Other Unusual Place-Names in Kentucky

Dwarf

At the intersection of State Routes 476 and 550 eighty miles southeast of Lexington

the Combs brothers were known in these parts for the tunnel Sam and Felix cut through 172 feet of solid rock using only hand drills and gunpowder. The tunnel carried water to their mill, and the hamlet's original name was Tunnel Mill. The Combses were ultimately even more widely known for the fact that a third brother, Jeremiah, or "Short Jerry," was a *dwarf.* The name dates from 1883.

Eighty Eight

On State Route 90 thirty-three miles east of Bowling Green

althoug *Eighty Eight* is about seven and a half miles from Glasgow, the nearest big town, one of the explanations residents like to give for the name is that it is *8.8* miles from there. Another explanation is that the first postmaster Dabney Nunnally either was a poor reader or had bad penmanship, and said that if the hamlet had a number for a name it would be easier for him. In either case, the Post Office Department stipulated that. the name be spelled out.

A remarkable coincidence occurred here on Election Day in 1948. When all the ballots had been counted, there were *eighty-eight* votes for Thomas Dewey and *eighty-eight* for Harry S. Truman.

Kelat

On State Route 1032 thirty-three miles north-northeast of Lexington

talk about accidental naming! When the townspeople learned the name Fairview was already taken, T. J. Smith, a geography teacher, cracked open a world atlas and let his index finger land on a town in Baluchistan (now Pakistan).

Mummie

On State Route 30 fifty miles southeast of Lexington

the name is said to have been chosen in 1915 to commemorate the discovery here of a *mummified* human body by the community's early settlers.

Oddville

On U.S. Route 62 seven miles north of Cynthiana and 30 miles north of Lexington

robert Rennick says that when storekeeper Hezekiah Whitaker applied for a post office in 1851, he passed along the Reverend J. C. Crow's recommendation that it be named Mt. Washington. The feds rejected the name, saying there were already enough Washingtons in the nation. So Crow, and perhaps others, desiring something peculiar (see *Peculiar*, Missouri), proposed *Oddville*. (See *Odd*, West Virginia, page 252.)

Ordinary

On State Route 32 forty miles southwest of Huntington, West Virginia

the townspeople were having trouble coming up with a name for their new post office in the summer of 1884, when one of them suggested that the word *ordinary* would be fitting. After all, it was just an *ordinary* place.

That's the legend, and Elliott County historian John Stegall says it may be true. But it's also true that his great-great-great-grandfather, George W. Carter, the first postmaster, came from Virginia, where *Ordinary* was already in use as a place-name. *Ordinary* was another word for "tavern" in Colonial times (see *Ordinary*, Virginia), and some have said that explains this name. But Stegall doesn't think there ever was a tavern here.

Pippa Passes

At the intersection of State Routes 899 and 1697 about 20 miles from the Virginia border

named for the poem by Robert Browning with the famous line: "God's in His heaven—All's right with the world!" *Pippa Passes* is the home of Alice Lloyd College, which was founded in the early 1900s with contributions from the Robert Browning Societies of New England. Lloyd herself was a devotee of Browning's poetry.

Dozens of American towns are named for literary characters or authors. *Pippa Passes* is one of a handful named for the literary work itself. *Ben Hur*, California, and *Ben Hur*, Virginia, which take their name from the hugely popular 19th century novel, are two other examples.

Quality

On State Route 106 twenty miles northwest of Bowling Green

Chosen in 1894, this name supposedly recognizes the high *quality* of both the people and the valley they settled.

Regina

On U.S. 460 twenty-five miles from the easternmost point of the state

no one but a Canadian would pronounce the woman's name *Regina* with a long *i*, so eastern Kentuckians believe the story that this village was named at the suggestion of a traveling salesman for his hometown in Saskatchewan.

Relief

On State Route 172 in eastern Morgan County 25 miles from the West Virginia border

This Appalachian hamlet got its own post office in 1859, and people thought it was a *relief* not to have to go all the way to West Liberty—thirteen miles away on a winding road—to get their mail. Another explanation is that this was a rest stop along the arduous wagon route between West Liberty and Paintsville.

Rowdy

On State Route 476 in northern Perry County 35 miles from the Virginia border

If you're looking for trouble, this is the place. *Rowdy* is on the *Rowdy* Branch of Troublesome Creek and only eight and a half miles up the road from *Hazard*. Locals like to tell strangers that the community was named not for the creek but for the character of its people. "We're a *rowdy* bunch, all right," chuckles former postmistress Erma Stacey.

louisiana

Fort Necessity

On State Route 4 about 33 miles southeast of Monroe

There was never a *fort* here, just Jesse Moore's store, which he named *Fort Necessity*. Moore, who came to Louisiana from Virginia soon after the Civil War, had in mind the Pennsylvania *fort* where George Washington suffered a gentleman's defeat in the French and Indian War, but he was also punning—the store was an outpost where you could buy *necessities*. He alluded to this in an ad he took out in the local newspaper when he opened the store with supplies he had purchased in New Orleans: "I've whiskey, rum and some little brandy. And something to please the children called sugar candy . . ." went his sales ditty.

Franklin Parish folks also point out that the post office in the store was a *necessity* in the days when the nearest other one was 11 miles away in Winnsboro.

Start

Fourteen miles east of Monroe in the northern part of the state

This tiny gas stop on I-20 didn't have a name until Hans Clausen got fed up with being postmaster of nearby Crew Lake. The year was 1918, and after trying hard to find a replacement, Clausen put all the mail in the mailbag, hung it where the train conductor grabbed it, and wrote a letter to Washington telling the postmaster general that he was quitting.

The mail started going to Jim Morgan's new store. When the Post Office Department told Morgan the new location needed a name, Morgan suggested Charleston for Charles Titche, a prominent landowner. (Another source says Charleston was the name of the manufacturer of the telephone in the store.) That was rejected because there already were 16 other Charlestons in the U.S. Morgan then proposed Morgantown, but that was rejected, too.

One day, Morgan's daughter, Rachel, asked her dad what he thought of the name *Start*— "since we're making a new *start* for the post office." Morgan tried the idea out on people who came into the store and they seemed to like it.

On July 26, 1918, the Post Office Department gave its official blessing to the name. Rachel was later appointed postmistress.

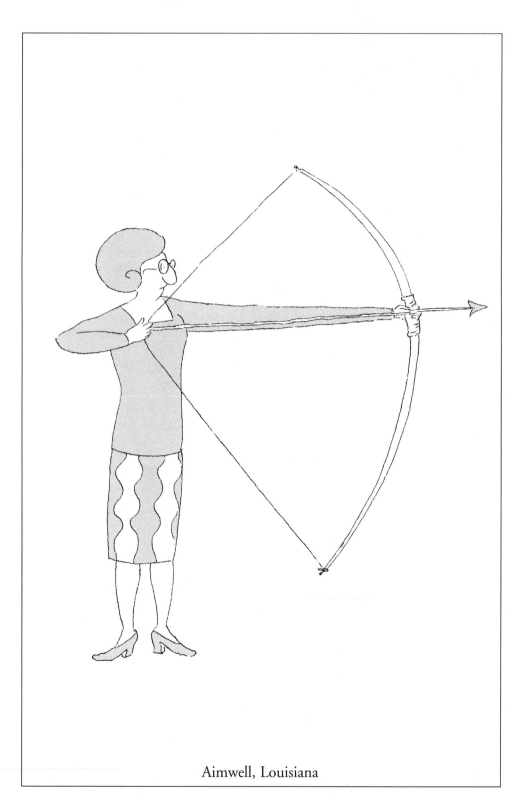

Aimwell, Louisiana

Waterproof

On State Route 570 fifteen miles north of Natchez, Mississippi, and within flooding distance of the Mississippi River

Like *Frostproof,* Florida (page 53), this name did not come with a guarantee. According to a Tensas Parish history, the entire town has been under two to three feet of water several times in its history. In fact, the town site had to be moved three times, because the Mississippi River wandered outside its banks and didn't go back. The town dates to 1830.

Early settler Abner Smalley loved to tell the story of how he chose the name *Waterproof.* He was standing high and dry on a strip of land surrounded by floodwater as far as the eye could see when a steamboat maneuvered toward the town dock to pick up a supply of cordwood, its fuel. The jovial captain saw Smalley, whom he knew well, and called out, "Well, Abner, I see you are *waterproof.*"

Twelfth President Zachary Taylor owned a plantation two miles east of *Waterproof.*

Other Unusual Place-Names in Louisiana

Aimwell

On State Route 126 forty miles northeast of Alexandria

This was the name of the eldest son of Joseph Willis, who is credited with organizing the first Baptist church west of the Mississippi at Bayou Chicot, Louisiana, in 1812. The *Aimwell* Baptist Church, which he organized here a few years later, is still standing. Willis was one of the first Protestant ministers to preach in defiance of the Black Code, which outlawed all religions except Catholicism in Louisiana when it was a colony of Spain.

Willis was 75 when his fourth wife gave birth to *Aimwell.*

Ajax

On State Route 174 near I-49 forty miles southeast of Shreveport

You know *Ajax* is a scouring powder, and you may know *Ajax* is a hero in Greek mythology, but you probably don't know *Ajax* was once a maker of industrial engines. According to Clare D'Artois Leeper in *Louisiana Places,* it was *Ajax* the engine-maker that inspired the name of this town. "Professor" Middleton, a school teacher here, had an *Ajax* engine in the sawmill he owned, and there also was one in the local cotton gin when the name of the town was changed from *Three Pines*.

Locals still say it was a good choice of names; *Ajax* stands for durability in their minds.

Baton Rouge

On I-12 seventy-seven miles west-northwest of New Orleans in the center of the state's "foot"

french explorer Pierre LeMoyne d'Iberville came upon a red post—a *baton rouge* in his native language—while mapping the lower Mississippi River Valley in 1699. The post marked the boundary between two Indian nations, the Bayogoulas and the Houmas.

A French fort built here in 1719 used the name, which was later adopted by the town that grew up around the fort. *Baton Rouge* became the state capital in 1849.

(See *Painted Post,* New York, page 169.)

Cut Off

On State Route 1 in south central Lafourche Parish in the southeastern part of the state

this town was named for the *cutoff,* or canal, linking Bayou Lafourche and Lake Salvador. The canal, which connected a number of natural and artificial channels, was intended to be a shortcut to New Orleans, but it was never developed sufficiently to be much more than a drainage for storm surges in this watery Mississippi delta landscape.

Stretching your legs in Cut Off: This is alligator country, and nearby Houma boasts more than a dozen alligator attractions, including Wildlife Gardens, a bed-and-breakfast where the gators slither around under guest cottages built out over the swamp and vie for raw chicken handouts each morning. A restaurant called the Bayou Delight serves diced alligator in a picante sauce. Swamp tours are popular, including one led by guitar-playing Ron "Black" Guidry (not the former Yankees pitcher) and his dog Gator Bait, a Catahoula hound (a Louisiana breed) with one brown eye and one blue eye. "Alligator Annie," aka Annie Miller, at 83 years old, is the grande dame of the tours. She ferries tourists through the swamps of Terrebonne Parish in a swamp boat and feeds whole chickens to the gators. For information on these and other Houma attractions, call the Houma-Terrebonne Tourist Commission at (800) 688-2732.

Frogmore

On U.S. Route 84 fifteen miles west of Natchez, Mississippi

Old-timers say that a railroad survey crew suggested the name, because the crew had never seen so many *frogs* in one place before.

Oklahoma has a *Frogville* that reputedly was named for the exceptionally large *frogs* found there.

Iota

Where State Route 98 crosses State Route 91 twenty-five miles west of Lafayette

the Southern Pacific Railroad needed a name for this small depot on the Eunice to Midland branch line, so a group of citizens met the train one morning and asked the conductor what he thought would be a suitable name. The conductor, an educated man with a quiet sense of humor, looked up and down the track and then beyond the station to the little settlement and said very clearly, pronouncing each syllable, "*Iota*"—a word in English meaning "a very small amount," derived from the Greek word *iota,* which is the name of the smallest letter in the Greek alphabet.

The railroad came through in the early 1890s. *Iota* became an incorporated village in 1907, and a town, by governor's decree, in 1919.

Jigger

On State Route 128 four miles east of Fort Necessity (see page 93)

the owner of the general store, who later became the first postmaster, had a five-year-old son who was nicknamed *Jigger* because he was much smaller than other children his age. He overheard the conversation in the store about choosing a name for the post office, and pestered, "Daddy, I want it to be my name. I want it to be *Jigger*. Please, Daddy. . . ."

This was told to me by Patsy Harris, the longtime postmistress of the *Jigger* Post Office and matriarch of Harris Hardware and Dry Goods (the general store). Little *Jigger* grew up to be her husband Charles. She says there were other names on the list sent to Washington in 1933, including Harrisville, but the feds chose *Jigger.*

Westwego

On U.S. Route 90 across the Mississippi River from New Orleans

The name was coined from the pioneer's cry, *"West we go!"* A hundred and fifty years ago, the town was on a major road west, and may have been a departure point for homesteaders or Gold Rush adventurers.

Money Names

MONEY IS SCATTERED ALL over the American landscape. **Money,** Mississippi, is named after Senator Hernando DeSoto *Money*. Both **Dollar's Corner**, Washington, and **Dollarville**, Michigan, were named for families named *Dollar*. **Dollar Bay**, Michigan, **Dollar Lake**, California, and **Dollar Lake**, Oregon, were all named for their shape—like a silver dollar. **Dollarhide**, Texas, toponymist Fred Tarpley says, may have been named for the fact that a drought killed most of the cattle, and their hides were sold for a *dollar* each. **Last Dollar Mountain,** Colorado, was probably named for a mining claim.

Greenback, Tennessee (page 222), was named for a political party that wanted to get off the gold standard. **Hardmoney**, Kentucky, took its name from the slogan of the opposing side of the same issue.

If you don't care what form your money comes in as long as it's **Cash,** look on the maps of South Dakota and Texas (page 227). **Cashtown**, Pennsylvania, is named, according to Myron J. Quimby in *Scratch Ankle, U.S.A.*, for a tavernkeeper's insistence that all customers pay with *cash*. **Hard Cash**, Mississippi, was named for the plantation of the same name whose original owner had bought with *cash*.

Two American towns and one lake give change: **Coin**, Iowa (page 81) and **Dime Box**, Texas (page 225), and **Tencent Lake**, Oregon. One used to take **Credit** (Arkansas) until it went belly up.

Finally, there is **Dinero**, Texas, *dinero* being the Spanish word for money.

maine

Convene

About 30 miles northwest of Portland in the southwestern part of the state

The name of this little village near Sebago Lake had to be changed from New Limington to something else if the community wanted a post office, because there already was a New Limington post office in Maine. A group of ladies discussing this matter hoped a new name could be decided upon quickly because it would be very *convenient* to have their own post office. "Let's name it *Convene,* then," one of the ladies suggested.

I'm not sure I believe this explanation, which comes from the *Dictionary of Maine Place Names* by Phillip R. Rutherford. I think the lady proposed *Convenient,* and a clerk at the U.S. Post Office Department changed it to the shorter *Convene.*

Kokadjo

On an unpaved timber company road just east of Moosehead Lake in the northwest-central part of the state

This is an abbreviated form of one of the longest place-names in the U.S.: *Kokadjeweemgwasebemsis,* which means a small kettle-shaped mountain lake in the Abenaki Indian language.

According to legend, recounted in *Indian Place-Names of the Penobscot Valley and the Maine Coast* by Fannie Hardy Eckstorm, the demigod Glooscap killed a big moose wading in Moosehead Lake, and then went after her calf. Lightening his load for the chase, Glooscap threw down his *kettle,* making *Kettle Mountain,* and then his pack, making *Sabotawan* or *Big Spencer Mountain.* He pursued the calf across what is now central Maine all the way to the coast, and when the moose took to the water near Belfast (Moose Point), Glooscap leapt across Penobscot Bay and killed the calf at what is now Cape Rosier.

And you thought Michael Jordan could jump!

Ducktrap, Maine

Other Unusual Place-Names in Maine

Amity

On U.S. Route 1 eleven miles south of Houlton and just a few miles from New Brunswick, Canada

People started settling Township No. 10 in 1825, five years after Maine was admitted to the union. Land cost 20 cents an acre, payable one half in cash and the other half in work on the roads. By 1836, the settlers were ready to give the village a real name. *Amity* was chosen as "a name which attested the harmony and peace obtaining among the early settlers," explains Ava Harriet Chadborne in *Maine Place Names and the Peopling of its Towns.*

Bingo

A few miles south of where State Route 6 crosses U.S. Route 1 in the eastern part of the state

Supposedly, this word jumped out of the mouth of an early resident when he told a shopkeeper that he had better be getting home, and the shopkeeper asked where he lived.

I thought that this place might have been named for a Saturday night *bingo* game at a V.F.W. hall. But when I mentioned this to the woman who answered the phone at the library in Lubec, the commercial center of Washington County, she reminded me that folks in this sparsely populated neck of the Maine woods near New Brunswick call this game of chance "beano"— like my mother did.

Coburn Gore

On State Route 27 fifteen miles east of the point where Maine, New Hampshire, and Quebec converge

Nothing unusual about the surname *Coburn,* but what's a *gore?* A surveyor's term, it turns out, for a wedge-shaped piece of land left over between two surveyed parcels. It is used in place-names here and there east of the Mississippi, especially in New England.

Cornville

On a town road four miles north of Skowhegan and 35 miles north-northeast of Augusta

This town was named for an unusually bountiful *corn* harvest. An Arizona town with the same name was meant to be Coaneville, after one of the early settlers, but the Post Office Department spelled the name wrong.

Ducktrap

On U.S. Route 1 halfway between Rockport and Belfast and 45 miles south-southwest of Bangor

The Penobscot Indians *trapped ducks* here when they were molting and couldn't fly. Today, motels and antique shops try to *trap* tourists with this quaint-sounding name.

Grindstone

Nine miles north of where State Route 11 meets I-95 in the east-central part of the state

This is where lumberjacks and Penobscot River drivers went to sharpen their axes.

Head Tide

On State Route 194 sixteen miles southeast of Augusta

Originally called *Head of the Tide*, this village is at the *head* of the Sheepscot River, where its *tidal* (salt) waters meet the freshwaters of Benny's Brook. Connecticut has a locale named *Turn of River.*

Northeast Carry

On the northeast tip of Moosehead Lake in the northwest-central part of the state

Carry is an old Maine woods word for portage. This is the place where canoes would be portaged between *North* Bay on Moosehead Lake and the West Branch of the Penobscot River.

Orient

On U. S. Route 1 in the southeastern corner of Aroostook County

This isolated town is on Maine's eastern border—and the U.S.'s; New Brunswick, Canada, is just across Grand Lake. When the town was incorporated in 1856, Americans used the word *orient* generically for "east"; it didn't necessarily mean Asia.

Starboard

About 11 miles south of Machias and U.S. Route 1 on the southeastern coastline

Sailors always say port and *starboard*, never left and right. This place is on the *starboard* side of Machias Bay—going out, that is.

Girdletree, Maryland

maryland

Accident

On U.S. Route 219 in the northwestern corner of the state

So many people ask about the origin of this name that the mayor and town council have authorized an official explanation that is printed on town stationary. It starts with "the legend most frequently told by the local citizens."

Around 1751, George Deakins received a grant of 600 acres of land in western Maryland from King George II of England. Deakins dispatched two independent survey parties to find the best tract. When they returned with their maps, Deakins discovered that, purely by *accident*, both parties had surveyed the same tract, even starting at the same tall oak. Deakins called his patent "The *Accident* Tract."

The other explanation on the handout was written by local historian Mary Miller Straus. She says that land records show that the naming took place a generation later, after Lord Baltimore opened the lands "westward of Fort Cumberland" in the Maryland Colony for settlement. Among the first land speculators to rush to the frontier were Brooke Beall and William Deakins, Jr. (George's son?), friends in Prince Georges County, east of what is now Washington, D.C.

On April 14, 1774, Deakins and his brother Francis finished surveying a fine tract of 682 acres with gigantic virgin timber bounded by the branches of Bear Creek. At the end of the day, they ran into Beall, who claimed that he and his party had surveyed the same tract, calling attention to the ax marks the surveyors had made on trees along the boundary lines. Deakins replied that it appeared that they had chosen the same acreage by *accident*, and land being in abundance, he conceded to Beall. On the survey that he submitted to Deputy County Surveyor John Hanson Jr., Beall named the tract *Accident*.

Basket Switch

On U.S. Route 113 in the southeastern part of the state

In the early 1890s, the village leaders petitioned the Maryland, Delaware and Virginia Railroad Company to establish a *switch*, or siding, here so that mine props, pilings for wharves, railroad ties, and other timber products could be shipped to market. Also pushing for the *switch* was a group of farmers who had organized to build a *basket* factory at the siding. They and other

Worcester County farmers needed the *baskets* for harvesting the peaches, tomatoes, and strawberries they grew. And there was good *basket*-making material—mostly gum and maple bark—nearby.

The *basket* factory eventually failed due to stiff competition both up and down the railroad line. A brick kiln was tried, but it failed, too; the local clay wasn't any good. Much later, about 1961, the *switch* building was occupied by a company that made candy molds whose freight moved by truck. Today, there are no *baskets* and no *switch* to be seen, just a name with a story to tell.

Dames Quarter

On State Route 363 in the southwest corner of Maryland's portion of the Delmarva Peninsula

The way that other Maryland and Virginia place-names use the term *quarter*—meaning a tract, district, or settlement—suggests that this one was named after a *Dame* family. But Robert I. Alotta makes a convincing case that the early watermen referred to this shore as *Damned Quarter* because the Indians still fished here—against the European settlers' will. Another of Alotta's sources for *Signposts & Settlers: The History of Place Names in the Middle Atlantic States*, says that the name may have something to do with the community's proximity to Deal Island, which was originally called Devil's Island. The *quarters* of the *damned*, therefore, were close to the Devil's island.

Anyway, by 1794, the local ministry had prevailed upon their brethren to sanitize the name to its present form, Alotta says.

Girdletree

On State Route 12 in the southeast corner of Maryland's portion of the Delmarva Peninsula

Someone *girdled* a *tree* here—cut away the bark and cambium in a ring around the trunk in order to kill it. Who, nobody knows for sure. Was it an Indian clearing for a garden plot? A surveyor being a little too aggressive in making his mark? Or was the girdler Charles W. Bishop, who is said to have killed a large beech *tree* before building his home. His farm was called *Girdletree* Hill and became the nucleus of the village, which by 1878 had a schoolhouse, two churches, two stores, a doctor's office, and a post office.

Two other noteworthy place-names in the immediate area are *Fleaville* and *Klej Grange*, neither of which is still on the map. The latter was named for the daughters of the Philadelphia financier Joseph Drexel: *Katherine, Louise, Elizabeth,* and *Jane.* Or were *Louise's* sisters *Kate, Emma,* and *Josephine,* as another source claims? As for *Fleaville,* this is another itchy-leg story, like *Scratch Ankle,* Alabama (see page 2), that you can probably figure out for yourself.

Parole

Just off U.S. Route 50 on the west side of Annapolis

during the Civil War, Union soldiers who had been court-martialed were sometimes *paroled* until such time as they could be exchanged for Confederate prisoners. At first the men were sent home to await exchange, but many of them circumvented the *parole* process by surrendering to the enemy, which usually meant being sent home for good. To discourage this practice, the government maintained *parole* camps where the men were kept under military discipline. This one was called Camp *Parole.*

Here, on the outskirts of Annapolis, is a little cemetery with row upon mournful row of white headstones, all exactly alike, hundreds of them—memorials to the men who died at Camp *Parole.*

Pekin (Nikep)

On State Route 36 in the northwestern part of the state

Some maps show *Pekin* on this spot, others show *Nikep.* The official state map has it "*Pekin* (*Nikep* P.O.)." What's going on here? Paul Dickson explains in *What's in a Name?*: *Pekin* worked fine until the community got a post office. Then letters meant for residents of *Pekin*, Indiana, started being delivered here—and vice versa. The problem was that *Md.* and *Ind.* could look nearly the same in longhand, and there was no zip code back then to serve as a referee. The U.S. Post Office Department had a tried-and-true method for solving such problems: spell the newer of the two names backwards.

Pekin takes its name from a coal mine.

Reliance

On State Route 392 at the Delaware border in the middle of the Delmarva Peninsula

it's not clear why the name *Reliance* was chosen for this hamlet in 1882, but it's easy to understand why local residents wanted to disassociate themselves from the original name, *Johnson's Crossroads.* The namesake, Joe Johnson, was the son-in-law and partner-in-crime of the notorious Lucretia "Patty" Cannon, the mastermind of a gang that kidnapped runaway slaves and free Negroes for their clients.

Joe and Patty also ran a tavern that "disappeared" customers.

Dex Nilsson relates in his book, *Discover Why It's Called . . . ,* that officials from both Maryland and Delaware raided the joint (the state line ran through the middle of it) one night, and Patty was arrested; Joe escaped. At her trial in Georgetown, Delaware, Patty confessed to nine murders and was sentenced to hang, but committed suicide in her jail cell.

Other Unusual Place-Names in Maryland

Bestpitch

On a county road in central Dorchester County on the Chesapeake Bay side of the Delmarva Peninsula

This is a family name—sorry baseball fans!—although one source suggests that the name might have originated in England from a cricket player with a live arm. Another source notes that there is no baseball field in this part of Dorchester County.

(See *Umpire,* Arkansas, page 24.)

Gratitude

On the Eastern Shore of the Chesapeake Bay across the Bay from and halfway in between Baltimore and Annapolis

First known as Deep Landing, this harbor town took its current name from a Philadelphia-based steamboat that docked here regularly in the late 1880s. The townspeople's *gratitude* for the business may also have contributed to the name change.

Issue

On the Potomac River in the southern part of the state about 40 miles south-southeast of Washington, D.C.

The name arose out of the *issue* of whether the post office should be at the north end of the village or the south end. The debate went on for months, and the Post Office Department began referring to the village as *Issue* in its correspondence, according to Hamill Kenny, author of *The Place Names of Maryland, Their Origin and Meaning.* The *issue* was settled when the post office was built in a compromise location—but the name stuck.

Ladiesburg

On State Route 194 thirty-five miles northwest of Baltimore

The story goes that when the village was founded in the early 1800s, someone took a quick census and counted seven *ladies* and one gentleman.

Rising Sun

On State Route 274 in the northeast corner of the state

Why would a town be named after an everyday occurrence—sunrise? It isn't; it's named for an early 19th-century tavern with a *rising sun* painted on its sign.

A road sign that gets the attention of northbound travelers on I-95 fifty miles north of Baltimore reads: NORTH EAST/RISING SUN (the names are stacked). *North East* is south on State Route 274; *Rising Sun* is north.

Why would a town be named after a compass point? *North East* and the river by the same name are at the *northeastern* end of Chesapeake Bay.

Delaware also has a *Rising Sun*.

Stretching your legs in Rising Sun: Herr Foods Inc. gives tours on weekdays of its high-tech potato chip factory seven miles north of here in Nottingham, Pennsylvania. At the end of the tour you get to taste warm chips direct from the production line; they literally melt in your mouth. Pretzel, corn chip, and tortilla chip-making also are part of the tour. Herr Foods was started 50 years ago by a 21-year-old Mennonite farmer who made potato chips in the kitchen of his home each morning and sold them door-to-door in the afternoon from his 1938 Dodge panel truck. The family still owns the business. Location: State Route 272, Nottingham, Pennsylvania. Telephone: (800) 637-6225. Admission free.

Secretary

On State Route 14 about five miles from U.S. Route 50 on the Chesapeake Bay side of the Delmarva Peninsula

Lord Henry Sewell, who served as *Secretary* of the Province of Maryland under Governor Charles Calvert (later Lord Baltimore), was granted 2,000 acres of land here in 1661. The stream flowing through the property became known as *Secretary* Sewell's Creek. Sometime in the intervening 330-odd years Sewell's name was dropped from both the creek and the town.

The governor coveted the grantee's wife, and when an appropriate time had passed after Lord Sewell's death in 1664, Lady Sewell became Lady Calvert.

Stretching your legs in Secretary: In nearby Cambridge you can tour the Wild Goose Amber Beer microbrewery. The tour, as you'd expect, includes a taste of the pale English-like ale with the beautiful label. Address: 20 Washington Street, Cambridge. Telephone: (301) 221-1121. Admission free.

T.B.

At the intersection of State Routes 5 and 373 twelve miles south-southeast of Washington, D.C.

People who guess this name had something to do with a *tu*berculosis sanitarium are not even close. *T.B.* are the initials of *T*homas *B*rooke (another source says *B*lanford), an early settler who carved the letters into trees all around the perimeter of his land. The initials gave the place an identity long before a village grew up here.

massachusetts

Loudville

On a local road in the southwest corner of the town of Northampton in the western part of the state

Clear Falls, which once supplied the power for the village's mills, gets *loud* and boisterous at times. There are reports of the crashing water keeping people awake at night. And a notable flood many years ago made the falls roar all the *louder* for a time. But while some people like to believe it was the falls' *loud* voice that gave the village its name, a more than 100-year-old copy of the *Daily Hampshire Gazette* pins the name on industrialist Caleb *Loud.*

What Andrew Carnegie was to steel and Pittsburgh in the 1890s, Caleb *Loud* was to mills and *Loudville* in the 1830s and 1840s. Between 1830 and 1846, he built and operated a button and button mold mill, a sawmill, a paper mill, and a cotton mill. He also built several churches and a silk mill in another town.

Sandwich

On State Route 6A just south of the Cape Cod Canal

i grew up on Cape Cod and played high school sports against *Sandwich* teams, so the name never was a mystery to me. But if you've never heard of *Sandwich*, England, or the Earl of *Sandwich*, you'd probably wonder about this one. It was named for the English town in 1637. The Earl didn't think to put his noonday ration of beef between two slices of bread until more than 100 years later.

One of the oldest towns in North America, *Sandwich* was settled by 13 families from Saugus (north of Boston) and either Plymouth or Duxbury at a time when the leaders of the Plymouth Colony were encouraging the formation of new towns. They hoped to catch up with the rival Massachusetts Bay Colony, which was growing by leaps and bounds.

The name may have been suggested by John Humphrey, the magistrate of Saugus, who owned a house in old *Sandwich,* then one of the embarkation points for the New World.

In the mid-19th century, *Sandwich* was known for its beautiful colored glass. The first pressed glass and lace glass in America was made here.

Loudville, Massachusetts

Stretching your legs in Sandwich: If you're traveling to *Sandwich* from points south, you'll pass close to the village of Onset as you approach the Cape Cod Canal. Housed there in the basement of an unassuming home overlooking a tidal pond is The World's Only Thermometer Museum. Richard Porter—"The Thermometer Man"—has amassed a collection of more than 2,800 thermometers from his travels around the world. It is said to be the largest collection in the world, and includes a thermometer from a radio station in the Yukon that goes down to minus 100 and a "Some Like it Hot" thermometer with a picture of Marilyn Monroe on it and a tendency to read a little high. Porter's Swiss Weather Houses not only tell the temperature but also give weather forecasts, signaling fair weather by sending Little Red Riding Hood outside, and rain by presenting the wolf.

Eight of Porter's antique thermometers appeared in the 1997 Oliver Stone movie *U-Turn.* Address: 49 Zarahemla Road, Onset. Telephone: (508) 295-5504. Admission free.

Sixteen Acres

Within the city of Springfield at the intersection of State Route 21 and Wilbraham Road

this location was known as *Sixteen Acres* as early as 1652, when Rowland Thomas petitioned for, and was granted, six acres of a *sixteen-acre* meadow on the banks of the Mill River. Researching old deeds, western Massachusetts historian Harry Andrew Wright also discovered a number of other *sixteen-acre* parcels in the area, leading him to conclude that this was a common unit of land in colonial Massachusetts. Wright notes in *The Story of Western Massachusetts* that *sixteen acres* is equal to one-tenth of the quarter-section unit so familiar to homesteaders of the late 19th century and their farmer descendants today.

Other unusual place-names in the Springfield area of Rowland Thomas's time include *Peggy's Dipping Hole, Necessity,* and *World's End.* In 1802, according to Wright, the main thoroughfare through *Sixteen Acres* was known as "the road to Dartmouth College." Dartmouth, 120 miles north in Hanover, New Hampshire, was then an Indian school.

Tree of Knowledge Corner

On State Route 3 within the town of Duxbury 35 miles southeast of Boston

two hundred years ago, an ancient oak *tree* stood at what is now the intersection of South Street and Summer Street (State Route 53). The huge *tree* had been there since before the Pilgrims landed in nearby Plymouth in 1620 and was the site of the first rural free delivery of mail in the New World, according to a local historian.

The post "runner" between the Plymouth Colony and the Massachusetts Bay Colony in Boston would leave messages and letters for Duxbury folk at the base of the *tree*. Later, when there was mounted service and a larger volume of mail, a wooden box was nailed to the tree. Still later the mail came by stagecoach three times a week. The box was left unlocked, and whenever someone from Duxbury proper was out that way, he'd retrieve his neighbors' mail.

This custom lasted so many years that the oak *tree* and the *corner* became known far and wide, and people began calling it *Tree of Knowledge Corner* because it was the place where important information was gathered and dispensed.

Later on, when there was regular mail service to Duxbury, and the box on the *tree* was abandoned, lovers would sometimes use it for *billets-doux*.

Sometime in the early 1800s, the *tree,* which had already had some of its limbs splintered by storms, was struck a fatal blow by a bolt of lightning. About that time, according to local folklore, a patriarch of the adjoining village of Tarkiln had a dream in which the spirit of the *tree* appeared before him and warned that if the site—which had seen so much of Duxbury's history, joys as well as sorrows—were ever left unmarked, a plague and other dire consequences would descend upon the town.

Since that day, local people have feared The Curse of the *Tree of Knowledge* and maintained a marker here. First it was a hand-painted sign, and there was much public fretting when it had to be temporarily removed in 1927 to widen the road. Since Duxbury's 300th anniversary in 1937, the site has been marked by a granite post.

Another section of Duxbury with a noteworthy name is *Tinkertown.* This locale had no real name other than "up around the pond" (Island Creek Pond) until about 1765 when it was named for Jeremiah Dillingham, a *tinker* from Pembroke, the town next door. He would set up shop here for days at a time to ply his trade. Dillingham had another reason for coming to Duxbury; his daughter lived here. And for a *tinker*'s daughter, she had a pretty fancy name, Princess.

White Horse Beach

A locale in the village of Manomet (on State Route 3A) about six miles south of Plymouth

acording to legend, this *beach* community was named for a 1778 incident in which a beautiful young maiden named Helen rode a *white horse* into the surf on a stormy August night and drowned. She was distraught because her father, a physician, didn't approve of her lover, a sailor named Roland Doane whom she had nursed back to health after his ship, the privateer *General Arnold*, went aground and broke up in Plymouth Bay the previous Christmas.

Helen was either looking for Roland along the *beach* when she fell off her *horse,* or she committed suicide because her father had run the young sailor off. To this day, people report seeing Helen's ghost perched on the big granite boulder in the bay called *White Horse* Rock.

Other Unusual Place-Names in Massachusetts

Brimstone Corner

In the town of Pembroke 22 miles southeast of Boston

the neighborhood takes its name from the *Brimstone* Tavern, a stagecoach stop on what the colonists called the Bay Path, the main road between Boston and Plymouth. Nobody knows for certain how the tavern got its name, but it's easy to imagine it being the butt of a Puritan minister's fire and *brimstone* sermon.

The tavern didn't get what the minister said it deserved until it burned to the ground in 1937.

Feeding Hills

Within the town of Agawam on State Route 57 five miles west of Springfield

the early inhabitants of Springfield kept their milking cows on the "inward commons" in what is now the town of Agawam and their calves and cattle on the rolling pastures a mile or so west of there known as the "outward commons," and later as *Feeding Hills.*

Piety Corner

Within the town of Waltham, a western suburb of Boston

this town was named for the *pious* nature of its inhabitants.

Teaticket

Just north of Falmouth in the southwest corner of Cape Cod

Since this town is in Massachusetts, I thought its name was somehow connected to the Boston *Tea* Party—that *ticket* was perhaps another word for tariff. But, no, this is one of those English spellings of an Indian word—the Wampanoag word for "the main course of a tidal river"—that totally strips it of its ethnicity. Earlier spellings, including *Teticket, Tataket, Tecticut,* and *Tehticut,* sound more like the real thing.

Bad Axe, Michigan

michigan

Hell

On County Route D 32 fifteen miles northwest of Ann Arbor

george Reeves was in a bad mood the day this little lake resort town was named—and he was hungry. His wife had just sent the family dog down the hill to the general store that Reeves operated; it was her way of telling him that supper was ready. As Reeves was going out the door, one of the men gathered around the pot-bellied stove stopped him. "George, we need to decide on a name for this place," the man said.

"You can call it *Hell* if you like," barked Reeves.

That story was passed down to the generation of folks who are now in their seventies and eighties by Puss Reeves Mann, Reeves's daughter.

The moralists in the community that Reeves built from scratch, and almost single-handedly, said *Hell* was living up to its name when a whiskey distillery and tavern opened its doors around the time of the Civil War. And they shook their heads in disgust again a few years later when a racetrack was built. When farmers went into town in search of these entertainments, a *Hell* Chamber of Commerce brochure points out, their wives could accurately say, "Our husbands are going to *Hell*!"

Nirvana

On U.S. Route 10 sixty-five miles north of Grand Rapids

in the Buddhist religion, *Nirvana* is the highest of heavens, the place you arrive when you've transcended all desire and become oblivious to care, pain, and external reality. This part of Michigan was, in the decade following the Civil War, a forest primeval of tall, straight white pines waiting for the first ring of an ax. It didn't have to wait long. Soon after Darwin Knight registered a plat of the town and was appointed the first postmaster in the spring of 1874, eleven sawmills were in full swing. When the slaughter of the pines was done, so was the town, though it still clings to the official map of the state.

Needless to say, there was plenty of "desire" and interest in "external reality" in *Nirvana* in those early years, especially of the kind that piles up in a bank account.

So what was Knight thinking of when he named this place, the heaven that he found here, or the kind that money can buy? Or was the name he chose an expression of a sincere interest in Asian culture?

The boom town's best hotel was named the Indra House, after Indra, the principal god of the Aryan-Vedic religion.

Stalwart

On State Route 48 in the southeastern part of the Upper Peninsula

this was a Republican outpost in 1881. When the citizens applied for a post office that spring, they wanted the postmark to bear the last name of the man they had helped elect president the previous November, James A. Garfield. Told by the Post Office Department that there already was a Garfield post office in their state, they presented the last name of his vice president, Chester A. Arthur, and were denied for the same reason.

Someone suggested that since Arthur represented the *Stalwart* faction of the Republican Party, that might be a good name for the village. The name was forwarded to Washington, D.C., and the Post Office Department gave its blessing.

Some people in the village must have had second thoughts about their choice that July when Garfield was shot in the back by an assassin who shouted, "I am a *Stalwart* and Arthur is President now!" Garfield died from the wound in late September.

The *Stalwarts* warred with the Half-Breeds, another Republican faction, over the spoils of office in those politically turbulent years, and ultimately were scorned for their patronage system. And Arthur, once the symbol of spoils politics, wasn't all that *Stalwart* as a president; he even reformed the Civil Service.

(See *Greenback*, Tennessee, page 222, for another place named for a political group of this period.)

Other Unusual Place-Names in Michigan

Bad Axe

On State Route 53 in the center of The Thumb

a survey party passing along one of the trails between Sebewaing and Harbor Beach in 1861 found a broken *ax* stuck in a tree. First known as *Bad Axe* Camp and then *Bad Axe* Corners, this place was just a small clearing in the forest until the county supervisors decided, after much discussion, to make it the county seat on October 15, 1872.

Before the Post Office Department banned "picture" addresses, letters were frequently delivered here with a drawing of a broken *ax* where you would expect to see a town name.

Bravo

On a county road 40 miles southwest of Grand Rapids in southwestern Michigan

first called *Sherman* in honor of either the Civil War general or an early settler, the name was changed in 1872 when the community applied for a post office and was told there already was a *Sherman,* Michigan. *Bravo* apparently brought to mind the bravery and spirit of the pioneers who cleared the dense woods to start a village.

Christmas

Thirty-three miles east-southeast of Marquette on the north coast of the central Upper Peninsula

Some *Christmases* are better than others, and Julius Thorson had a truly bad one here on the south shore of Lake Superior. He asked Santa to help him build a *Christmas* theme village here on a tract of land he purchased shortly before World War II, and all he got in his stocking was coal. The first step in his dream, a toy factory called *Christmas* Industries, burned to the ground on September 18, 1940, only a year after it opened. Thorson talked about rebuilding in 1941, but then the war interfered with his plans. The name lived on.

(See *Christmas,* Arizona, page 14.)

Germfask

On Route 77 in the east-central part of the Upper Peninsula

this odd name has nothing to do with *germs,* although it was created by a man who knew a lot about them. Dr. W. French used the first letter of the surname of each of the eight founding settlers: *G*rant, *E*dge, *R*obinson, *M*ead, *F*rench (the good doctor himself), *A*ckley, *S*hepard, and *K*naggs.

This is explained in *Michigan Place Names* by Walter Romig, a very valuable source of information about Michigan place-names.

Mass City (or Mass)

Near the intersection of State Routes 26 and 38 in the northwestern part of the Upper Peninsula

this name has nothing to do with the Catholic church service, although there are quite a few Catholics in this neck of the Upper Peninsula woods. The town takes its name from the *Mass* Mining Company. Walter Romig says copper was discovered here in 1848 by Noel Johnson, a runaway slave from Missouri, who later sold his claims to *Mass* Mining.

Samaria

On a county road that connects U.S. Route 23 with I-75 a few miles north of Toledo, Ohio, in the southeastern corner of Michigan

i thought this was one of the hundreds of Biblical names on the map of the U.S.— for *Samaria* in the parable of the Good Samaritan (Luke 10:30-37). No, this little community was named by (and for) *Sam* and *Mary* Weeks, who probably were well aware of the Biblical connotation.

Schoolcraft

On U.S. Route 131 a few miles south of Kalamazoo

this name doesn't have anything to do with a philosophy of education. Founding father Lucius Lyon named the town in 1831 for his friend Henry Rowe *Schoolcraft* (1793–1864), a well-known Indian agent and ethnologist, who also had an Upper Peninsula county and a Livonia, Michigan, college named after him. *Schoolcraft* was one of the first Americans to study and write about Indian life and customs.

Temperance

On a county road nine miles north of Toledo, Ohio

this unincorporated settlement was named in 1880 by Marietta Hayden Ansted, founder of the local chapter of the Women's Christian *Temperance* Union, and her teetotaler husband Lewis, the first postmaster. Lewis ran a general store and sold land. Every deed had a clause that prohibited the sale of alcoholic beverages.

In 1935, an ad hoc group called the *Temperance* Law and Order Society forced a storekeeper to stop selling liquor. The group was led by Harriet Ansted Brunt, Marietta and Lewis's daughter.

(See *Temperanceville*, Virginia, page 240.)

Wooden Shoe

On State Route 61 six miles east of Gladwin and 45 miles northwest of Saginaw

a handwritten note kept in a file at the Gladwin County Library says that this village on the Tittabawassee River was named for a brand of beer drunk by loggers from Ohio who worked in the area many years ago. Beer bottles with the *Wooden Shoe* trademark are still found here from time to time.

Young America, Minnesota

minnesota

Sleepy Eye

At the intersection of State Route 4 and U.S. Route 14 eighty miles southwest of Bloomington

People here are as wide awake and with it as anywhere else. The name honors Dakota Chief Ish-Tak-Ha-Ba (*Sleepy Eyes*), a friend of the first white settlers who started arriving when the railroad came through in 1872. His grave is near the old railroad station. Ish-Tak-Ha-Ba's name is also on a beautiful lake on the north side of town. In fact, the town's original name was *Sleepy Eye Lake*.

In 1879, the citizens became uncomfortable with the derogatory connotation of the name and went to the state legislature to have it changed to *Loreno*. But everybody continued to call it *Sleepy Eye*, so another trip to St. Paul was made to change it back.

Twig

Ten miles west-northwest of Duluth on U.S. Route 53

This village on the main road to Duluth got its start in 1908 when S. N. Peterson filled in a frog pond and built a general store. The next thing the farmers in the area wanted was a post office, so they wrote a letter to the Postmaster General in Washington, D.C. He wrote back, requesting that the citizens select a name of not more than four letters. *Twig* was one of several they sent in, and the one they thought had the least chance of being chosen.

A *Twig* postmaster once suggested that the reason *Twig* was chosen was because the bureaucrats in Washington were enchanted with the idea of a *twig* being the smallest branch of the national network of post offices.

Young America

On State Route 5 about 35 miles west-southwest of Minneapolis

Young America was a catchphrase of expansionist-minded people back when this town was being settled, starting in 1856. After the Civil War, the town became a magnet for German immigrants, who wanted to change the name to *Teuteburg* once they were in the majority. The Germans and the Yankees compromised on *Florence*—the daughter of the town's first dentist, R. M.

Kennedy, but reverted to *Young America* when it was discovered there was another town named *Florence* in Minnesota.

There is an Indiana town named *Young America* that is said to be named for the nameplate on a piece of sawmill machinery.

Other Unusual Place-Names in Minnesota

Ball Club

On U.S. Route 2 on the Cass-Itasca County line in the north-central part of the state

The Ojibway Indians invented the *ball* game we know today as lacrosse. This community is at the southern end of *Ball Club* Lake, which is shaped something like a lacrosse *club* or racket. The name is a translation of an Ojibway word.

(See *Ball Ground*, Georgia, page 61.)

Castle Danger

On the Lake Superior shore about 26 miles northeast of Duluth

Some say this place was named for a *castle*-like structure along the shore that warned ships of some nearby *danger*. Rocks? Shallow water? Others say it was named for a ship, the *Castle,* which sank here. No evidence of the wreck has ever been found.

Outing

On State Route 6 in the north-central part of the state

William H. Andrews, who platted this hamlet on the southeastern shore of Crooked Lake in 1907, hoped the name would draw city people and fishermen for *outings.*

Tenstrike

On U.S. Route 71 in Beltrami County in the northern part of the state

When a party of homesteaders arrived here in the 1890s, one man was bowled over by the natural beauty of the area—the virgin forests, the pristine lakes and streams, the deep, rich soil. "I think we've made a *tenstrike*," he exclaimed, borrowing the bowling term for throwing a perfect ball.

Another version of the story has it that a Mr. Brown from Crookston, Minnesota, opened a trading post here. Business was so brisk that he compared it with throwing a *tenstrike*.

Warroad

On the southwestern shore of Lake of the Woods a few miles from the Manitoba border

This name makes more sense if you break it into two words, its original form—*war road*. And if you substitute *path* for *road*.

This was the front of the long-running *war* between the Chippewa and the Sioux over the wild rice on the shores of Lake of the Woods, according to the *Warroad* Heritage Center.

Hot Coffee, Mississippi

mississippi

Hot Coffee

On State Route 532 about 30 miles north-northwest of Hattiesburg

before Hattiesburg outstripped it, Ellisville was the commercial hub of south central Mississippi. Farmers traveled there by mule or horse-drawn wagon to trade their crops for dollars and hard-to-get staples. In the late 1880s, an enterprising businessman named L. N. Davis saw the need for a place to stop along the way for refreshment, and opened a general store on what is now Highway 532, about twelve miles northwest of Ellisville. Davis hung a sign in the shape of a *coffee* pot outside the store, and soon travelers marked the progress of their journey by the distance to his store: "It's just a few more miles until we reach that store that sells *hot coffee*," they would say. And later, as the stop became more familiar, ". . . just a few more miles to *hot coffee*."

And so the little stop on the farm-to-market road became known as *Hot Coffee*. By the 1920s, the name began appearing on maps and road signs.

Davis's grandson, R. J. Knight, moved the store across the road in 1929, and today the R. J. Knight General Merchandise Store is operated by Herbert Harper, R. J.'s son-in-law. Ten years ago, Harper put up a sign on the shoulder of Highway 532 that says "Downtown *Hot Coffee*" and another one two hundred yards away that greets travelers coming from the opposite direction. The store is in between the two signs, and it's still the place to get a cup of *coffee* in *Hot Coffee*. "I make it every morning," Harper says.

Stretching your legs in Hot Coffee: Near the back of the general store on the left, hanging on the wall above some shelves of hardware, is a six-foot-long stuffed sturgeon. It's been there since 1938, when the 198-lb. fish was taken from the nearby Leaf River. According to an account R. J. gave to a local historian, area fishermen were fed up with having their lines broken by the unseen monster, so they put up a fence across the stream and started shooting into the water. Pretty soon the sturgeon floated to the surface. R. J., then 27, rolled up his pants and dragged the big fish to shore. It was such a good big-fish-that-*didn't*-get-away story that soon afterward both *Life* and *Field & Stream* magazines sent reporters to *Hot Coffee* to get the details.

For a memento of your visit to *Hot Coffee*, Herbert Harper sells T-shirts, baseball caps, and "Baby Aboard" signs that say "I've been to downtown *Hot Coffee*." The mugs say (what else?) "*Hot Coffee*."

Midnight

On U.S. Route 49W thirty-six miles southeast of Greenville

One night about a hundred years ago, a cotton planter was playing poker on a steamboat wheeling up the Mississippi River. He was on his way back to Humphreys County from New Orleans, where he had gone to sell his crop. He had a cold hand all night, and eventually lost all his cash—a year's income. So he put up his plantation as his final bet—and lost it, too.

The winner pulled out his pocket watch with one hand as he laid his cards down on the table with the other, and announced that the plantation's new name would be *Midnight*. When a village sprung up in the area, it seemed natural—and perhaps lucky—to name it after the plantation.

Poker played a hand in the naming of at least two other U.S. towns: *Plush*, Oregon (page 195) and *Corydon*, Iowa. Judge Seth Anderson named *Corydon* for his hometown in Indiana after winning a game whose prize was the privilege of naming the town.

Three Aces Oil Field in Callahan County, Texas, was named when the first well came in, interrupting a poker game, according to a story told by Fred Tarpley in *1001 Texas Place Names*. All the players threw down their cards and ran outside, except for one man who yelled after them to finish the hand. After losing all night, he had just been dealt *three aces*.

(See *Show Low*, Arizona, page 15, for a place that takes its name from another card game.)

Whynot

On State Route 19 thirteen miles east of Meridian (near the Alabama border)

When I asked locally about this name, I was soon led to Jim Dawson, the Lauderdale County archivist, who wrote a history of his hometown in 1992. This is what he discovered: *Whynot* started out as *Whitesville* when W. H. White established a post office in his store in June 1852. But that didn't last long. By December, the U.S. Post Office Department had notified him that the name had to be changed; there was already a post office named *Whitesville* in the state. What happened next nobody knows for sure, but local legend and a genealogical branch reaching back to Randolph County, North Carolina, give some pretty good clues.

At that time, there were Spinks and Needhams living in the area around W. H. White's store. They had originally come from a village in North Carolina that, according to legend, got its name in an accidental way. Sometime in the late 1700s, the good people of the village gathered at the meeting house to choose a name for the place. The meeting dragged on and on, with suggestion after suggestion. "*Why not* name it this . . . ? *Why not* name it that . . . ?"

Finally, an old man, cranky from sitting on a hard bench for three hours, stood up in the back of the room and said, "I'm tired of all this *why not* this name and *why not* that name talk, as I'm sure the rest of you are. Let's name our village *Why Not* and be done with it, so we can all go home."

So in 1852, when the Spinks and the Needhams needed a name for their adopted village, they did what many American pioneers did back then, they named it after the village they originally came from.

And *why not?*

(See *Wynot*, Nebraska, page 145, and *Why*, Arizona, page 18.)

Other Unusual Place-Names in Mississippi

Alligator

Just off U.S. Route 61 fifty miles north-northeast of Greenville

randfathers here in northern Mississippi tell their grandchildren that the early settlers put *alligator* skin on their wooden plowshares so they wouldn't wear out too quickly. The *gators* came from nearby *Alligator* Lake, which is shaped somewhat like the reptile.

Chunky

On a county road eight miles west of Meridian

this town was named for *chunka*, a Choctaw Indian stickball game still played each summer at the Choctaw Indian Fair in Philadelphia, Mississippi.

Ecru

On State Route 15 eighteen miles west-northwest of Tupelo

this town takes its name from the color of the paint on the railroad station. For another town that was named for a paint color, see *Grayburg*, Texas.

Graball

On a local road north of Sumner, county seat of Tallahatchie County, in the northwestern part of the state

the captain of the steamboat that docked at the Tallahatchie River landing here collected odds and ends in a *grab* bag. He charged 50 cents a fistful. One day, a giant of a man with hands the size of catfish paid his four bits and emptied the bag in one *grab*.

It

On U.S. Route 51 between Brookhaven and Hazlehurst in the southwestern part of the state

Several stories are told about the origin of this name. The one I like best is this one, told to me by Mississippi place-name collector Jim Brieger:

In the 1920s, *It* was the last stop before Jackson for the bus headed north from the Gulf coast—the last chance to freshen up before being met by a relative or sweetheart. "This is *It*," the driver always announced.

Reform

On State Route 15 twenty-two miles north of Louisville and 18 miles west of Starkville as the crow flies

The story is told that the man who established the first rural mail route in the community declared that he'd use his position to *reform* its uncouth patrons. (See *Reform*, Alabama, page 6.)

Zero

A few miles south of Meridian on the Clark County line

Jim Brieger says this locale was named in 1880 by Press Mason, the first postmaster, who exclaimed: "Let's name it *Zero* for this surely must be the jumping off place for the rest of the world."

A man with the opposite perspective named a western Massachusetts village *World's End* in the early 1600s.

missouri

Ink

On a county road in central Shannon County halfway between Springfield and the Mississippi River

In 1886, the U.S. Post Office Department notified the states that it wanted short town names—just three letters if possible. Missouri towns named *Map, Nip,* and *Not* were approved that year, according to historian Margot McMillen (see *Tightwad,* Missouri).

People in an isolated hamlet in Shannon County, she goes on to say, held a meeting in the one-room school to choose a name. Getting nowhere fast, someone picked up a children's spelling book and read aloud the three-letter words. Ark? Bat? Cat? . . . The meeting dragged on and on until someone spilled a bottle of *ink.*

"*Ink!* That's a three-letter word!" someone gushed. "Let's name the town *Ink.*" Everyone agreed it was a great idea.

That's not the only explanation McMillen uncovered. Someone else told her that the postmaster named the town after receiving a parcel whose contents had been spoiled in transit by spilled *ink.* Another *Inkite* explained that the postmaster wrote down all the three-letter words he could think of, sent the list to Washington, D.C., and let the feds choose.

(See *Ink,* Arkansas, page 21.)

Novelty

A mile west of where State Routes 151 and 156 intersect in Knox County in the northeastern part of the state

Dr. Richard Thomas Pendry named this town on a whim in the mid-1850s after the wide assortment of merchandise he carried in his frontier store. Perhaps that is where the term *novelty* store comes from.

A local historian notes that the store was on a hill, and Doc Pendry put up a high pole with a red flag flying from it to guide people to the store. Another account says the flag was to guide people to his medical office, and that Doc Pendry's wife gave the place its name because she thought the flag was such a *novel* idea.

(See *Novelty,* Ohio, page 186.)

Reform, Missouri

Peculiar

An exit off U.S. Route 71 about 30 miles south of Kansas City

Yes, there is a place called *Peculiar*. I've been there. There's nothing *peculiar* about it, that I could tell. I ate lunch at Dianne's, whose parking lot fills with farmers' pickup trucks every weekday noon, and where you can smoke at any table in the restaurant. Dianne smokes. The hamburger I ordered was just what you'd expect in a small town eatery; the fries were above average.

After lunch I walked across the street to the post office to buy an envelope stamped with the "*Peculiar*, Missouri" postmark. On the way out of town I noted all the *Peculiar* businesses: *Peculiar* Hardware and Lumber, *Peculiar* Pizza and Subs, *Peculiar* Drive-In (a convenience store with gas pumps), *Peculiar* Farm Supply. Passing the West *Peculiar* Fire Protection District station on my left, I got back out on the divided highway and drove to Harrisonville, the Cass County seat.

According to the Cass County Historical Society, *Peculiar* was named in the spring of 1868, when the pioneers scattered along the east branch of the Grand River applied for a post office. Their application, which was filled out by first postmaster Edgar Thomson, says there were 51 families living within a two mile radius of the post office, which would be housed in Thomson's store.

Thomson proposed the name Excelsior, but a letter arrived from Washington, D.C., a few weeks later, saying that name had already been taken in Missouri. He sent in another name and another, and each time got the same reply. Finally, Thomson sent a letter to the postmaster general himself with his final proposal. "If that won't do, please assign a name to our post office," he wrote. "We don't care what name you give us so long as it is sort of *peculiar*." He put quotation marks around the word *peculiar*.

In early June of that year, Thomson heard back from Washington. He had been commissioned postmaster of the *Peculiar* Post Office.

Stet

On County Road K in eastern Ray County 45 miles east-northeast of Kansas City

Stet is a proofreaders' term meaning "let it stand." Proofreaders and editors write it above a word, or in the margin of a manuscript to signal the typesetter *not* to make a previously indicated change. So it is hard for me, a magazine editor who has used the term hundreds of times, to believe that the town was named by Ed Mansur, a storekeeper, as a county history says. More likely it was named by the editor of a newspaper published in the town, because no one outside of publishing uses the term.

Nonetheless, "let it stand" is a pretty good motto for a community trying to get its footing as an economic hub.

Tightwad

The owner of the first store in this tiny crossroads community is said to have sold a prize-winning, 60-pound watermelon to a mailman for $1.50 one hot August morning. The storekeeper agreed to hold the melon until the mailman finished his route and was on his way home.

A few hours later, a city fellow in a car (the mailman was in a horse-drawn wagon) stopped at the store, saw the melon, and offered $2 for it. The storekeeper took the man's money without batting an eye, and went out to his garden to get another melon for the mailman.

When the mailman came back for his melon, he saw that it wasn't the one he had paid for. He protested angrily, but the storekeeper wouldn't give him his money back. The mailman took the smaller melon, but as he was pulling away from the store he shouted at the top of his lungs, *"Tightwad! Tightwad!"*

This is the legend Margot Ford McMillen retells in her book *Paris, Tightwad, and Peculiar: Missouri Place Names*. A simpler version was told to me by the keeper of the current store in town, *Tightwad* Treasures Convenience Store and Flea Market, where I stopped for a cup of coffee. She says that a customer asked the storekeeper to cut a "plug" from a watermelon to see if it was ripe. The storekeeper refused. When the customer got home and discovered that the melon was not ripe, she took it back to the store to get her money back, and was refused again.

Whatever really happened, the storekeeper must have been one miserly SOB, and there must have been many such incidents, for the place to be named after his unpleasant behavior.

The *Tightwad* Bank, before it closed in the late 1980s, had hundreds of out-of-town depositors, for the simple reason people loved having the name on their checks.

Other Unusual Place-Names in Missouri

Blue Eye

The story is told that first postmaster Elbert N. Butler's neighbors suggested the name because of his striking *blue eyes*. He also had jet black hair.

Clever

On State Route 14 fifteen miles southwest of Springfield

frank Netzer's store was the gathering place in this crossroads community in the late 1890s, and it was here that word was received from back East that the Post Office Department had rejected Netzer's name for the new post office. The storekeeper turned the problem over to his customers, who didn't even get close to agreeing on a name until Tom Lentz proposed *Clever*. To him the word meant not only adroit and witty but friendly and accommodating. Lentz obviously liked his neighbors.

Competition

Twenty-two miles southeast of Lebanon in the south-central part of the state

the name comes from the *competition* among three tiny settlements over which one should have the school—and, perhaps, the post office.

Fairdealing

On U.S. Route 160 about 17 miles southwest of Poplar Bluff and 22 miles north of the Arkansas border

according to local legend, a stranger arrived in town one day many years ago with a lame horse. A horse trader made him an offer for a good horse that the stranger thought exceedingly *fair*. He promised to spread the word that there was *fair dealing* at this location.

Foil

A mile off State Route 95 forty-five miles southeast of Springfield in northwestern Ozark County

first postmaster Jack Blair is said to have named this Ozarks hamlet after a small town in Oklahoma (now vanished) where he had once worked. A *foil* against what—the Indians? Or was this a place where the buffalo roamed—*foil* being an old word for animal trail? The store and post office and the house that Jack built in 1909 are still standing.

Stretching your legs in Foil: The Ozark Mountains region is dotted with old grist mills, and three historically interesting ones are all within a short drive of *Foil*. The Dawt Mill, a three-story frame building on the North

Fork of the White River, features a stone millrace. Location: 12 miles northeast of Gainesville on State Route PP. The Aid-Hodgson Mill is in the community of Sycamore, a half mile east of State Route 181. The spring there is said to flow at the rate of 12 million gallons per hour. Closest to *Foil* is the Zanoni Mill, a two-story frame building with an overshot wheel. Location: Ten miles north of Gainesville on State Route 181. The village of Zononi, by the way, was named for a pre-Civil War novel. There are signs directing tourists to all three mills.

Protem

On State Route 125 near the Arkansas border 20 miles east-southeast of Branson

This Ozarks hamlet split into two factions over the question of what to call itself. One Saturday, men from each faction drove their wagons to a meeting that everyone sensed could turn into a showdown—all carried shotguns. Violence was averted when the richest, best-educated, most respected man in the hamlet, C. C. Owen, persuaded his neighbors to call the place *Protem* from the Latin *pro tempore*, meaning "for the time being." "We can petition the government to change it later if it doesn't work out," he said. Nobody ever did.

Owen became the first postmaster in 1875.

Reform

At the intersection of County Roads O and CC twenty-four miles northeast of Jefferson City

Some say this town was named for a religious group called the *Reformites*. Others say it was so-named because its early settlers were bible-quoting Christians who had all *reformed*.

One of them was Reverend William Coats, who organized most of the Baptist churches in Callaway County. Locals like to tell the story of how his grandson "drowned" his cholera in 1833 by drinking a barrel of water in 24 hours.

Rescue

On State Route 96 about 35 miles west of Springfield

The story is told that the village was named for the *rescue* of a destitute family by postmistress and general storekeeper Martha Arthur. The time was the 1890s.

(See *Rescue*, Virginia, page 242.)

Sharp

On County Road CC in northeastern Ozark County near the Howell County line about 70 miles southeast of Springfield

Second postmaster J. J. Swain boasted that he was the *sharp* one in a trade he made with first postmaster Andrew J. Hensley—perhaps for the post office. The post office lasted from 1890 to 1915, when the mail started going to *Cureall* in Howell County, according to postal records. *Cureall* was a health resort.

Udall

Three miles north of the Arkansas border on the east side of Norfolk Lake in southeastern Ozark County

Originally called St. Ledger, postmaster Riley Compton changed the name in 1885. The theory is that the name is derived from the teamster's call to his horse—"Get up there, *you doll*"—that Compton heard all day long out on the street.

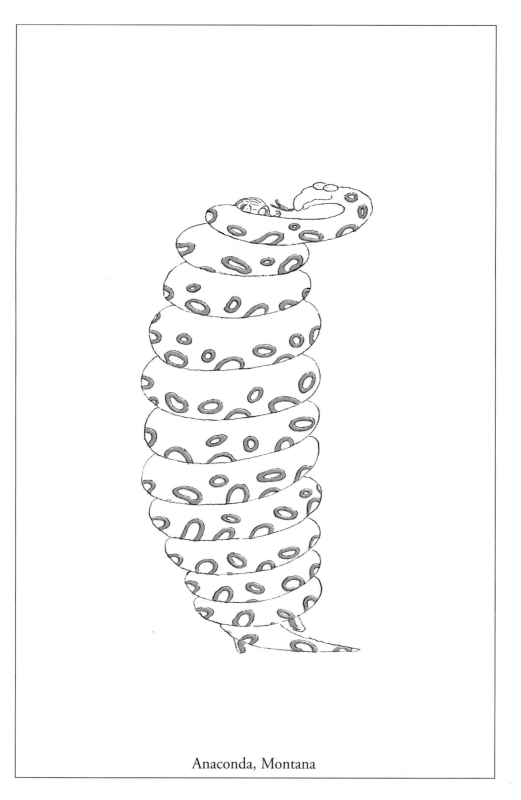

Anaconda, Montana

montana

Checkerboard

On U.S. Route 12 fifteen miles east of White Sulphur Springs and 89 miles east of Helena

When Dale McAfee left home in 1943 to seek his fortune in New York City, his hometown was named Delpine. When he came back in 1985, it was called *Checkerboard.* The current generation accepts the explanation that the real estate in and around the town is *checkerboarded* between U.S. Forest Service land and privately owned land. But McAfee says the land isn't all that broken up—not like other places in Montana; and, besides, the stream that runs through town has always been known as *Checkerboard* Creek. "The name probably had something to do with somebody playing *checkers* by the creek," he surmises.

McAfee, who, like a lot of Montanans, never met a government agency that didn't make him angry, blames the Forest Service for the name change. "The Forest Service probably did it to satisfy its own whim," he says.

Emigrant

On U.S. Route 89 twenty miles south of Livingston and a 46-mile drive southeast of Bozeman

at least two groups of *emigrants* passed through the beautiful Paradise Valley at a time when, for the sake of convenience, gold and silver prospectors were naming land features and specific locales. One source says a wagon train traveling either the Bozeman or Bonanza Trail came through on August 28, 1864. Two days later, three of these *emigrants* climbed up into the mountains and found gold.

Another source says that on June 1, 1887, Morman *emigrants* from Utah passed through here on their way to forming a new settlement on Lee's Creek near what is now Cardston in Alberta, Canada. There were eight families in the party, and they carried all their belongings in six wagons. The wagons were pulled by oxen that would pull their plows once they got to Canada. The *emigrants* also brought their cattle, horses, and chickens, which were in crates in one of the wagons.

Stretching your legs in Emigrant: Just a few minutes south of *Emigrant* is Chico Hot Springs Lodge, an unpretentiously charming Old West hotel with a lobby that has hardly changed since the hotel opened on June 20, 1900. The lodge has a gourmet restaurant with walls lined with paintings by landscape artist Russell Chatham (a frequent diner), a rowdy saloon

Nameless Places

WHAT WITH STUMPS to pull and wagon wheels to fix and winter coming on, the pioneers weren't always up to naming the places they inhabited and the geographical features that they used to orient themselves, give directions, and predict the weather. So they left them *nameless*, as in **Nameless Cave**, South Dakota, and **Nameless**, Texas, a town that gave up on having a real name after the U.S. Post Office Department rejected six submissions, and **Nameless**, Tennessee, an Appalachian Mountains hamlet that hardly tried to think of an appropriate name. Or, with tongue in cheek, they gave the place *no name* at all, as in **No Name**, Colorado; **No Name Glacier**, Washington; **No Name Mesa**, Arizona; and **No Name Brook**, Maine.

In all, the U.S. Board on Geographic Names has 1,115 features and a couple dozen towns in its database that have *No Name* or *Nameless* in their name.

A variation on this theme is the use of the Spanish word for "nothing," *nada*. A town in Colorado County, Texas, called **Nada** is said to have been named by immigrants after Nadja, Czechoslovakia, but as George R. Stewart points out in *American Place Names*, it's not likely the namers would not have been aware of the meaning of the word to the many Spanish-speaking people in the region.

Will C. Barnes includes a **Nadaburg** in *Arizona Place Names* that was sometimes called **Nada** for short. It was so named because there was absolutely nothing there, he says.

Other variations are expressed in the names **Nowhere**, Oklahoma; **Unnamed Wash**, Nevada, and **Unnamed Wash**, California; and **None** (for *no name*), Missouri, what people called *Enon* at first.

The irony of these "nameless" places, of course, is that they were all important enough to be given a name.

where you can rub elbows with real cowboys, and two outdoor pools filled year-round with mineral water from the hot springs, one 94 degrees for playing and one 104 degrees for soaking away your urban troubles.

Twodot

On U.S. Route 12 ten miles west of Harlowton in central Montana

*t*wo Dot was the brand of open-range rancher George R. "*Two Dot*" Wilson. At first, Wilson used the king pin from his wagon to sear *two dots* side by side on each hip of his cows. Today the brand is owned by Emma Freeser, and it has a bar under the two dots: •• . If you can't find any of her cattle roaming about, you can get a look at the brand at the saloon in town; it's embedded in the door.

Twodot is still very much the ranching community it was when the saloon, the town's first structure, was built just before the turn of the century. When I called in mid-March, postmaster Rick Schuler told me that the chances of getting rancher/historian John Whelan to call me back anytime soon were slim. "It's a pretty busy time of year; everybody's out calving," Schuler said. Whelan is the present occupant of the old George R. "*Two Dot*" Wilson homestead.

Other Unusual Place-Names in Montana

Anaconda

On State Route 1 twenty-seven miles northwest of Butte

What does a copper mining town have in common with a bone-crushing South American snake? Nothing, really. The town was named for the copper mine in nearby Butte, which, in turn, was named by a man who had read a Civil War account that described Grant's army encircling Lee's like a giant *anaconda.*

The town was first called *Copperopolis.*

Stretching your legs in Anaconda: Get out of the car anywhere in town and look up, up, up at the world's tallest smokestack—at the Anaconda Smelter.

Garryowen

An exit off I-90 halfway between Billings and the Wyoming border

Only a handful of U.S. place-names are a person's first and last names combined—and this isn't one of them. *Garryowen* is the name of an ancient Irish song that was the regimental tune of the U.S. 7th Cavalry; and the town overlooks the spot where, on June 25, 1876, cocky Lt. Colonel George A. Custer and 265 cavalrymen made their deadly last stand against a combined force of Sioux and Cheyenne Indians.

Intake

On State Route 16 twelve miles north of Glendive in the eastern part of the state

this community was on the *intake* side—that is, the reservoir side—of the Lower Yellowstone Irrigation Project dam the federal Bureau of Land Management started building in 1908. Sometimes it was called "the Dam Town."

Quietus

On a gravel road in the southeastern part of the state near the Wyoming border

f rank Brittain sent a list of fifteen names with the town's application for a post office in 1917, and all of them were rejected by the officials in Washington. "Well, I guess they put a *quietus* on that," Brittain said to his wife. She immediately saw the opportunity to have some fun at the feds' expense and dashed off a letter. A few weeks later the name *Quietus* was approved. This anecdote is told in Roberta Carkeek Cheney's *Names on the Face of Montana*.

Quietus is near Hanging Woman Creek, but that's another story.

nebraska

Alliance

On U.S. Route 385 in the northwestern part of the state

In the late 1800s, dozens of eastern place-names were repeated in the new towns rising up along wagon trails and railroad tracks west of the Mississippi River. The name *Alliance* arrived here in the Sand Hills from Ohio via the Burlington and Missouri Railroad and one of its engineers, J. M. Paul. *Alliance*, Ohio was his hometown.

The parent town was also named by a railroad man, J. S. Robinson, for the intersection of the Pittsburgh, Fort Wayne and Chicago, and the Cleveland and Pittsburgh Railroads, which Robinson and local business leaders hoped would soon form an *alliance*.

Stretching your legs in Alliance: A few miles north of town on U.S. Route 385 you may wonder if you've been driving too long and if you're beginning to see things that aren't there. Off to the right of the highway, rising out of the dry, brown prairie, 29 junk cars from the 1950s and 1960s point heavenward, buried up to their back windows in the ground. Nine others, familiarly horizontal, form crude arches over pairs of "planted" cars. All 38 cars are painted gray to look like stone. The cars are configured in a big circle—100 feet in diameter—with a horseshoe of cars in the middle of the circle whose open end faces northeast. Welcome to Carhenge!

Modeled after Stonehenge in England, whose builders used 20 and 30-ton stones instead of two-ton cars, Carhenge is the brainchild of Jim Reinders, an electronics engineer who gathered 35 friends and family members together in 1987 to build a memorial to his father on the old family farm. Carhenge is expanding as a Car Art Reserve. Recent additions include an installation depicting salmon spawning made entirely of car parts, and Ford Season, a sculpture made up entirely of Fords that suggests Nebraska's changing agricultural landscape through the four seasons. Location: On U.S. Route 385 two and a half miles north of *Alliance*. No phone. Admission free.

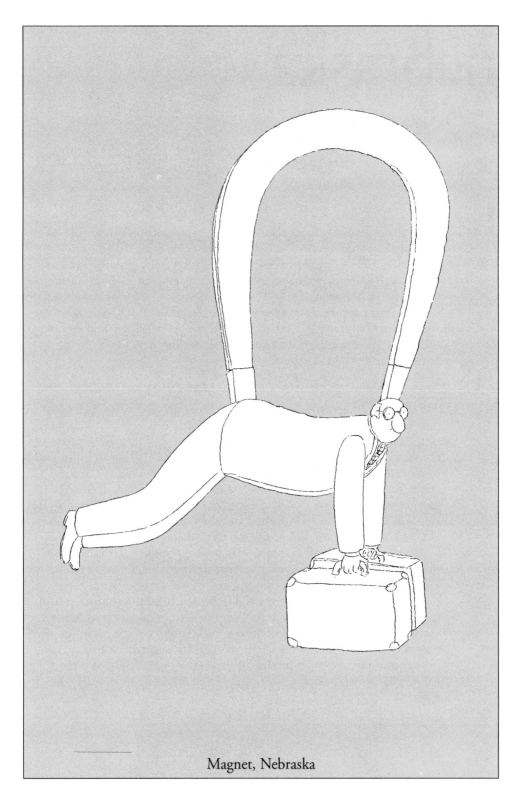

Magnet, Nebraska

Hazard

At the intersection of State Routes 2 and 10 twenty-seven miles north of Kearney in the central part of the state

There's half a handful of explanations for how *Hazard* got its name. Some say it was named for a Mr. *Hazzard* (two *Z*s), who drilled a well for the Grand Island and Wyoming Central Railroad depot that was the tiny town's first building. Others say it was for a dangerous marshy area along the track, which prompted the townspeople to put up a warning sign: "*HAZARD.*" Or was the *hazard* the big pothole on Main Street in the late 1880s?

One account says the first settlers wanted to name the place Bunnell. When they learned that there already was a Bunnell in Nebraska, they held a meeting to choose another name. A number of names had been proposed and rejected when a frustrated citizen stood up and announced loudly, "I'll *hazard* a name you won't dismiss." But before he could say it, he was cut off by another man, who exclaimed, "*Hazard.* That's it. We'll name it *Hazard.*"

Whichever explanation is true, the town, whose population never reached 300 and now hovers around 70, has had its share of *hazards.* The Blizzard of '88 nearly buried the town alive before it really got going. Two huge fires destroyed big chunks of the business district. The Depression knocked out both of its banks in 1929, and the droughts and dust storms of the 1930s drove off many of its farmers.

Wynot

Just off State Route 12 two miles south of the Missouri River in the northeastern part of the state

The St. Paul Townsite Company purchased the land for this stop on the Chicago, St. Paul, Minneapolis and Omaha Railroad in 1906 from an elderly German man named Willibold D. Schulte. The question of what to name it came up soon afterwards at a public meeting. The story goes that when someone suggested a named that struck Schulte's fancy, he shouted gustily, "Ja, *Vy not?*" And the proposed name was quickly forgotten. (See *Whynot,* Mississippi, page 128.)

If this seems like a flimsy hook on which to hang a place-name, it wasn't the only one in Nebraska. One early settler who was having trouble coming up with a name for a post office sent in the name *Trouble.* Another hoped that *Okay* would be O.K., and it was. One naming committee was totally stumped until one of its members noticed a Uneeda Biscuit box. Pretty soon Nebraska had a post office and a town named *Biscuit.*

(See *Uneeda,* West Virginia, page 253.)

Other Unusual Place-Names in Nebraska

Bee

On a spur of State Route 15 thirty-four miles northwest of Lincoln and eight miles north of Seward

The name has nothing to do with an insect that stings, or with a prairie social gathering for the purpose of doing work. This was Township *B* on the plat of Seward County made near the turn of the century.

Broken Bow

At the convergence of State Routes 2, 21, and 70 in the central part of the state

First postmaster Wilson Hewitt sent in three different names to the Post Office Department in 1879, and all three were rejected. Then one day, his sons, Fred and Erwin, came home with a *broken* Indian *bow* they found along the banks of Muddy Creek. Hewitt went straight to his desk and wrote a letter to Washington.

Magnet

On State Route 59 two miles west of U.S. Route 81 and 30 miles north of Norfolk in the northeastern part of the state

In almost every state west of the original thirteen colonies you find "*magnet* towns," places with names designed to attract people to them. This one stands out because it is so incredibly blatant. And as the librarian up the road in Hartington told me, it didn't work; *Magnet* never amounted to anything.

Magnet Towns

HERE ARE SOME OTHER examples of magnet towns: **Enterprise**, Alabama, Kansas, Oklahoma, Illinois, Indiana, North Dakota, and Utah; **Carefree**, Arizona and Indiana; **Security**, Colorado; **Eden**, Idaho; **Advance**, Indiana and Wisconsin; **Success**, Missouri; **Delightful**, Ohio; **Tranquility**, California and Ohio; **Paradise**, California, Kentucky, and Illinois; **Ideal**, South Dakota and Minnesota; **Progress**, Indiana and Texas; **Opportunity**, Montana and Washington; **Excel**, Alabama; **Prosperity**, Indiana and South Carolina; **Prosper**, Michigan; **Prospect**, Pennsylvania and Illinois; **Commerce**, Georgia, Oklahoma, and Texas; **Energy**, Illinois and Texas; **Endeavor**, Wisconsin; **Acme**, Wyoming; **Paragon**, Indiana; **Confidence**, California; **Utopia**, Ohio; and **Eminence**, Indiana.

There also are numerous towns named **Harmony**, **Independence**, **Freedom,** or a name based on one of those words, all of which expressed the outlook of the founders and were meant to lure people hoping to start a new life.

Surprise

On State Spur Route S-12E forty miles northwest of Lincoln

All the historical accounts mention George Miller, who along with his wife and two sons were the second family to settle in the area. One account has it that Miller, who arrived in 1881, was *surprised* to find a river (the Big Blue) with enough water flowing between its banks to turn the wheel of the grist mill he wanted to build. Other accounts say that as new settlers came over the gentle hills to the north and south, they were *surprised* to see an operating mill so far from civilization—the nearest towns were two days away. It soon became known as the *Surprise* Mill, and when enough settlers had arrived to establish a town, *Surprise* was the obvious choice for a name.

Searchlight, Nevada

nevada

Cal-Nev-Ari

On U.S. Route 95 near where California, Nevada, and Arizona converge

The name is self-explanatory once you look at a map, but finding out how and when this little desert community of 450 got its name took a while. It wasn't in *Nevada Place Names*, and the Las Vegas Library couldn't help.

Border Names

CAL-NEV-ARI IS NOT UNIQUE; you find these cut-and-paste names along the borders of many states. But the seams aren't always visible.

Sitting on the point of land where Kentucky, Ohio, and West Virginia come together is **Kenova**, West Virginia. Another three-state name is **Texarkana**, which straddles the Texas-Arkansas border 30 miles north of the Louisiana border (and thought to be even closer when the city was settled in the early 1870s). The name was conceived when a railroad surveyor nailed a board to a tree and painted "Tex-Ark-Ana" on it.

Another Arkansas border town was named before the border was with a state. **Arkinda** combines *Ark*ansas with *Ind*ian Territory.

Texas rubs elbows with Oklahoma at the panhandle town of **Texhoma**, Texas, and with New Mexico at **Texline**—a more utilitarian border name of a type found in a dozen states. All the way on the other side of the state, Texas waves to Louisiana from the western bank of the Sabine River at **Texla**.

Maryland keeps its border with Delaware straight with **Delmar**, **Marydel,** and **Mardela Springs**. State Street, the main street in **Delmar**, runs right along the border. On its Pennsylvania border, Maryland has **Sylmar** and **Pen Mar**, which, by the way, is one of the best places in the East to watch hang gliders take off.

Other border names include: **Illmo,** Missouri; **Monida**, Montana; **Idavada**, Idaho; **Florala,** Alabama; **Kanorado**, Kansas; **Texico**, New Mexico; **Texola**, Oklahoma; **Tennga**, Georgia; **Tennemo**, Tennessee; **Uvada**, Utah; **Michiana**, Michigan, and **Virgilina**, Virginia, by far the most graceful sounding of all these border names.

California is the cut-and-paste leader with five names, not all of which still appear on maps: **Calneva** and **Calada** on the Nevada border, **Calor** opposite Oregon, **Calzona** on the Arizona border, and **Calexico**, just across the international border from **Mexicali**, Mexico, itself a border name.

Neither could the state Board on Geographic Names.

So I called the fire station—the most promising number that the information operator had to offer—and talked to a woman who, without really saying it, indicated she could help me but *not* on the emergency line.

An older man answered, "Casino," when I called the non-emergency number, but I also heard the woman's voice in the background. Fire station? Casino? The post office also was under the same roof, Ellis Squire told me.

Squire explained that, during World War II, General George S. Patton's tank drivers trained where the casino now stood. Nearby is a mile-long airstrip the Army built to move equipment in and out of the training camp.

Nancy Kidwell and her husband "Slim," a pioneering aviator from California whom Squire claims knew Amelia Earhart, homesteaded the abandoned camp in 1965. They punched a well and grew barley for a few years to get title to the land, and then reopened the airstrip as Three Corners Airport. When Slim died in the mid-1980s, it was renamed Kidwell Airport. Slim is buried on the airport grounds; Nancy is still alive and owns the casino.

So what about the name *Cal-Nev-Ari*, I asked Squire. That's what Slim and Nancy called their homestead, "right from the beginning." And it's what they named the Casino and the post office, too, he said.

Locals pronounce *Cal-Nev-Ari* as if there were no hyphens. It rolls off the tongue smoothly after you've said it a few hundred times, and sounds faraway and exotic.

Dinner Station

On State Route 225 twenty miles north of Elko in the northern part of the state

a two-story stone building here once housed a hotel that was a meal stop for stagecoach passengers headed for ranches and mines in northern Elko County.

Jackpot

On U.S. Route 93 on the Idaho border

this isolated town of 500 was named on April 7, 1959, by the Elko County commissioners for that exhilarating ringing of silver that casual gamblers hope and pray will be their reward for pumping quarters into a slot machine all night. Could there be a better name for a town in the original gambling state?

Before 1959, *Jackpot* was referred to as *Unincorporated Town No. 1*. Obviously, the county commissioners knew what they were doing when they got their hands on a gambling license.

Other Unusual Place-Names in Nevada

Contact

On U.S. 93 in the northeastern corner of the state

the community that grew up here around the turn of the century took its name from the *Contact* Mining District. The name was descriptive, referring to a geological zone where limestone made *contact* with granite.

Contact was a station on a branch of the Union Pacific Railroad running between Wells, Nevada, and Twin Falls, Idaho.

Jiggs

On State Route 228 twenty miles south of Elko

the citizens were forever arguing about what to call their town—until someone suggested they name it after the husband who was always bickering with his wife in the popular comic strip "Maggie and *Jiggs*."

Searchlight

Where U.S. Route 95 and State Route 164 cross 50 miles south of Las Vegas near the southeastern point of Nevada

gold prospector Floyd *Searchlight* is remembered with this name, but locals would rather tell you that the town takes its name from a remark made long ago: "Yes, there's gold in these hills, but you'd need a *searchlight* to find it." Or that two brothers lighting a campfire here in 1898 named the location for the brand name on their box of matches.

Seven Troughs

On a remote dirt road in western Pershing County northeast of Reno in the northwestern part of the state

around the turn of the century, local ranchers placed a series of *seven troughs* below some springs to collect water for their stock, according to *Nevada Place Names* by Helen S. Carlson, a principal source of information about Nevada place-names. Water from the springs collects behind a massive natural dike of black basalt that cuts across a canyon.

A mountain range, the canyon, and a mining district also go by the name. Gold was discovered here in 1905; now tungsten is mined.

Shantytown

On the western shore of Ruby Lake 45 miles south-southeast of Elko

This little supply center for hunters and fishermen was named for its shabby appearance.

Sly Surnames

IN EVERY CORNER of the country there are places that seemingly are named for actions, animals, objects, descriptive terms, or abstract ideas but turn out to be surnames. Here are some I stumbled upon while doing research for this book: **Admire**, Kansas; **Honor**, Michigan; **Spades,** Indiana; **Tiger**, Washington (*Cougar*, Washington, is named for the real thing); **Amble**, Michigan; **Ponder**, Texas; **Covert**, New York; **Bachelor**, North Carolina; **Ransom**, Michigan; **Slick**, Oklahoma; **Smock**, Pennsylvania; **Cheek**, Texas; **Waltz,** Michigan; **Ebony**, Texas; **Riddle**, North Carolina; **Bankers,** Michigan; **Drums**, Pennsylvania; **Suit**, North Carolina (near a town once called *Vest*); **Pray**, Montana; **Severence**, Colorado; **Kite**, Georgia (a simplification of *Kight* requested by postal authorities); **Startup**, Washington, **Birthright**, Texas; **Love**, Arizona; **Deputy**, Indiana (the name originated in England when an infant was abandoned and left on the doorstep of a *deputy*); **Coffee**, Georgia; **Pancake**, Texas; **Guntown**, Mississippi (for James *Gunn*); **Rule**, Texas; **Silent,** Arizona; **Register**, Georgia; **Hasty**, Colorado; **Fedora**, South Dakota; **Kitchen**, Ohio; **Searchlight,** Nevada; **Barwise**, Texas; **Roulette**, Pennsylvania; and **Dull**, Texas.

That last one is pretty good, but my favorite is **Boring**, Maryland, an address that has made its residents the brunt of a lot of ribbing over the years. The town was named in 1880 for its first postmaster, David J. *Boring*.

new hampshire

Breakfast Hill

On a local road six miles north of Hampton (between I-95 and U.S. 1) and three miles from the Atlantic coastline

b*reakfast Hill* is a village in the town of Rye, the site of the first permanent settlement in New Hampshire, a fishing camp with about ten inhabitants (all men) established in 1623. Eight years later, a band of 80 colonists, including 32 women, arrived from England and spread out along the coast between here and what is now Portsmouth.

The Indians whom the colonists encountered were at first friendly and cooperative, according to a local history, but friction between the two cultures inevitably developed. By the early 18th century, the Indians felt they were being squeezed off their rich fishing and shellfishing grounds at the mouth of the Piscataqua River and started fighting back.

On one raid, the Indians killed or captured 21 colonists on the Portsmouth Plains, what is now Brackett Road in Rye. Another time, they killed 14 and took four hostages before retreating to the top of a *hill* to eat *breakfast*. While the Indians were resting, militiamen from Portsmouth surprised them and rescued the captives. Since then this locale has been known as *Breakfast Hill*.

City slickers staying at the Furnace Creek Inn dude ranch in Inyo County, California, eat *breakfast* in pretty *Breakfast* Canyon after an early morning ride.

Stretching your legs in Breakfast Hill: Near the entrance to Straw's Point Road in Rye is a little cemetery with headstones marking the graves of many of the settlers killed in the Portsmouth Plains Massacre. There is also a boulder with a plaque on it commemorating John Locke. Locke had slashed the Indians' canoes while they were resting on *Breakfast Hill*, and he paid for it with his life and his scalp.

Cowbell Corners

Two miles north of downtown Salem and 15 miles northeast of Nashua

t*he town was named for the *bell* that hung in the belfry of a woolen mill that has long since been torn down. Salem reference librarian Debbie Berlin didn't

Breakfast Hill, New Hampshire

know that until she looked it up for me in a town history, but she remembered that up until 1960 there was a bridge over nearby Route 28 that people called The *Cow* Bridge. It was used by the dairy *cows* at Tenney Farm. The area is now "all shopping malls," according to Berlin.

Another humorous place-name in this neck of the woods is *Hitty Titty Brook*.

Towns and villages with *corner(s)* in their name date back to Colonial times, making them among the oldest place-names on the map of the U.S. These names are common in New Hampshire, Massachusetts, and Delaware.

Deerfield Parade

About 20 miles east-southeast of Concord and 20 miles northeast of Manchester

Whenever anyone in the Deerfields —*Deerfield, Deerfield Center, South Deerfield,* and *Deerfield Parade*—has a local history question, they call Joanne Wasson. So that's what I did when the library in *Deerfield* couldn't help me. Wasson said she "assumes" the triangular-shaped common in the largest of these four villages was used as *parade* ground for the state militia and perhaps for the colonial militia before that, but she's never seen it written down anywhere. It may also have been used as a muster field, or training site, for firing cannons.

Wasson is certain that there once was an inn overlooking the common where, in the early 1800s, the Order of the Cincinnati (officer veterans of the Revolutionary War) held its annual meeting every Fourth of July. And they almost certainly *paraded* around in their uniforms, she says.

Parade, South Dakota, is the only other *parade* I found on the map of the U.S.—and it's a fake. The town was named for George *Paridis*, an early settler, but that changed after the namers learned there already was a *Paradis* in the state.

Fish Market

On a town road eight miles east of Lebanon and 50 miles northwest of Concord

According to a Letter to the Editor in the Friday, August 9, 1907, edition of *The Enfield* (New Hampshire) *Advocate*, Amos French, an early settler, placed ads in newspapers from Burlington, Vermont, to Boston promoting the village as a *fish market*, hoping this would deliver more customers to the door of his general store. There was, perhaps, a fin of truth to his claim; locals had been catching two-, three-, and even five-pound pickerel in Crystal Lake and making extra income by shipping them by stage to buyers in Hanover and Concord.

The letter does not say whether French's scheme worked.

Other Unusual Place-Names in New Hampshire

Happy Corner

On U.S. Route 3 at the northern tip of the state—between First Connecticut Lake and Lake Francis

This gas stop on the road to Quebec is said to have been named for a store where local men gathered to gab and joke and play cards.

Harts Location

On U.S. Route 302 in the White Mountain National Forest in the north-central part of the state

You won't find this term—*location*—used in place-names in any other state. This hamlet in the White Mountains was named for George *Hart* and his cousin Richard *Hart,* who bought a total of 2,440 acres of timberland from Thomas Chadbourne in 1772. Chadbourne was granted the land by King George III of England as reward for service in the French and Indian War.

Horse Corner

On a town road three miles east of Concord

The story goes that a Revolutionary War soldier garrisoned in Portsmouth deserted and stole a *horse* to ride home to Concord. Some forty miles later, he abandoned the *horse* in a cellar hole and continued his journey on foot. The Town of Chichester History Committee claims that the second word of this place-name comes from the fact that the *horse* was later found in the *corner* of the cellar hole. More likely, the namers used the word generically; *corner(s)* was a common term for a crossroads community back then.
(See *Cowbell Corners*, New Hampshire, page 153.)

Lost Nation

On a town road six miles northeast of Lancaster and 20 miles northwest of Mt. Washington

White Mountain lore has it that this little settlement was named by an itinerant preacher. When he called the faithful together for worship, only one person showed up, inspiring a sermon in which he likened the local population to one of the *lost* tribes of Israel.
Allan Wolk writes about a *Lost Nation,* Iowa, in his book *The Naming of America.* He tells of a happy, prosperous *nation* of Indians that, according to legend, was completely wiped out one devastatingly cold and snowy winter.

new jersey

Bargaintown

Near Atlantic City on the Garden State Parkway

Local historians point to two legends, both of which sound plausible:

> 1. David Howell, a Colonial-era blacksmith, had his smithy on the site of the village; he also owned land there. Whenever a customer came into his shop to have work done, he is said to have *bargained* trying to sell them a house lot as hard as he labored over the anvil.
>
> 2. James Somers made a *bargain* with his slaves. He offered them their freedom if they would build a road around what is now called *Bargaintown* Lake. The slaves took him up on it, and Somers proved more than true to his word. He not only granted the slaves their freedom, he gave each one of them a parcel of land to till in the *bargain*.

Double Trouble

On a county road about four miles southwest of Tom's River and 55 miles east of Philadelphia

The name has to do with the mill dam on Cedar Creek in the early 19th century. Either because of faulty engineering or structural damage caused by muskrats burrowing through it, the earth and wattle dam washed away twice within a single week. The first time it happened, the miller, according to local legend, cried, "Here's *trouble!*" But he was up to it, and he rebuilt the dam. When it washed away a second time a few days later, the miller cried, "Here's *double trouble!*"

No one knows whether the miller rebuilt the dam after the second catastrophe.

Locals like to point out that Cedar Creek rises near Mount Misery, flows past *Double Trouble*, and empties into Barnegat Bay at Good Luck.

Double Trouble, New Jersey

Ongs Hat

On a local road in central Burlington County halfway between Camden and the Atlantic coastline

In the Gay Nineties, this village (now abandoned) was the center of social life in the Pine Barrens. Saturday night dances drew people from miles around to step to the music of country fiddlers. A young flame named *Ong* was a regular at these dances, and his handsome face and shiny silk top *hat*, worn with a rakish air, made him the center of attention.

Ong had many jealous admirers, according to New Jersey historian Henry Beck, and one night one of them felt *Ong* hadn't given her sufficient attention. So she snatched the top *hat* from *Ong's* head and stomped on it in the middle of the dance floor.

Another naming legend says that *Ong*, having had a considerable amount to drink on a memorably raucous Saturday night, tossed his caddish topper high into a tree at the center of the village. There, beyond the reach of even the most daring tree-climber, it hung in the wind and rain for many months.

Penny Pot

On U.S. Route 322 roughly halfway between Camden to the northwest and Atlantic City to the southeast

Penny Pot is on the old stagecoach route from Philadelphia to Absecon, on the New Jersey shore. In 1762, Isaac Dole was granted a license to operate a tavern here. People referred to it as Smashed Hat Tavern, because when someone got rowdy and broke a window, Dole stuffed the hole with an old hat to keep the cold out.

Smashed Hat might well have been the village's original name, although it has been suggested that the village got its name from another tavern, the *Penny Pot* in Philadelphia. Or was it from the pub in Bristol, England, where good ale could be had for a *"penny a pot"*?

Another source offers what sounds like a traditional storyteller's invention: A traveler from Cape May, New Jersey, stopped at the inn for a fresh mount and then proceeded on to Philadelphia. When he returned to the village to pick up his horse and settle his account, the innkeeper called to his wife to bring him some change. Rachel called back that there was not *"a penny in the pot."*

Yellow Frame

On State Route 94 straddling the Sussex-Warren county line in the northern part of the state

Since 1786, a *frame* church, painted *yellow* with white trim, has stood on a heavenly hill in this rolling countryside near the Pennsylvania border. Grace Van Horn, historian for the *Yellow Frame* Presbyterian Church and a lifelong resident of the community, says that before the dairy farms dwindled after World War II, and trees grew up in the pastures, you could see this bright *yellow* place of worship from five miles away in any direction.

The original church was replaced in 1887 with the present Queen Anne-style structure, which, heretically, was painted in a Victorian color scheme of cream, rust, orange, and brown, according to church records. That lasted only a few years.

"I guess they had their fling at not being *yellow*," says Van Horn.

Other Unusual Place-Names in New Jersey

Bivalve

On a local road near the point where the Maurice River flows into Delaware Bay

This unlikely place-name, found here and in Maryland, celebrates the oyster, a mollusk, like the clam, with a two-*valved* shell.

Califon

On a local road 35 miles west of Newark and 35 miles north of Trenton

This may be the only town in the United States whose name didn't get recorded right because the men painting the sign on the railroad station botched the job. It was supposed to say *California*. Rumor has it the painters were not sober by the time they ran out of space.

Why *California? Califon* Historical Society President Dan Freibergs has heard two stories. In one of them, miller Jacob Neighbor gets gold fever, goes to California, makes his fortune, and then comes home and names the town *California*. In the other, Neighbor makes a *California*-size fortune with a new method of grinding corn.

Cheesequake

Near where State Route 34 joins U.S. Route 9 about 20 miles south-southwest of Elizabeth

It's said that the New York *cheesecake* they make here in northern New Jersey is so rich it will make your stomach *quake*. That would be a good story if it were true. In fact, *Cheesequake* is an English translation of a Lenni-Lenape Indian word, and locals pronounce it as if it were spelled C-h-e-s-s-q-u-i-c-k.

Ho-Ho-Kus

An exit off the Garden State Parkway about ten miles north-northeast of Paterson

This is not hocus-pocus, but a real New York City bedroom community whose name is buried in the name of the *Chihohokies* Indians and their largely forgotten language.

Pie Town, New Mexico

new mexico

Truth or Consequences

On I-25 a little more than halfway between Albuquerque and El Paso

This was the name of a popular radio show in the 1940s and 1950s. On March 31, 1950, the small city of Hot Springs voted to accept host Ralph Edwards's nationally broadcast offer of free publicity to any town that would change its name to the name of his show. For many years, Edwards led a group of Hollywood stars to *T or C*, as it is locally known, for the annual *Truth or Consequences* Fiesta. People in *T or C* showed that they were grateful for

Gimmick Names

MOVE NOW FROM Truth or Consequences, New Mexico, in 1950 to eastern Montana in 1993 and you find tiny Ismay, Montana, population 28, changing its name to **Joe, Montana,** in a publicity stunt dreamed up by a disc jockey in Kansas City. *Joe Montana*, the great San Francisco 49ers quarterback had just joined the Kansas City Chiefs for his last hurrah. Ismay—I mean *Joe*—got its old name back after the 1994 Super Bowl.

If a town in a state with the right name can do it, a town with the right name in the right state can do it, too. The city council in Troy, a central Texas town of 1,400, voted to call the place **Troy Aikman**, after the Dallas Cowboys star quarterback. Again, it was only until the 1994 Super Bowl.

The only other U.S. town to change its name for a major sports figure is **Jim Thorpe**, Pennsylvania, formerly Mauch Chunk—but that's no gimmick. The name has been official since 1954, when the town fathers crossed paths with the 1912 Olympic hero's widow while looking for a tourist attraction to stabilize the town's yo-yoing coal mining economy.

Mauch Chunk, by the way, is Algonquian for "bear mountain."

Two hoax names, **Goblu**, for "Go Blue!" (University of Michigan), and **Beatosu**, for "Beat OSU!" (Ohio State University), were secreted onto Michigan's official state transportation map in 1979-80, only to be removed the next time the map was issued. The University of Michigan and OSU are Big Ten football rivals.

Then there is **Hamilton!,** Ohio, whose city council voted in 1986 to add an exclamation point to the city's name. It seemed like a good way to draw attention to this factory town of 61,000, which is always being overshadowed by Cincinnati. Mapmakers, even the official state ones, ignored the gimmick.

the attention by naming the city's biggest park for Edwards.

Waters, Arkansas, changed its name to *Pine Ridge*, the fictitious setting of the *Lum and Abner* radio show in 1936. Chester Lauk and Norris Goff, the show's creators and star performers hailed from nearby Mena, Arkansas, and they based their characters on people in the Waters area.

Stretching your legs in Truth or Consequences: Before the white men drove them off, Indians of various tribes traveled to the hot springs here to bathe wounds they had suffered in battle. It was considered neutral territory, and was a favorite retreat of Geronimo. Today, the hot springs still attract thousands of people each year. Bill Kaysing, in his now classic guide, *Great Hot Springs of the West*, mentions the Charles Motel and Bathhouse as one of several hot springs resorts within the city limits.

Wagon Mound

An exit off I-25 in east-central Mora County in the northeastern part of the state

The community that officially became *Wagon Mound* in 1882 was a long-established water stop on the Santa Fe Trail. It was first known as *Los Cuernos* and then *Santa Clara,* when it was a Mexican customs station (starting in 1836). In 1881 and 1882, the outpost had a fling with the name *Pinkerton* after Pinkerton detectives set up shop to guard some railroad equipment stored here.

The name *Wagon Mound* comes from the butte just east of town that resembles a covered *wagon.*

Wagon Mound was the hometown of Fray Angelico Chavez, the Franciscan priest and writer who celebrated and chronicled the early history of New Mexico. He died in 1996. In his later years, Fray Angelico—a name he took from a famous 15th century Italian priest and artist—was a familiar figure in the cafes on the Santa Fe plaza, always wearing a black beret and smoking a cigar.

Other Unusual Place-Names in New Mexico

Brilliant

On a dirt road a few miles northwest of Raton and a few miles south of the Colorado border

The name referred to the *brilliant* sheen of the coal mined in nearby Tin Pan Canyon. The coal had a luster that was superior to most coals. The town called itself *Swastika* for a few years during World War II, in defiance of Hitler. That's not as contradictory as it sounds: What locals had in mind was the Indian swastika, which symbolized being blessed with good luck from all four compass directions.

Highway

On State Route 206 thirty-seven miles south of Clovis in the eastern part of the state

This gets my vote as the least imaginative place-name in the U.S. I can imagine a conversation taking place between two ranchers back in the early years of this century, when *Highway* was named. One of them has just returned from Portales (the Roosevelt County seat, 26 miles north) with a letter postmarked "Washington, D.C."

"What's it about?" asks the other rancher.

"The government says we've gotta have a name for this place," says the first rancher. "We can't have a post office until we have a name. What do you think we should call it?"

"Oh, gosh, I don't know . . . It's right on the *highway*. Tell them to call it *Highway*."

Lingo

In southern Roosevelt County in the eastern part of the state about three miles from the Texas border

This is probably a family name, but it is sometimes said that this place was named for the *lingo* used by locals, who talked more like Texans than New Mexicans.

Originally called *Need* (see *Needmore*, West Virginia), the Post Office Department said the name was too much like Weed in Otero County and had to be changed. *Need* lasted only 19 months, from July 26, 1916 to March 5, 1918, according to *New Mexico Place Names*, edited by T. M. Pearce.

Pep

On State Route 206 in Roosevelt County 35 miles south of Clovis in the eastern part of the state

This town was named during the Depression (1936), supposedly for the breakfast cereal *Pep*, which was supposed to give you the energy you needed to survive tough times.

Stretching your legs in Pep: Eight hundred tourists a day stop in Roswell, in the next county west, to take in the sensational exhibits at the International U.F.O. Museum and Research Center. They come to see walls covered with clips from tabloid newspapers reporting on alien visitors, abductions, and U.F.O. sightings, to read personal sighting letters, to view documentary movies, and to gawk at a model of an alien stretched out on a hospital gurney. For $2.50, you can be photographed with the extraterrestrial, a prop in the Showtime movie *Roswell*. Visitors claiming to have been abducted by aliens can be debriefed by museum officials. Some visitors to the museum travel 30 miles north of town to visit the site of the Roswell Incident, where in 1947 a shiny silver spacecraft carrying five alien passengers supposedly crashed in the desert, only to be covered up by the military. Museum address: 114 North Main Street, Roswell. Telephone: (505) 625-9495. Admission charged.

Pie Town

On U.S. Route 60 in northern Catron County 67 miles from the Arizona border

a prospector failed to find any gold on his small claim, so he turned to a skill he had practiced earlier: *pie*-making. He put up a sign on the highway advertising his *pies*, which were deep with filling and had a light, flaky crust. Word spread among workmen and travelers that this was the place to buy a delicious *pie*.

(See *Pie*, West Virginia, page 252.)

Turn

On State Route 304 about eight miles south of Belen and 35 miles south of Albuquerque

h ispanics have been calling this place Casa Colorada since it was a stagecoach stop in the mid-18th century. That an unimaginative Anglo came along in 1927 and named it for a *turn* in the road has been a source of resentment ever since.

White Signal

On State Route 90 twenty miles south of Silver City in the southwestern part of the state

O ld West pioneers and prospectors got their bearings from an immense vein of *white* quartz in the side of a mountain they called the *White* Dyke. This *signal*, which a Silver City newspaper reporter described in 1908 as "resembling an immense stone wall which has been newly whitewashed," could be seen for miles around.

new york

Fresh Kills

On the west side of Staten Island

Those *kills* you see on maps of New York, Pennsylvania, and Delaware—Cats*kill*, Fish*kill*, Bush*kill*, to name three —are, like cottage cheese and the gambrel roof, a legacy of the Dutch settlers who came to the New World by the thousands in the 17th and 18th centuries. *Kill*, from Dutch *kil*, means creek or channel. This one, a *fresh*water creek and locale, shows how messy place naming can get when two different languages get hinged together, like a Dutch door, in one word.

Not knowing any of this, you'd guess there was a slaughterhouse here or a marsh where gangster hit men dumped their "clients." In truth, it is the site of the biggest garbage dump in the world, New York's *Fresh Kills* Landfill.

Stretching your legs in Fresh Kills: In 1996, the New York Sanitation De-partment started offering tours of the 2,200-acre dump. The tour starts at the visitors center with an 11-minute video on the trash biz and includes a trip up Trash Mountain. Other attractions are the garbage barges, the big crane that unloads them, the little sweeper boats that pick up the spillage, the containment pit, and the Hitchcockian cloud of seagulls that hover overhead. The *Fresh Kills* Landfill may not be on a par with the Museum of Modern Art or the Statue of Liberty for New York City attractions, but it's pretty amazing nevertheless. And it doesn't smell all that bad. Location: On Muldoon Avenue, an exit off the West Shore Expressway, Staten Island. Telephone: (212) 788-4057.

Horseheads

On State Route 14 six miles north of Elmira and 85 miles southwest of Syracuse

Animal rights activists won't like this story. This industrial center was named for the rows of *horse* skulls found here by the first settlers. In August 1779, Revolutionary War General John Sullivan ordered his troops to kill all their worn-out nags and serve them for dinner. The Indians arranged the skulls in rows along the trail long after the soldiers moved on, and named the locale The Valley of the *Horseheads*. One source says that pioneer children

Painted Post, New York

played a game in which they stepped from *head* to *head*, trying not to touch the ground.

Sullivan's Army, 4,000 strong, was returning from the western front where it had gone to crush the Iroquois Nation for supporting the British. The soldiers burned Indian villages and destroyed crops everywhere they found them.

Painted Post
On I-390 about 90 miles south-southeast of Rochester and just north of Corning

Visitors to *Painted Post* have received a sculptural greeting since before the Revolutionary War. Today, it comes from the bronze figure of an Indian warrior with upraised arm at the corner of Hamilton and Water Streets. In the late 18th century, what caught your attention was more warning than greeting: a hewn tree stump inscribed with 58 human stick figures—30 of them headless and all of them red.

Historians say the Iroquois Indians made pictographic markers to record important events. British General Freegift Pachen speculated that this one may have documented a skirmish in the French and Indian War. He said the headless figures represented the body count, and the remaining 28 the number of captives. The *painted post* must have had special significance for Pachen, who witnessed it as a captive of the American forces in April 1780.

According to local folklore, the *post* was spirited away to Centerville, New York, in 1801. When it was returned, it was kept in the village tavern until about 1810, when it disappeared again after a brawl. Another story says the *post* eventually rotted and was carried away by one of the Conhocton River's notorious floods.

A local history goes on to say that a new oak *post* was erected in 1803, which later was destroyed by a combination of the elements and the jackknives of souvenir seekers. Then in 1824, a local artisan received a commission of one cow to create a sheet iron weathervane depicting a warrior with a plumed headdress. The sculpture stood atop a 30-foot pole. A second sheet iron Indian was dedicated in 1880 to replace the first.

The bronze figure was erected on Memorial Day in 1950 and moved from the middle of the street to a corner in 1972. The warrior stands before a reproduction of the original *painted post.*

(See *Baton Rouge,* Louisiana, page 96.)

Other Unusual Place-Names in New York

Accord

On U.S. Route 209 in eastern Ulster County about 50 miles from West Point

When the residents of this Shawangunk Mountains community were fed up with squabbling over what to name their post office, they wrote a letter to the U.S. Post Office Department in Washington, D.C., suggesting it be named *Discord.* Some smart postal official, who evidently knew a bad name choice when he saw one, wrote back that the postmark should read *Accord.*

Conquest

On State Route 38 twenty-five miles west-northwest of Syracuse

Paul Morrell at the Lang Memorial Library in nearby Cato explains that when the "super towns" on the western frontier of New York were being broken up in the early 19th century, people in this tiny hamlet between the Finger Lakes and Lake Ontario were jubilant over their *conquest* of the town of Cato. They had won local control, and an end to six-mile walks through the snow to attend town meetings or to worship. *Victory*, six miles north of *Conquest*, was named for the same reason. Both towns were established in 1821.

(See *Victory*, Vermont, page 236.)

Endwell

On a local road four miles west of Binghamton

The town was named in 1921 for the *Endwell* shoe, "the shoe that *ends well* on your foot." Shoe manufacturer and Broome County mover and shaker Henry B. Endicott may have rearranged the letters in his son *Wendell*'s name to create the shoe's name. No rearrangement was required when the small city next door was named *Endicott* for the old man.

Holland Patent

On State Route 365 ten miles east of Rome and 50 miles east of Syracuse

This town was named for Lord Henry *Holland*, who held a *patent* (from King George of England) on 20,000 acres on the western side of the town of Trenton.

Neversink

On State Route 55 in northern Sullivan County 35 miles north of the point where New York, New Jersey, and Pennsylvania come together

neversink, like most places, has had ups and downs, but its name has nothing to do with its knack for survival. Translations of the original Algonquian word suggest that the name had something to do with the nearby river of the same name, but probably nothing so literal as the explanation suggested by a *Buffalo News* reporter a few years back: that the water between the river's banks rushes turbulently onward—*never sinking*.

Paradox

Eleven miles west of Ticonderoga and about 100 miles north of Albany on State Route 74

this hamlet in the Adirondacks is named after *Paradox* Lake, which, according to Dorothy Cole, curator of the nearby Schroon Lake Historical Museum, is well-known locally for tilting northward, so that spring run-off flows south to north, instead of the expected north to south.

Penn Yan

On State Route 54 about 30 miles north of Elmira at the outlet of Keuka Lake

the coinage of this name settled a dispute over what to call the town. It had split into two proud and unyielding factions: the settlers from *Penn*sylvania and the settlers from New England, called *Yan*kees.

Protection

On State Route 16 about 25 miles south-southeast of Buffalo

this place never needed special *protection;* the name comes from a popular tavern called *Protection* Harbor.
(See *Protection*, Kansas, page 85.)

Toast, North Carolina

north carolina

Black Jack

On a local road about ten miles south of Greenville in the eastern part of the state

It had nothing to do with the card game or a rogue; this town was named with a hatchet. The story goes that when the carpenters were putting the roof on the Free Will Baptist Church (around 1831), the question of what to name the community came up. One of the men threw his hatchet, and it landed in a *blackjack* oak. "Why not name it for these trees that grow around here," he said. And everyone agreed that was as good as any other name.

The church was burned during the Civil War when Union troops stationed 12 miles away in Washington raided *Black Jack*, killing nine Confederate soldiers who were hiding in the church. Several others were wounded and several were taken prisoner. The only Union losses were a few horses.

Democrat

On State Route 197 north of Asheville in the western part of the state

Judy Dillingham, who with her husband Hoyt runs D & Ds, the restaurant and grocery store that is *Democrat*'s nerve center, sent me a clipping from the Raleigh *News and Observer* that explained the origin of the name and discussed the name *Republican* in Bertie County. *Democrat*, it seems, was named in the early 1800s by a staunch *Democrat* at the suggestion of a disgruntled Whig (*Republican*). Since that day, everyone in *Democrat* has lived up to the town's name on Election Day, although Judy worries that may soon change. A lot of Floridians are moving in, and she suspects they're *Republican*.

No one is certain how *Republican* got its name. One story that locals tell is that the name honors Joe Barnum, a farmer who was the only registered *Republican* in the county. Another theory is that there was a public meeting house here and *public* somehow became *Republican*. Both stories sound unlikely.

What is certain is that no one in *Republican*—whose citizens you can count on your fingers—votes *Republican*.

Democrat is in Buncombe County, which gave us the slang word "bunk."

Back in 1820, North Carolina Congressman Felix Walker delivered a long-winded and pointless speech in the House of Representatives that seemed irrelevant to the issue being debated, the Missouri Compromise. Asked why he did this, he replied that he was not speaking for the benefit of his fellow Representatives but for his constituents in Buncombe. Soon, "speaking for Buncombe" became a popular expression for a long-winded, non-sensical speech. Over time, it was shortened to "bunkum" and finally to "bunk."

Jugtown

On a local road near the Randolph-Moore county line about 65 miles southwest of Raleigh

jugtown was named in the 1920s for the simple but graceful pottery made by Ben Owen, who was famous for his extraordinary glazes—"tobacco-spit brown," "frogskin-green," and "Chinese blue," for example.

Rich deposits of clay enticed English potters to this area in the 18th century, and for generations afterward people came here in their wagons to buy *jugs*, crocks, and other domestic pottery. But it was at *Jugtown* that Owen, with the high-minded sponsorship of Raleigh artist Jacques Busbee, started making pottery as much for its beauty as its function.

Stretching your legs in Jugtown: Vernon and Pam Owens (first cousins who hang an "s" on the end of the family name) carry on Ben Owen's tradition at *Jugtown* Pottery. Ben Owen III, the master's grandson, throws pots nearby at Ben Owen Pottery. These potters and a dozen others in the Asheboro area are collectively known as the Seagrove Potters. You can pick up an inexpensive guide to their shops at the Friends of the North Carolina Pottery Center, 124 Main Street, Seagrove. If you hope to visit them all, plan to spend the weekend. Address: Jugtown Pottery is at 330 Jugtown Road, halfway between Seagrove and Robbins. Telephone: (910) 464-3266.

(One of the towns on the Seagrove tour is *Why Not*, an accidental place-name whose story is told in the Mississippi chapter, page 128.)

Tar Heel

On State Route 87 twenty-five miles south of Fayetteville

a number of stories are told to explain why North Carolina is nicknamed the *Tar Heel* State, from which this town of a hundred-odd souls takes its name. One says that it dates to the Revolutionary War, when British troops crossed a river that had had *tar* dumped into it and came out with *tar heels*.

Another story, which is retold in the *Encyclopedia of the South* by Robert

O'Brien, says that the name originated during the Civil War, when the state militia was fighting alongside the regular Confederate Army. When the going got rough, the regulars retreated, leaving the militia to fend for itself against the Union Army. After the shooting stopped, the North Carolinians vowed that the next time they went into battle with the Confederate regulars, they would put *tar* on their boots so they would stick to their positions until the battle was won.

Whatever the origin, North Carolina was synonymous with *tar* for 150 years, leading in world production of the black goop from 1720 to 1870. In the 18th century, seven out of ten barrels of *tar* exported from the colonies to England came from North Carolina.

Other Unusual Place-Names in North Carolina

Alert

On a local road in northern Franklin County 40 miles northeast of Raleigh

natives like to tell people passing through that their ancestors believed that it was a good idea to be *alert* at all times. The man I talked with at the Franklin County Library didn't have anything more authoritative than that to offer. He did say, however, that if you pronounce *Alert* the way the dictionary tells you to pronounce it (with the "a" pronounced as "uh"), "everybody will know you're not from Franklin County."

Bandana

On State Route 80 less than 20 miles from the Tennessee border in Mitchell County

two folk explanations have been passed down through the years. One says that a railroad brakeman was told to find a suitable location for a station. When he found it, he marked the spot with his *bandanna*. The other folktale says that twenty years before the coming of the railroad, a politician named Thomas Johnston campaigned in the area wearing a red *bandanna*.

Take your pick.

Bughill

On State Route 905 about 40 miles north-northeast of Myrtle Beach, South Carolina

richard Wright, a lawyer in nearby Tabor City who is an expert on the history of the township, says *Bughill* is not much of a *hill*—maybe thirty or forty feet above sea-level, but it's crawling (and flying) with every kind of *bug* imaginable—mosquitoes, no-see-ums, roaches, and others with names known only to low-country natives. This is a very swampy region that was a hideout for General Francis Marion—"the Swamp Fox"—during the Revolutionary War.

Justice

On State Route 581 thirty miles northeast of Raleigh in eastern Franklin County

People called this place *Bowden's Store* back a hundred years ago. It seemed natural to continue calling it that after the community got its own post office. But there already was a Bowdens in the state, so the name had to be changed. Mrs. Bowden, who ran the store with her husband, J. L., remarked that while it would have been nice to have their name on the postmark, she believed in *justice* for all. Her neighbors liked the sound of that.

Anyway, it was easy for the Bowdens to be conciliatory; they got all the business that came with having the post office in their store.

Kill Devil Hills

On State Route 12 near Kitty Hawk on the Outer Banks

Local legend has it that the name comes from a brand of rum so potent it could *kill* the *devil* himself.

Stretching your legs in Kill Devil Hills: Wilbur Wright made aeronautical history here on December 17, 1903, when he kept a motorized bi-wing glider aloft for 59 seconds. Brother Orville watched with sheer delight as the flimsy wood and fabric aircraft skimmed over the sand dunes the length of one, two, nearly three football fields (852 feet). You can find out about the genius of these two bicycle mechanics from Dayton, Ohio, at the Wright Brothers National Memorial. The 60-foot granite pylon itself is on Big Kill Devil Hill, a 90-foot dune. Below it is the visitor center that houses full-scale reproductions of two Wright Brothers gliders. On the grounds are reconstructions of the hangar and the building they used as a workshop and living quarters in the fall of 1903. Location: U.S. Route 158, Kill Devil Hills. Telephone: (919) 441-7430.

Nags Head

Opposite Roanoke Island on the Outer Banks

the name probably came from England where there are three similar ones, but that hasn't stopped locals from making up stories. The best is that "land pirates" would hang a lantern from the neck of a *nag* on a stormy night and lead it slowly along the beach. Ship captains would see the bobbing light, and thinking that it was another vessel, conclude that they, too, could safely move closer to shore. When the ship beached, the pirates were waiting for it.

Old Trap

On a local road off of U.S. Route 158 seventeen miles southeast of Elizabeth City near Albermarle Sound in the northeastern part of the state

a man who stopped in this village on his way to sell a day's catch of fish or to take grain to the gristmill could expect to catch hell from his wife that night, because the grog shop that operated here in the mid-1700s was considered a *trap* for temptation. The chief temptress was West India rum, which flowed through the village like the tide.

By the end of the Revolutionary War, the village was being called *The Trap; Old Trap* came into use after 1800. There also is a *Trap* in Bertie County, North Carolina.

Scuffleton

On State Route 903 in Greene County in the eastern part of the state

marie Eastman, who works at the Greene County Public Library in Snow Hill, says she's never seen anything in writing that explains the name, but when she was a little girl (60 years ago) her father told her that this crossroads was named for the wrestling matches—the *scuffles*—held there on Saturday nights.

Silk Hope

On a local road in north-central Chatham County 30 miles southwest of Durham

it was *hoped* that the cultivation of *silkworms* would catch on here as a cottage industry. It never did. The name was in use starting before 1870.

Toast

Off of U.S. Route 52 just west of Mount Airy and 38 miles northwest of Winston-Salem near the Virginia border

This is one of those totally accidental names. It was chosen by the U.S. Post Office Department from a list of names suggested by the community. E. P. Mc-Leod, the school principal, supposedly thought of it while buying groceries in Hutchens Store one evening in 1927.

The center of town looked like burnt *toast* the day after Hutchens Store and the post office caught fire in 1932. Sparks from the fire ignited Grover Snow's garage across the street. Joe Simmons's grocery store and Lewis Dowell's barber shop also burned.

north dakota

Zap

On State Route 200 twenty-six miles west of Stanton in the west-central part of the state

Zap got on the map on May 9, 1969, when several thousand college students, bikers, and flower children converged on this town of 300 for a mini-Woodstock dubbed "The Zip to *Zap*." The townspeople were patient with the revelers until they started breaking up one of the town's two bars to get more wood for the bonfire they had built in the middle of Main Street. Around midnight, Mayor Norman Fuchs called in the National Guard, a decision that resulted in *Zap* making national newspaper and television headlines the next day.

The name *Zap* was adopted on May 29, 1913, after the owner of the townsite, Joseph Kraft, declined the honor of having the post office and the community named for him. Beyond that, there is little agreement on the origin of the name.

Douglas Wick, author of *North Dakota Place Names*, explains that after Kraft withdrew his name from consideration, a man named *Zap* stepped forward. Edward *Zapp*, a prominent St. Cloud, Minnesota, banker of the time, is also mentioned. An information sheet City Auditor Cindy Peterson sent me says *Zap* was named by Lee C. Pettibon, a Northern Pacific Railroad official who said the lignite coal mine on the edge of town reminded him of a coal mining town in Scotland called *Zapp*.

Wick says that many people in this area are of Russian extraction, and the name may be short for the name of a Russian town.

Zapites get a little misty-eyed talking about their 15 minutes of fame in 1969—the only riot in the history of North Dakota that had to be put down by the military and mentioned on all three major television networks. About 1,000 aging baby boomers gathered in *Zap* in May 1994 for a mellow 25th anniversary of the Zip to *Zap*. The biggest hunk of wood they burned was a wooden match.

The zip for *Zap* is 58580.

Cando, North Dakota

Other Unusual Place-Names in North Dakota

Backoo

Seven miles northwest of Cavalier and 75 miles north-northwest of Grand Forks in the northeastern corner of the state

this is one of those places where, when the time came for giving it a name, someone closed his eyes and pointed at a map of the world. Some say it was pioneer John Mountain, whose finger landed on the *Barcoo* River in Australia. Wick writes that others contend the town was named for *Baku,* a port on the Caspian Sea.

Cando

On U.S. Route 281 in Towner County in the northern part of the state

Prosper Parker headed a group that, on February 14, 1884, selected this emerging farm center as the county seat. When another prominent Towner County citizen questioned the group's authority, Parker, a county commissioner, responded, "We *can do* this, and to show the world we'll name the town *Cando.*"

To this day, *Candoans* think of themselves as people of action who never say "can't." The official municipal slogan is "You *can do* better in *Cando.*"

Stretching your legs in Cando: Cando isn't far from the Geographic Center of North America. The legend on the U.S. Geological Survey marker says that this is "the point on which the surface of the area [North America] would balance if it were a plane of uniform thickness." Location: The marker is at the intersection of U.S. Route 2 and State Route 3 just west of Rugby.

Cannon Ball

On State Route 24 in Morton County 35 miles south of Bismark

this unincorporated place was named for a stream whose bed and banks were littered with boulders said to resemble *cannon balls.* Over the years, many of them have been carried away in the trunks of tourists' cars.

On the east side of town, the boundary line between Mountain Time and Central Time goes *cannonballing* right down the middle of the Missouri River.

Concrete

On the Cavalier-Pembina county line a mile south of State Route 5 in the northeastern corner of the state

a University of North Dakota professor named Earle Babcock discovered a deposit of cement-making clay here in 1891. The first settlement to rise up near the mine was called McLean. It was renamed *Concrete* in 1908 by the wife of Webster Merrifield, president of the university, who had an interest in the mine.

(See *Concrete*, Washington, page 245.)

Donnybrook

On U.S. Route 52 thirty-five miles northwest of Minot

n ope, no one got into a big brawl here on the banks of the Des Lacs River; the town was named after the annual *Donnybrook* Fair in Ireland, which *is* famous for its brawls.

Seroco

On a county road nine miles northeast of Center and 35 miles northwest of Bismark in Oliver County

t he people who named this rural community in 1908 depended on *Sears Roebuck & Company*, the Chicago-based mail order giant, for much of their household and farm goods. So they coined a name using the first two letters of each word in the company's name.

Another good North Dakota acronym name is *Grenora*, which stands for the *Great Northern Railroad*.

ohio

Circleville

On U.S. Route 23 about 20 miles south of Columbus

In 1810, the Ohio General Assembly directed the Pickaway County commissioners to lay out a county seat that preserved a large prehistoric "enclosure"—a *circle* nearly a quarter mile in diameter—and several round, grassy mounds. So instead of a town square, they made a *circle* and then ringed it with circular streets and alleys. Four cross streets radiated from the hub like spokes on a wagon wheel. An octagonal county court house was erected at the center of the town *circle*.

By 1838, the townspeople had tired of going around in *circles* and started squaring off their streets, a job that took the *Circleville* Squaring Company many years to complete and completely obliterated the town's archaeological endowment.

People in "Old Roundtown" like to boast that their forebears had accomplished the geometrically impossible: they had "squared a *circle*."

Stretching your legs in Circleville: This is the site of one of the biggest fall festivals in the East: the *Circleville* Pumpkin Show, which draws more than half a million people to this small city of 12,000 each October. The show opens at noon on the third Wednesday of the month with the pumpkin weigh-in and runs through Saturday. There are seven parades, performances by bands, dance troupes and magicians, 12 city blocks of arts and crafts, two beauty pageants—Miss Pumpkin and Little Miss Pumpkin—and, of course, pumpkin kitsch and foods aplenty. Dorcas Smalley, who works at city hall and is on the Pumpkin Show committee, listed pumpkin burgers, whoopie pies, soda pop, doughnuts, fudge, pizza, and cream puffs as some of the more unusual pumpkin delicacies you can sample at the festival. Her favorite? "The whoopie pies. Oh, my God, they're luscious."

Getaway

On State Route 243 about four miles north of the Ohio River and Huntington, West Virginia, in Lawrence County

This was the first stop in the free state of Ohio—"the *get-away* point"—for runaway slaves headed north from slave states Kentucky and West Virginia, both of

Circleville, Ohio

which are just across the Ohio River. From here the slaves were escorted by members of the Underground Railroad to another frontier settlement about 15 miles north that was considered a safe distance from the slaves' former masters and the professional slave hunters who prowled free state border towns. The runaways were guided along ten trails that wound maze-like through the forest north of *Getaway*—designed to throw off anyone in pursuit.

Veto

On State Route 339 west and north of Belpre in southeastern Ohio

this crossroads village was proud of Washington County native son Judge Ephraim Cutler, who was a prominent member of the state's constitutional convention, held in Chillicothe in November 1802. Cutler was revered for his successful *veto* of a clause in the constitution that would have allowed slavery in Ohio when it entered the Union as the 17th state in 1803.

Veto was the second place in the county to get its name from Cutler's noteworthy presence at the state's constitutional convention. Eight years earlier (1842), one of the old judge's neighbors suggested the name *Constitution* for the next village east when it applied for a post office.

Cutler, then 75, was appointed postmaster, a position he held until his death at age 86. The post office was in the judge's store. His annual federal salary in 1848 was $19.80.

The judge's surname ended up as the moniker for another Washington County name, but the town wasn't named for him. The place-name honors William Parker *Cutler,* a promoter of the first railroad in this area.

Other Unusual Place-Names in Ohio

Chagrin Falls

On the Cuyahoga-Geauga county line in Cleveland's eastern suburbs

the name probably came from the Indian word *shagrin* or *shaguin,* meaning "clear water"; or, less likely, from *shagreen,* a colloquialism for the sycamore tree. But the story Ohioans like best is this: When Moses Cleaveland (one of the founders of Cleveland) arrived at the headwaters of what is now called the *Chagrin* River, he was *chagrined* to learn that it was not the headwaters of the Cuyahoga, his destination. Some published sources attribute the name to Harvey Rice, one of Cleaveland's surveyors.

Charm

On State Route 557 about 15 miles west of Dover in east-central Ohio

When the village applied for a post office in 1886, the government sent a list of names from which to choose. The story goes that the villagers chose *Charm* because of the connection they made between the name and one of their own, Yone Yoder. He was the village jeweler and watch repairman, and as was the fashion at the time, he wore a large watch chain with both a watch and a *charm* (ornament) hanging from it.

Stretching your legs in Charm: It is said that half the Amish in the world live in eastern Holmes County. In nearby Berlin, you can study the Behalt, a cyclorama that traces the social history of the Amish, Mennonites, and Hutterites from their heretical beginnings in Zurich, Switzerland, in 1525 to the present. The giant painting is ten feet tall by 265 feet long. Address: County Route 77, Berlin. Telephone: (330) 893-3192. Admission charged.

Jumbo

On State Route 67 about 14 miles west of Kenton and 65 miles northwest of Columbus in western Hardin County

This don't-blink-or-you'll-miss-it crossroads was named in 1885 by the proprietor of the general store, according to William Daniel Overman, author of *Ohio Town Names*. He was searching for a name when he read in the newspaper of the death of *Jumbo*, P. T. Barnum's "Biggest Elephant on Earth," which had been hit by a train in Canada.

Nearby is another tiny place named *Jump*, and another named *Round-head*, after an Indian chief.

Novelty

On State Route 306 a few miles east of Cleveland

First postmaster Henry Hill felt obligated to come up with a *novel* postmark in 1899.

Once, a letter arrived at his post office addressed: Unusual, Ohio.

(See *Novelty*, Missouri, page 131.)

Outville

On a local road about 15 miles east of Columbus

Outville is in the *out*back of Licking County, but it is named for a Mr. *Out*coult, the first station master for the C. & O. Railroad, which came through in 1853.

Seven Mile

On U.S. Route 127 about seven miles north of Hamilton and 24 miles north of Cincinnati

Seven Mile Historical Society President Jim Martin says General "Mad Anthony" Wayne had a temporary headquarters here known as *Seven Mile* Camp. President George Washington had sent Wayne to the territory to crush an Indian revolt. The camp was *seven miles* north of Fort Hamilton, today the site of the Butler County Courthouse. A road that runs through *Seven Mile* is named Wayne's Trace.

Torch

On State Route 7 about 11 miles west-southwest of Belpre in the southeastern part of the state

according to local legend, the town's early settlers carried pine *torches* when they walked to evening church services.

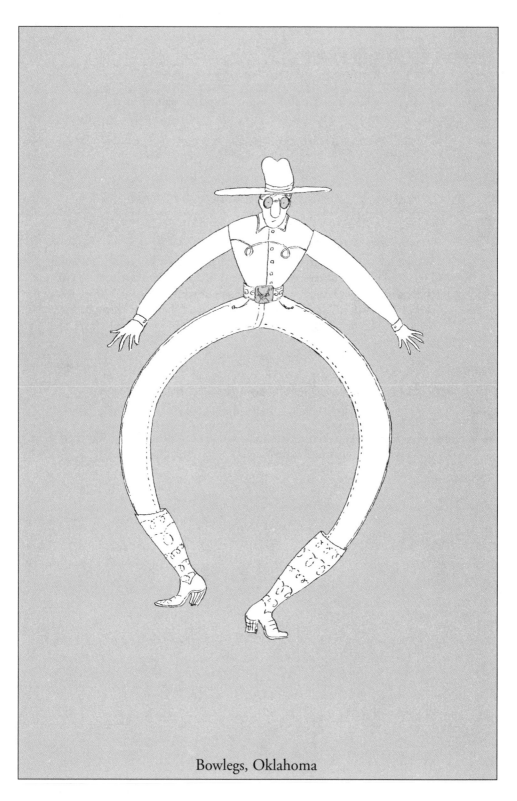

Bowlegs, Oklahoma

oklahoma

Gene Autry

On a spur of State Highway 53 northeast of Ardmore in the southern part of the state

The people in this small community (population 97) were so proud to have a celebrity in their midst that they changed the name of their town after *Gene Autry* bought the Flying A Ranch in 1938. *Autry* and his band sang from the back of a railroad car at the naming ceremony.

Autry, the singing cowboy of Western movie fame who later in life owned the California Angels baseball team, planned to settle down on the ranch, but then World War II abruptly changed his plans. From then on he visited the ranch infrequently.

The town had been called *Berwyn* since the late 1880s. It was given that name by the men laying that stretch of the Santa Fe Railroad, who hailed from *Berwyn,* Pennsylvania.

Stretching your legs in Gene Autry: Elvin Sweeten opens his *Gene Autry* Museum on Saturdays and Sundays, or by appointment. The museum is dedicated to the singing cowboys of the Western B movies and includes posters, 78 rpm record albums, films, photographs, two of *Gene Autry's* guitars, and other memorabilia. Location: The museum is in the old *Gene Autry* School at the west end of Main Street. Telephone: (405) 294-3047.

Slapout

On U.S. Route 270 near the eastern end of the Oklahoma Panhandle

In 1932, Tom Lemmons moved two old frame buildings to a plowed field beside a dusty road and opened a grocery store. He called the place *Nye.* Tom's sister, Artie, helped out in the store, and she had a funny way of responding whenever a customer asked for an item that had sold out. "Sorry, we're *slapout* of that," she'd always say. That stuck in people's minds, and pretty soon *Slapout* is what everyone called the place—except Tom.

He put a sign above the store's entrance that read "Nye Mercantile," and until he sold the store in 1944, he kept up a friendly rivalry with Joe Johnston, who operated a store on the other side of the road and always referred to the little business community as *Slapout.* When someone stopped on Tom's side of the road and asked for directions to *Slapout,* he would point towards Johnston's store and say, "That's *Slapout* over there; this is Nye. Can I help you with something?"

A similar story is told to explain the origin of *Slapout,* Alabama.

Stretching your legs in Slapout: Slapout is in Beaver County, whose mascot is Big Beaver, a 12-foot-tall statue on the main drag in the town of Beaver. For pure country kitsch, it ranks right up there with the Prairie Chicken statue in Rothsay, Minnesota. Big Beaver is holding a symbol of the inhospitable country the pioneers called No Man's Land—the cow chip. Because there were few trees, the early settlers burned dried cow dung for cooking and heating. Pioneer families made a game of tossing cow chips into their wagons when they collected them in the fall. Those days are relived each April in Beaver at the World Championship Cow Chip Throwing Contest, which has been held continuously since 1970. The chips fly on the last day of the Cimarron Territory Celebration, which begins on the Saturday closest to April 15 and continues through the next Saturday with music, a classic car show, bike race and parade, the crowning of the Pioneer Queen, a horseshoe pitching tournament, and a dance at the American Legion hall.

At the big event, each contestant gets two tosses, and selects his or her own cow chips from a wagon loaded with them. They must be at least six inches in diameter. The record toss is 182 feet 3 inches for men and 132 feet for women, set by a woman from Wisconsin, who has won at least ten times over the last 20 years.

Other Unusual Place-Names in Oklahoma

Bowlegs

Just off U.S. Route 377 sixty miles east-southeast of Oklahoma City in Seminole County

This town was named for Billy *Bowlegs,* the Seminole Indian chief who led his tribe on the infamously sad exodus from Florida to Indian Territory as part of the so-called Indian Removals to the West in the 1840s. *Bowlegs* was a bad translation of the Seminole name *Bolek.*

Centrahoma

Just off State Route 3 twenty miles southeast of Ada in west-central Coal County

The name was coined from *central Oklahoma* by someone with an imprecise sense of geography. Just look at the map!

Cookietown

At the junction of U.S. Route 277/281 and State Route 5A twenty-four miles south of Lawton

Years ago, there was a friendly farmer who traded at the general store in this unincorporated community. The storekeeper never let him leave without giving him a *cookie*. The farmer told his young son about this, and the next time the farmer went to *town*, the boy pleaded, "Daddy, please, can I go to *Cookietown* with you?"

Grainola

On State Route 18 forty miles northeast of Ponca City and four miles south of the Kansas border

this town was named in 1910 for the bounty of *grain* grown by local farmers. (The hippie breakfast cereal with the big chunks of oatmeal in it has a slightly different spelling—*granola*. I looked it up.)

Hominy

Where State Routes 99 and 20 cross in Osage County 40 miles northwest of Tulsa

more cereal? Well, maybe, but locals say there once was a mission here named *Harmony* whose name got twisted out of shape by the cowmen who followed the clergymen to these parts.

Another theory is that the town was named for an Osage Indian hero called *Ho Moie.*

Stretching your legs in Hominy: Since 1990, Native American artist Cha Tullis has painted more than two dozen dramatic and colorful murals on the walls of downtown stores.

Loyal

Fifty miles northwest of Oklahoma City in the ranchlands of western Kingfisher County

this was one of a number of U.S. towns that changed their German names during World War I. The ranchers here evidently didn't want to leave any doubts about whose side they were on when the name was changed from *Kiel* in 1918.

The story goes that the name change took place shortly after a man ran down Main Street yelling, "The Kaiser's going to win. The Kaiser's going to win." He was tarred and feathered.

Stretching your legs in Loyal: People say Turner's Cafe serves the best chicken-fried steak in Kingfisher County—maybe even all of central Oklahoma. Coraletha Turner has had the diet-busting Western dish on the menu since the cafe—Loyal's only restaurant—opened in 1954. Location: Main Street. Telephone: (405) 729-4225.

Nuyaka

Off State Route 56 ten miles west of Okmulgee and 25 miles south of Tulsa in the east-central part of the state

The name is thought to be a white man's phonetic spelling of the way that the Creek Indians pronounced *New Yorker.* It was brought back to Creek country in Alabama (*Nuyaka* Town) after President Washington invited 26 Creek leaders to New York to sign a 1790 treaty designed to keep Spain from encroaching on our infant republic's southwestern frontier. The name was later transferred to Oklahoma when the Creeks were exiled to the West. The first settlement was known as *Nuyaka Mission,* a Presbyterian outpost established in 1884.

All this may be true, but native Bostonians, like myself, will tell you that *Nuyaka* is what someone from Southie (South Boston, that is) calls a person who roots for the Red Sox's oldest rival.

Okay

On State Route 251 fifty miles southeast of Tulsa and just north of Muskogee

The town was named for the *OK* Truck Manufacturing Company, which had a plant here. *Okay* was the last in a long parade of names for this town of five hundred, which got its start as an Arkansas River trading post in the early 1800s. One of those names was *Sleepyville.*

The last word from the mouth of the librarian in nearby Wagoner who helped me was, *"Okay?"* I, of course, responded, *"Okay."*

oregon

Helix

On a local road about 12 miles northeast of Pendleton in the northeastern part of the state

This is one of the oddest explanations for a place-name in the U.S. The town apparently is named for the *helix* of the human ear; that's the curved rim that forms the top of the lobe.

The story that has been passed down through the Oregon medical community is that the town was named in the spring of 1880 by a man who had an infected *helix*, and was sent by his doctor to a specialist in Pendleton. The patient was told the medical term for the location of his ailment and decided it would be a dandy name for the town's new post office.

Was this guy running a fever?

Irrigon

On the Columbia River and U.S. Route 730 ten miles west of Hermiston

This quiet farming community was called Stokes until the Bureau of Reclamation dug reservoirs and *irrig*ation canals to draw farmers to the area. Ready water transformed a twenty-mile swath on either side of the river from a desert to a lush area of cropland, pastures, and ponds. The name was changed to *Irrigon*—a melding of the words *irrigation* and *Oregon*—even before the first shovelful of dirt was dug, probably because of the influence of visionary agriculturist Addison Bennett, who began publishing *The Oregon Irrigator* in Stokes in 1904.

Another Oregon town named to attract farmers was *Freewater*, now Milton-*Freewater*.

Noti

On State Route 126 sixteen miles west of Eugene

In February 1926, *Noti* Postmaster H. G. Suttle told this story to Lewis L. McArthur, author of *Oregon Geographic Names* (a principal source of information about Oregon place-names): In the early days of the Oregon Territory, a white man and an Indian were traveling together in the Willamette River Valley. They only had one horse between them, so they

Sublimity, Oregon

did what was known as "riding and tying." One man would ride ahead a distance, tie the horse, and proceed on foot. When the other man reached the horse, he mounted it and rode a distance beyond where he passed his walking companion and tied the horse again. And so forth.

It is said that the white man agreed to tie the horse at the point where a certain creek joins the Long Tom River—where the town of *Noti* is now located. Instead, he continued on to Eugene, leaving the Indian to walk the rest of the way. So *Noti* is the spot where there was *no tie*.

Plush

On a county road near the National Antelope Refuge in Lake County in the southern part of the state

The story is told that this desert outpost was named for a Paiute Indian who knew how to play poker but couldn't get his mouth around the word for a hand containing five cards of the same suit, a *flush*.

There's a mean side to the story: In the game that gave *Plush* his nickname, his white friends dealt him a *flush* and let him keep raising his bets until he lost all his money to another player to whom the cheaters had dealt an even better hand.

(Card games also played a hand in the naming of *Midnight*, Mississippi, and *Show Low*, Arizona.)

Sisters

On U.S. Route 20 fifteen miles northwest of Bend

This town was named in 1888 for three imposing peaks in the Cascade Range known as the Three *Sisters*. Up until early in this century they were known individually as Faith, Hope, and Charity.

As if to show that it does not discriminate on the basis of gender, Deschutes County also has a town named *Brothers*. It's on the same road, U.S. Route 20, about 40 miles southeast of Bend.

There are two explanations for how *Brothers* got its name. One says that there were several bands of *brothers* among the early homesteaders, the most prominent of which were the Stenkamp *brothers*. The other explanation is that a ranch hand, sitting at idle on his horse and looking at the Three *Sisters*, some 50 miles away to the northwest, noticed three similar hills in the foreground and dubbed them the Three *Brothers*. The name was adopted by the ranch, Three *Brothers* Sheep Camp, and in September 1913 by the *Brothers*, Oregon, post office.

Other Unusual Place-Names in Oregon

Drain

On State Route 99 halfway between Eugene and Roseburg

I once passed through here on my way to interview the mayor of Elkton, the next town west, and I must admit I was disappointed to learn that the name is a surname (no funny story to tell). But my spirits were lifted when a local woman told me that *Drain* High School sports teams are sarcastically referred to as the Drips; and that a woman from elsewhere in Douglas County who goes out with a man from *Drain* (a *Draino?*) who turns out to be a creep might be inclined to call him a "drip."

I read somewhere that there also is a *Sink* in this part of Oregon, but I haven't been able to find it on a map.

Greenhorn

On a local road in the mountains a few miles north of where U.S. Route 26 hits State Route 7 and west of Baker City

This locale was not named for the gold mining novices who flocked here in the 1860s, as you might expect, but for a prominent serpentine (mottled *green*) rock.

Greenhorn was one of five incorporated towns in the U.S. where the 1990 census takers couldn't find anyone to count.

Halfway

On State Route 86 fifteen miles from the Idaho border in eastern Baker County

halfway isn't *halfway* to anywhere—but it used to be. Lewis L. McArthur says the first post office (about 1887) was on the Alexander Stalker ranch, midway between Pine and Cornucopia, both now ghost towns. Later, the post office was moved much closer to Pine, taking the name *Halfway* with it. Since then, people have tried to justify the name by saying the town is *halfway* between Pine and Carson, or Baker City and Cornucopia, or some other combination, none of which has been correct.

Paisley

On State Route 31 eighty miles east-southeast of Crater Lake in the southern part of the state

This place was settled by Scottish immigrants who wanted to remember their home in the old country, *Paisley*, a city near Glasgow. One of them was first postmaster Samuel G. Steele, who sold his first stamp on May 12, 1879.

Remote

On State Route 42 in eastern Coos County in the southwestern part of the state

Situated midway between I-5 and the coast, this tiny town is still as *remote* as it was when it was named by the early settlers in the 1880s.

Sublimity

On a county road about 12 miles southeast of Salem

First postmaster James M. Denny is said to have named this place in 1852 for its *sublime* scenery. Gazing at the foothills of the Cascades from his cabin on the east side of town was a transcendental experience for him. A *National Geographic* writer who visited here in 1946 described the area as "a mountain fairyland of majestic timber, white water, and wild flowers."

Tangent

On State Route 99E thirty miles south of Salem and seven miles east of Corvallis

This town was named for a long (20-mile) stretch of straight track—a *tangent*—on the Southern Pacific Railroad.

Tollgate

On State Route 204 a few miles east of the Umatilla Indian Reservation in the northeastern part of the state

Oregon's first cross-country roads were privately owned *toll* roads. This *tollgate* was on what was known as the Woodward Road, which crossed the Blue Mountains in the 1870s.

Wagontire

On U.S. Route 395 in the wide-open spaces of the south-central part of the state

The town was named for nearby *Wagontire* Mountain, where a *wagon* wheel lay by the side of the road for many years. It was a well-known landmark a hundred years ago.

Name Cleansing

NAME CLEANSING HAS BEEN GOING ON throughout our nation's history. **Hell-to-Pay** sounded much too rowdy to a new generation of residents who were trying to project a dignified image of their central Washington town, so they changed it to *Eltopia*. *Avondale*, Rhode Island, was called **Lotteryville** for more than a hundred years until the townspeople petitioned for a post office in 1893. The feds said the name had to go; gambling was illegal.

The clean-up movement became national policy in 1890 when President Benjamin Harrison created the U.S. Board on Geographic Names to rule on the appropriateness of new and existing names. Some have complained the board took all the fun out of place naming, changing raunchy **The Nipples**, Arizona, to innocuous **College Peak**, for example.

In 1971, the board approved the U.S. Geological Survey's proposal to change **Whorehouse Meadow**, Oregon, to **Naughty Girl Meadow.** The Oregon Board on Geographic Names got wind of this 11 years later (it's a remote grassland in Harney County) and petitioned to reverse the decision because the original name had historical significance (see page 33).

Either way, **Whorehouse Meadow** or **Naughty Girl Meadow**, it's a fun name.

In 1963, the U.S. board systematically changed all the geographic features and the handful of "populated places" with *Nigger* in the name to *Negro*; and around 1967 changed all the places with *Jap* in the name to *Japanese*. The latest offender is *Squaw*, according to Roger Payne, the board's executive secretary. As of early 1997, at least three state legislatures had addressed the issue, and the U.S. Board on Geographic Names had, for starters, approved the renaming of **Squaw Gulch** in Siskiyou County, California, to **Taritsi Gulch**, substituting another Indian word for "woman."

pennsylvania

On State Route 340 eight miles east of Lancaster and 50 miles west of Philadelphia

adolescents have been giggling over the name of this Lancaster County village for generations. But in 1814, when the village was named, the name would not have stirred even the dirtiest mind. Back then the word *intercourse* meant nothing more intimate than friendly intermingling among neighbors.

There are three theories on the origin of the name. The first has to do with an old race track just east of town. It was very popular starting in Colonial times, drawing riders and bettors from miles around. The track was a mile long and straight as an arrow (look at this stretch of U.S. Route 340 on any map); races were run east to west, with the finish line in the village proper. The starting line was known as the "enter course," and believers in this highly plausible theory say that by 1814 this had evolved into *intercourse*.

The second theory holds that the village was named for the *intercourse*, or crossing, of two well-traveled roads in the village, the Old King's Highway (Old Philadelphia Pike) and the Newport Road. They crossed in front of a tavern called the Cross Keys, which one source says was the village's original name.

The third theory is the simplest: that this was a place both of commerce and social gathering—a place of *intercourse*.

Stretching your legs in Intercourse: Twenty minutes north of *Intercourse* on State Route 772 is the small town of Lititz, where you can find out what a good pretzel means to a Pennsylvania Dutchman. Sturgis Pretzel House, the first pretzel bakery in America, makes those big, puffy, golden brown figure eights that connoisseurs slather with mustard. Bakers twist them by hand, as Julius Sturgis did when he opened the bakery in 1861, and bake them in the original oven, circa 1784. And you get to twist a pretzel, too, on a tour of the bakery. Address: 219 East Main Street, Lititz. Telephone: (717) 626-4354. Admission charged.

Bird in Hand, Pennsylvania

Scalp Level

A few miles south of Johnstown on State Route 160

There are any number of stories concerning the origin of this name, most having to do with Indian attacks—a subject that could cause a pioneer's imagination to run wild. However, the most likely explanation is that the name comes from the Appalachian mountaineers' expression for a *leveling* off (*skelping*) of something—for instance, the land between two ridges (as in this case) or the trunk of a tree.

Some say the people who named the town had a particular *skelping* in mind: the day in 1830 when Jacob Eash, the German immigrant who was the first settler, gathered his neighbors together for a "frolic" at which the men cut all the trees and laurel *level* to the ground while the women cooked supper and minded the children.

I like the story of the old mountaineer who would get drunk on Saturday and threaten to "*scalp* them all off *level*." "Them?" His detractors, I assume.

Other Unusual Place-Names in Pennsylvania

Academia

On a local road about seven miles south of Mifflintown and 40 miles northwest of Harrisburg

In 1754, this town was named for the Tuscarora *Academy*, a school for training ministers and teachers. The original *academy* building is now the home of the Mifflintown Historical Society.

Bird in Hand

On State Route 340 five miles east of Lancaster and 53 miles west of Philadelphia

The town was named for a Colonial-era inn on the Old Philadelphia Pike. The inn had a swinging sign out front with a *bird* and a human *hand* painted on it. Underneath this image were the words of the old adage: "A *bird in hand* is worth two in the bush."

This reminds me of the time we were driving across Nebraska on I-80 late at night with lightning flashing all around us and our two small boys frightened and overtired. We foolishly turned down the *bird-in-hand* of a cheap but clean motel bed in North Platte, only to discover there were no vacancies between there and Grand Island.

Blue Ball

On State Route 23 eleven miles northeast of Lancaster and 50 miles west of Philadelphia

about 1766, Robert Wallace opened a general store and tavern here with this name. According to *Pennsylvania Place Names* by A. Harvey Espenshade, an old book that is still the best source on the subject of Pennsylvania place-names, travelers asking for directions would be told to stop "at the sign of the *Blue Ball*."

This is not to be confused with the tavern (and later town) at the sign of the *Blue Bell* on the outskirts of Philadelphia, where General "Mad Anthony" Wayne slept the night before his court martial trial.

Brogue

On State Route 74 about 14 miles southeast of York and 12 miles north of the Maryland border

a long, long time ago someone placed a worn-out *brogue* (a heavy, coarse shoe with a hobnailed sole) atop a pole outside a tavern. Five roads converged at this spot, so the shoe was seen by many people, especially the Scotch and Irish settlers of the area. They, of course, are responsible for bringing this style of shoe to America, as well as the lilting way of speaking English we call a *brogue*, although the two words are not linguistically related.

Compass

On State Route 340 between Lancaster and Coatesville in the southeastern part of the state

this is yet another Lancaster area town named for a tavern. It was on the Lancaster Road (now Route 340) at the sign of the Mariner's *Compass*. It is said that William Penn and a crew of surveyors stopped here to take *compass* readings, because they thought they were getting off course for Philadelphia. John Miller hoped to capitalize on that fact—kind of a "George-Washington-slept-here" marketing strategy—in naming the tavern and inn.

Coupon

On a local road about eight miles west of Altoona in the southwest-central part of the state

the coal company that operated here in the late 1800s paid its employees in scrip or *coupons* that could be redeemed only at the company store. This infuriated the first postmaster, who also ran a general store, and he retaliated by recommending this peculiar name to the U.S. Post Office Department.

Eighty Four

At the intersection of State Routes 136 and 519 six miles east of Washington and 20 miles south of Pittsburgh

the name was chosen by the townspeople because the post office opened in *1884*. *Eighty Four* is the corporate headquarters of *84* Lumber, which takes its name from the town.

Fairchance

On State Route 857 six miles south of Uniontown and eight miles north of the West Virginia border

this borough of 2,000 was founded in 1792 by John Hayden, who built the Fairfield Furnace, an iron smelter. He sold the business in 1805, and the new owner renamed it *Fairchance* Furnace, stating that he wished to give all his employees a *fair chance* to make a decent living.

Frugality

On State Route 53 twelve miles northwest of Altoona

a sesquicentennial (1804–1954) history compiled by the Cambria County Historical Society says this mining town was named in 1888 for a land grant made to Revolutionary War veterans. Evidently, they had no illusions about getting rich off their free land. The name might also apply to the lives of the early coal miners.

Purchase Line

Just off State Route 286 sixteen miles northeast of Indiana (the town) and 65 miles northeast of Pittsburgh

according to a 1995 history of Indiana County, this community is near the line of demarcation between lands claimed by the Six Nations Indians and the Province of Pennsylvania in the First Treaty of Fort Stanwix, signed November 5, 1768. The line was surveyed the next spring, and trees were razed on both sides, leaving a 50-foot-wide no-man's-land. The line ran west from Cherry Tree to a point on the Allegheny River north of Kittanning.

Wampum

Indians of the Algonquian Nation used *wampum*—beads made from shells—for money. This village, which was started by Irish brothers Robert and John Davidson in 1796, was close to the Delaware Indian village called Kus-kus-kee, and there apparently was quite a bit of trade between the two.

After it got a post office in 1832, the village had a brief fling with the name *Irish Ripple* before reverting back to its original name.

Dick Allen, the moody infielder who was baseball's bad boy in the 1960s and 1970s (like Albert Belle in the 1990s), hails from *Wampum.*

rhode island

Watch Hill

On the shore of Block Island Sound at the Connecticut state line

With its commanding view of Block Island, Fishers Island, and the Atlantic Ocean beyond, this was a strategic location for the colonists and probably was a lookout and signal station for the Indians who preceded them. A *watch* house was erected during the French and Indian War, which the local militia occupied during the Revolutionary War to *watch* for British warships. The *Watch Hill* Lighthouse was built in 1806.

Jonathan Nash, the first lighthouse keeper, rented rooms in his house. His entrepreneurial spirit led to the building of a hotel, the *Watch Hill* House, in 1833. After a new railroad linked the Rhode Island and Connecticut shores with Boston in the late 1830s, new hotels were built in the village at the rate of one every five or six years. By the 1870s, *Watch Hill* was a major oceanfront resort, with five big hotels—the Narragansett House, the Atlantic House, the Plimpton House, the Larkin House, and the "new" *Watch Hill* House—lining the beach, and catboats catching the breezes on Little Narragansett Bay.

Nearby *Avondale* was originally called *Lotteryville* because of its gambling houses. A 1943 history of *Westerly* (another nearby town) says that the Post Office Department demanded that the name *Lotteryville* be changed when the community applied for a post office in 1893 (see "Name Cleansing" on page 198). Another interesting place-name in the area is *Varietyville*.

Other Unusual Place-Names in Rhode Island

Arctic

A neighborhood in the town of West Warwick on State Route 33 in the central part of the state

When the Sprague Manufacturing Company took over the Wakefield Mill in 1852, the new owner was told that this neighborhood was a "frost pocket," so he renamed the mill *Arctic* so it would rhyme with his three other textile mills in Warwick, Natick, and Quidnick.

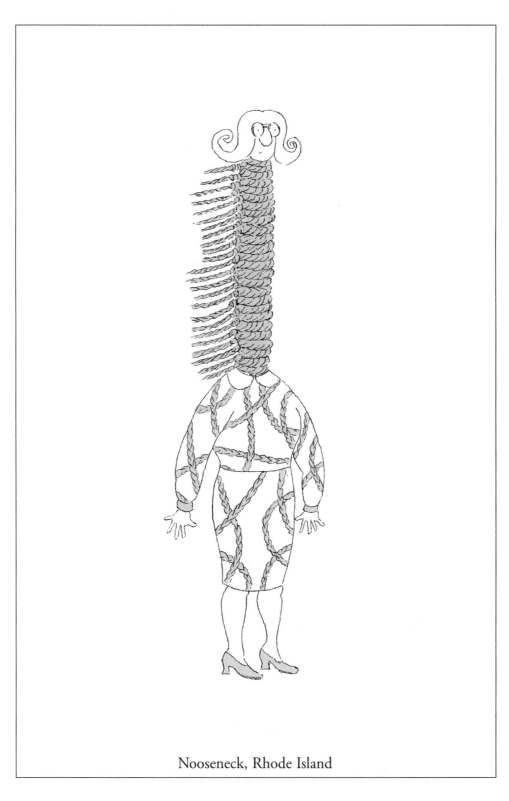

Nooseneck, Rhode Island

Chopmist

On State Route 102 north of the western part of Scituate Reservoir

the English-speaking colonists who inhabited the Eastern Seaboard frequently adopted Indian place-names. Since the Indians had no written language, the colonists wrote the names as they heard them. Different listeners came up with different spellings, and the names often went through so many permutations they didn't sound much like the original anymore. This is one such name. The original meaning of *Chopmist* was "dividing place" or "dividing of the hills," and earlier spellings were *Chapumiscook* and *Chapompamiskkok.*

Nooseneck

On State Route 3 fifteen miles west-southwest of Warwick in the southwest-central part of the state

the Narragansett Indians came to the valley of the Big River—the *Nooseneck* Valley—every fall to hunt deer. They hung "running *nooses*" from birch saplings and then drove the deer into them. One source says that the Indians came from 20 to 30 miles away for this annual venison harvest.

Another colorful old place-name in the vicinity is *Hell's Half Acre*, where the owner of the Ovenbird Tavern had his female employees dance in Congdon Mill Road to attract customers, according to local historians Blanche Albro and Roberta Bacon. Inside, the tavern was notorious for gambling, prostitution, and even a few murders.

Prudence

A village on Prudence Island in Narragansett Bay

roger Williams, Rhode Island's founder, bought three islands in Narragansett Bay from the Indians and renamed them for three of the "virtues": *Prudence, Patience,* and *Hope.* He later sold the islands to pay off debts in England.

Williams, a charismatic man who was banished from the Massachusetts Bay Colony in 1636 for his subversive ideas, also named *Providence,* the state capital, for God's *providence* in guiding him to a new life in the wilderness that Rhode Island then was.

Tarkiln

On Colwell Road on the east side of the town of Burrillville and five miles southwest of the city of Woonsocket in the northern part of the state

This was the site of Burrillville's first industry, a *kiln* for making *tar* from pine pitch. New Englanders, for some reason, are pretty loose about the spelling and pronunciation of this place-name. Here it's "Tarkhill," "Tarkill," "Tarklin" or "Tarklyn," as well as *Tarkiln*, according to Sue Giquerl at the Jesse M. Smith Memorial Library in Harrisville, Rhode Island. In Orleans, Massachusetts, where I did part of my growing up, we all said "Tarkin" Road, though it was spelled *Tarkiln*.

south carolina

Honea Path

On U.S. Route 178 fifteen miles southeast of Anderson in the northwestern part of the state

This odd-sounding name is the result of a spelling mistake. According to the Anderson (South Carolina) *Independent-Mail*, the town was named for William *Honey*, an early trader and landowner. The 1885 town charter and early deeds bear the name *Honey Path*. But when the town was incorporated in 1917, the "y" in *Honey* somehow became an "a," and the mistake has been repeated on legal documents ever since.

Why *Path*? Perhaps one of the early trade *paths* crossed *Honey's* land. It might even have been the legendary Cherokee *Path*, the 18th-century route along which deerskins moved from the backwoods of South Carolina to the port of Charles Town (now Charleston) and then on to England, where deerskin coats and hats were very much in vogue.

Ninety Six

On State Route 34 nine miles east of Greenwood and 65 miles west of Columbia

In the spring of 1730, a surveyor named George Hunter and the Indian Trade Commissioner for the colony of South Carolina, George Chicken, traveled on horseback from Charles Town to Keowee in what is now Oconee County. Keowee was then the center of the Lower Cherokee Nation. They followed the Cherokee Path up the Congaree River valley, and then the Saluda and Savannah River valleys. Hunter drew a detailed map of the route that shows every stream crossing along the way. Near where the Saluda and Savannah River valleys fold into each other, and about four miles from the present-day site of *Ninety Six*, Hunter wrote the number *96*.

Merchants in Charles Town who saw the map, or had heard deerskin traders talk about a place called *Ninety Six* on the Cherokee Path, assumed the name stood for the distance (*96* miles) from there to Keowee. And that is how the name has been explained ever since.

The only real competition for the distance explanation came from a romantic legend that became popular in the 1890s and had a 30-year run before fading away after World War I. In the legend, a Cherokee maiden rides from Keowee to the fort at *Ninety Six* to warn her British lover of an impending Indian attack. While on the trail, the girl kept a count of the

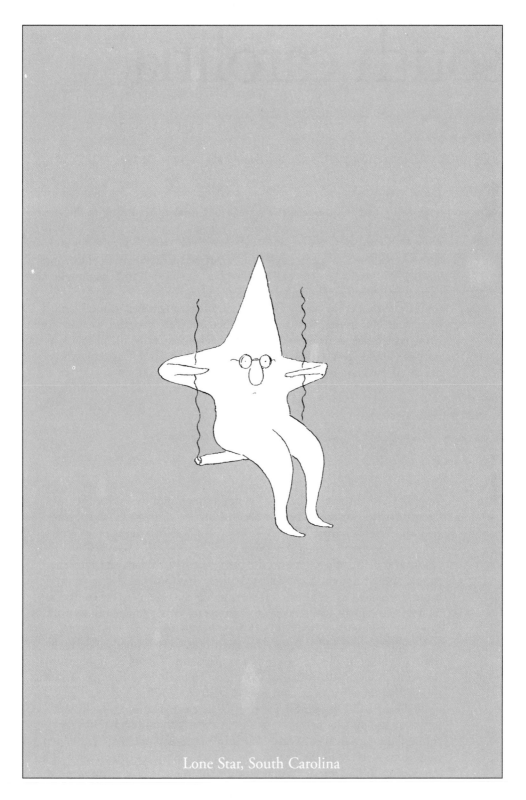

Lone Star, South Carolina

stream crossings, and the total was *96*. The flaw in this tale is that George Hunter drew his map on May 21, 1730, and there wasn't a British fort at that location until 1759.

David P. George, a local historian, dismisses the Cherokee maiden legend out of hand and has serious doubts about the distance explanation. He tells why in "*Ninety Six* Decoded," a pamphlet he published in 1992. First of all, Keowee is only 78 miles from *Ninety Six* by the Cherokee Path, he claims. And even though distance measurement was crude in those days—George Hunter used his watch and an estimate of the speed of his horse to make computations—an experienced surveyor wouldn't be off by that much. George also analyzed the way the deerskin traders counted miles (by the streams along the route), and found that *96* miles didn't add up there either.

So he turned his attention to the streams themselves. He knew that the descriptive names of them—Apple Tree, Beaver Dam, Hen Coop, for example—were the traders' signposts and mile markers. One of the creeks was called *Ninety Six*, same as the town. Why? Studying topographic maps of the area, George noticed that near where Hunter wrote "*96*" on his 1730 map, the streams along the Cherokee Path change direction. *Six* streams north of this location flow south into the Savannah River, while another *nine* streams south of the location flow northeast into the Saluda River. Separating the groups is *Ninety Six* Creek.

George concluded that when these backwoodsmen talked about their travels along the Cherokee Path in Charles Town they were misunderstood. They were referring to "the *nine*" and "the *six*"—the location where the streams changed course, not "*96*."

(See *Nine Times*, South Carolina, page 212.)

Other Unusual Place-Names in South Carolina

Centenary

On State Route 41 twenty-five miles southeast of Florence in the eastern part of the state

The Methodists who settled here gave their church (and later the town) this name because it was built in 1836, the 100th anniversary of the founding of Methodism in England. *Centenary* is another word for centennial.

Due West

At the intersection of State Routes 20 and 184 between Anderson and Greenwood

What began in the early 1700s as *Dewitts' Corner—Dewises* and *Duets'* are other recorded spellings—now rolls off the tongue as *Due West*, and is spelled that way. Confusing the issue is the fact that when the first boundary between South Carolina and the Cherokee Nation was drawn in 1765, it started at *Dewitts' Corner* and ran west to the Savannah River, although more southwest than *due west*. Today the line divides Anderson and Abbeville counties.

Some people in town have the impossible address of *East Due West*.

Lone Star

At the intersection of State Routes 267 and 33 thirty-six miles southeast of Columbia

according to Debbie Roland, director of the Calhoun County Museum, this crossroads was named soon after the railroad came through. An engineer commented that when he approached it at night, the solitary little store at the crossroads looked like a *lone star* in the sky. People living in the immediate area liked the sound of this, and the name stuck.

Nine Times

On State Route 133 about eight miles northwest of Pickens and 28 miles west-northwest of Greenville in the northwestern corner of the state

according to the Pickens County Museum, the name comes from an old Cherokee trade path that crossed a stream *nine times*.

(See *Ninety Six*, South Carolina, page 209.)

Prosperity

On U.S. Route 76 eight miles south of Newberry and 32 miles northwest of Columbia

Prosperity is a common commendatory place-name that is found in a number of states. This one is interesting because it replaced an earlier name—*Frog Level*—that became an embarrassment for a town that in 1873 saw itself as up-and-coming.

Local legend has it that the name *Frog Level* derived from an incident in which an old man got drunk and passed out at the edge of a frog pond. Waking in a stupor, he imagined the frogs were croaking, "*Frog Level! Frog Level!*"

Rains

On State Route 576 thirty miles east-southeast of Florence in the northeastern part of the state

It *rained* and it *rained*, day after gray day, during construction of the railroad (now the CSX) through here in 1941, so when a name was needed for the new station, *Rains* seemed fitting.

Round O

On U.S. Route 17 eight miles east of Walterboro and 40 miles west-northwest of Charleston

Local legend has it that the first white settlers were confronted one day by an Indian warrior with a large circle, or *"O"* painted on his chest.

Society Hill

Where U.S. Route 52 crosses U.S. Route 401 twenty-four miles north of Florence

This name isn't as upper-crust as it sounds. The St. David's *Society* of Welsh Baptists built a church and an academy on a *hill* here in the late 1770s. The town overlooks the Pee Dee River in the Carolina Sand Hills.

Tea, South Dakota

south dakota

Igloo

One mile off State Route 471 in the southwestern corner of the state

etween 1928 and 1943, the U.S. Army built 802 *igloo*-shaped structures for storing munitions at the Black Hills Ordnance Depot. They were laid out on nine city blocks next to the Burlington Northern Railroad track. Each *igloo* had a rounded concrete roof and exterior walls that were bermed with earth to contain an accidental explosion. On August 25, 1942, with the World War II mobilization effort in full swing, the J. A. Terteling and Sons construction company set a world record for pouring concrete by completing 32 *igloo* roof arches within a twenty-four-hour period.

The combined military and civilian population of the government housing community just outside the depot's gates grew to nearly 5,000 by 1944, when a contest was held to give the community a name. The winning name was submitted by 14-year-old Donald Kolkman; the prize was a $25 war bond.

Tea

An exit off I-29 just south of Sioux Falls

y 1902, when the town was incorporated and got its own post office, postal officials in Washington were telling all applicants to choose a short name. There were already enough long, confusing, and misspelled place-names on the map of the United States. With this in mind, fifteen citizens met in the general store one afternoon to decide on a name. A number of short names were proposed, but none that a majority could agree upon. Suddenly, one of the citizens looked at his watch and announced, "It's *tea*-time." Another said, "That's it. Why not call the town *Tea*." A vote was taken, and the result was unanimous.

Usta

On State Route 73 in the northwestern part of the state

aCcording to *Usta's* only remaining resident, Jane Hauser, a cattleman named Ed Lemmon and his Sioux Indian friend were passing through the area when they stopped at the little store on the main road. They joined a discussion going on around the potbelly stove on the subject of what name to put on the community's application for a post office. Lemmon looked around the store, shrugged, and suggested a Sioux word that sounds something like *usta* and means lame or crippled.

Hauser and her husband ran the store from 1954 until they closed it for lack of business in 1972. "My husband always said it [the store] has been lame or crippled all the time we've had it," Hauser says.

Lemmon left a prouder legacy—his own name—to another South Dakota town. *Lemmon* is about fifty miles north of *Usta*, near the North Dakota border.

Other Unusual Place-Names in South Dakota

Midway Stores

On U.S. 81 eighteen miles north of Yankton in the southeastern part of the state

mIdway between Yankton to the south and Freeman to the north is a group of *stores* and gas stations locals know simply as *Midway*.

Porcupine

On a local road eight miles north of Wounded Knee in the southwestern part of the state

sOme pine trees on a nearby butte of the same name make it sort of look like a crouching *porcupine*, especially if you squint your eyes.
(See *Monkeys Eyebrow*, Kentucky, page 89.)

Rockerville

On U.S. Route 16 twelve miles south-southwest of Rapid City

tHe *rocker* system of gold mining was used where the ore was found in dry placer beds. The gravel was placed in a cradle-like contraption made of wood and *rocked* back and forth until the gold particles settled to the bottom. Once called "the prettiest little mining camp in the Black Hills," *Rockerville* produced $150,000 worth of gold in its first year (1876) and $250,000 in its second, according to the WPA writers program sponsored by the University of South Dakota in 1941.

The camp was also known for having the rowdiest saloons in the Black Hills.

Sanator

On State Route 89 six miles south of Custer and 50 miles south-southwest of Rapid City

The name is short for *sanatorium.* The South Dakota *Sanatorium* for Tuberculosis opened here in April 1911 and closed in June 1963 for lack of patients, the battle with the deadly respiratory disease having been won.

Stretching your legs in Sanator: Everybody knows about Mt. Rushmore and the four presidents' heads carved into the side of it. But few people seem to know about nearby Thunderhead Mountain (about 15 miles north of *Sanator*), where a colossal statue of Chief Crazy Horse, the great leader of the Ogalala Sioux, is being blasted out of granite. His head will be about 87 1/2 feet high, nearly a third higher than the heads of Washington, Jefferson, "Teddy" Roosevelt, and Lincoln; and the feather in his still-to-be-carved flying hair will be 44 feet long. His pointing left arm will be 263 feet long, and the head of his horse will stretch out beyond that. It's the largest mountain statue in the world. The statue has been 50 years in the making, and it will probably be another 50 years before it is completed. But Crazy Horse's emerging face is worth seeing now, and a one-thirty-fourth scale model at the Crazy Horse Memorial here gives you an idea of what is to come. Location: U.S. Route 16/385 about five miles north of Custer. Telephone: (605) 673-4681. Admission charged.

Spot, Tennessee

tennessee

Bell Buckle

On a county road about eight miles northeast of Shelbyville and 45 miles south-southeast of Nashville

This is one of the oldest place-names in Bedford County, as evidenced by a deed recorded in 1807 naming *Bell Buckle* Creek as one boundary. There are at least four plausible accounts of the origin of the name in local histories, and they all have to do with a cow *bell* and a *buckle*.

One account says that the local Indian tribe carved a cow *bell*, belt, and *buckle* into a tree as a pictographic warning to settlers looking for new grass for their cows to keep out.

Another source says that the first white men to survey the area carved the same symbol to signify that the land would be good for pasture. Other symbols were used for other types of land.

Still another version of this story attributes the carvings to traders who made a deal with Indians here, and then recorded the transaction by carving symbols in the bark of a tree, including a *bell* and *buckle*.

Most residents of the town go by the only account describing an actual cow *bell*, which hung from a belt *buckled* around a beech tree. The *bell* supposedly came from a cow an Indian had killed.

The town sprung up less than a hundred yards from the storied beech tree and the creek.

Gilt Edge

On State Secondary Route 59 thirty-two miles north of Memphis and just a few miles from the Mississippi River and Arkansas border

I could not tell the story behind this place-name better than Tom Siler did in his 1985 book *Tennessee Towns: From Adams to Yorkville*, so here it is: "This little town claims to be well over 100 years old, a fact that may explain: 1) why no one can remember the origin of the name *Gilt Edge* and 2) why no one can agree over whether the name should be spelled as one word or two. Good-naturedly, the residents talk, but they come to no decision and seem not to care. W. T. Fletcher, a present-day local historian, thinks the townspeople like the meaning of *Gilt Edge*, i.e. 'of high quality,' or 'classy.' Others insist the name came from a shoe polish of long ago. The second issue is hopelessly muddled, the name being written as one word here and as two there throughout the tiny settlement. *Gilt Edge* was incorporated in 1908."

Only

At an exit off I-40 ten miles east of where it crosses the Tennessee River

this sleepy little village sprouted in the early 1880s near an old log fort. Close-by was a spring that still marks the center of the village. One of the early settlers, Tom Sutton, operated a general store and, according to a county history, he had an idiosyncratic way of quoting the price of an item in his store. When asked the price of a sack of hard candy or a plug of tobacco or a harness—any item—he would always reply, "*Only* five cents," or "*Only* seventeen cents," or "*Only* twenty-three dollars. . . ."

Sutton's patrons jokingly referred to the store as the *Only* store. A later proprietor, Allen Hunt Brown, saw to it that the name became official when he became the village's first postmaster. The post office is still in the old store, although longtime postmistress Alice Dyer stopped stocking the store's shelves in 1993.

Only was considered an improvement over the village's original name of *Dreamer*, which some citizens thought would stigmatize the place. How could the town expect to be taken seriously with a name like that? they complained.

Topsy

Just off State Secondary Route 99 in northern Wayne County in the south-central part of the state

this may be the only town in North America (or even the world!) named after a mule. This is how it happened: One day in 1901, Lewis Whitehead, "Cage" Sprinkles, Ira Luna, and Jim Tom Meredith were outside Johnny Wisdom's general store discussing what to name the new post office. Will Lafferty rode up on his old mule *Topsy* and joined the conversation. The men told him how the feds said the village couldn't keep the name *Greenbrier* if it wanted its own post office, because there already was a post office with that name in Tennessee. Lafferty promised to think about a name.

"Maybe we ought to name it after old *Topsy* there," Whitehead then said, chuckling. The other men took him more seriously than he had meant it, and the village soon had a new name.

Whitehead also made a name for himself as an inventor, according to a local history. Experimenting with mustard gas, he accidentally killed three cows when a shell filled with mustard seed exploded after he shot it from a .22 rifle. His formula was used to propel torpedoes in World War I. After the war, he invented a coupling for railroad cars.

Other Unusual Place-Names in Tennessee

Calfkiller

A few miles south of Monterey (an exit off I-40) halfway between Nashville and Knoxville

This little settlement was named for an Indian chief who didn't look kindly upon the white men who joined the Cherokees and the buffalo on the Holston Trace (an aboriginal trail) starting in the late 1780s.

Katherine Goodwin, the librarian at the Monterey Branch Library, wrote me a note about a different explanation for the name: "A lot of folks around here say that it was only part on account of the Indian chief, because the *Calfkiller* [Creek] originates at a spring near the top of the Cumberland Plateau and then comes a-roaring down a very steep hollow. When spring and fall rains come, the creek gets up in a hurry and takes everything in its path."

Curve

Seven miles north of Ripley in Lauderdale County in the western part of the state

This town was named for the big *curves* here in both the main road and the Illinois Central Railroad.

There is an old ditty about *Curve* and four other place-names along this stretch of Tennessee Secondary Route 209. It goes like this: "Down the *Halls*, through the *Gates*, around the *Curve*, and *Flippin* into *Ripley*."

Difficult

North of the Cumberland River and about 55 miles east-northeast of Nashville

In the early 1870s, the residents of Williams Cross Roads petitioned the federal government for a post office. The letter was almost impossible to read due to bad penmanship and poor spelling, causing a frustrated Post Office Department clerk to write "this is *difficult*" across the top of it. Those words *were* legible, and as the letter moved up the chain of command, *Difficult* became the new post office's name.

Less likely is the story of the postal inspector who had a *difficult* time finding the post office. He was told to go by way of *Angel Hill, Devils Elbow,* and *Defeated* on unmarked and crisscrossing roads.

Defeated was named for the March 2, 1786, *defeat* of a surveying party by Cherokee raiders led by Chief Hanging Maw.

Frog Jump

Six miles northwest of Humboldt and 25 miles north-northwest of Jackson on State Route 54

This little hamlet in the western part of the state was supposedly named for its natural endowment of bull *frogs*. The name didn't go uncontested: Another faction wanted to name the place *Lightning Bug Hollow* or *Blister Bug City*.

Greenback

On State Secondary Route 95 about 15 miles southwest of Maryville and 31 miles south-southwest of Knoxville

Jonathan Tipton, a candidate for the state senate in 1886, is said to have persuaded the residents to name their town after the populist *Greenback* Party, whose supporters were opposed to a tight federal monetary policy based on a strict gold standard. The policy was making it hard for farmers to pay back their debts and was driving farm prices down. The party and the Agrarian Revolt petered out by the late 1890s, but the name became a permanent fixture on the map of Loudon County.

(See *Stalwart,* Michigan, for another place named for a political group, page 118.)

Spot

Just off I-40, about 12 miles east of where it crosses the Tennessee River and 50 miles west of Nashville

Local legend has it that an early resident, Lewis Mathey, was registering at a hotel in Chicago when a big splotch of ink dropped on his address. The amused hotel clerk looked down at the registration card and condescendingly asked him if he hailed from *Spot*. Mathey, who managed the general store and lumberyard in town, returned home and told his neighbors the story, and the name stuck.

texas

Cut and Shoot

On State Route 105 six miles east of Conroe and 40 miles north of Houston

numerous stories have been told to justify this peculiar place-name. One tells of patrons in a saloon who "took to fighting" with knives and pistols, *cutting and shooting* each other. Another says the *cutting and shooting* resulted from an argument over the design of a church steeple. The least likely story has to do with *cutting* cattle (changing their direction) toward a *shute*.

The story that is told most frequently, albeit with many variations, centers on a dispute over the use of the community hall. It seems that the Missionary Baptists, Hardshell Baptists, and Methodists in town went in together to build the hall for use as a combination church and school house, with the understanding that all denominations were welcome to worship there—except Mormons and Apostolics.

In July 1912, an Apostolic preacher named Stamps appeared in town and was invited by a group of citizens to hold a meeting at the hall. When this got around, the town split into two factions—one that was willing to relax the rule and let Stamps preach and one that said absolutely not. The latter's position had been hardened, no doubt, by the rumor that Stamps occasionally visited saloons and liked to dance.

On July 20, the day before the meeting was to take place, R. B. Mann sent his son Clark to Archie Vick's house to get the keys to the community hall so he could lock the doors. When the other side got wind of this, they threatened to break down the doors if necessary. Hearing this, Mann saddled his horse and rode Paul Revere-style through town alerting the anti-Apostolic faction.

The next morning, both sides met at the hall with their knives and guns at the ready, according to a version of the story recounted in a history of Montgomery County published in 1952. Accusations flew back and forth, with Mann and George King getting into a red-hot argument that threatened to end violently before King withdrew to a grove of shade trees. After everyone had cooled down a bit, Stamps stood under a tree and delivered a sermon to his sympathizers and supporters, who listened from their buggies and wagons.

The next day, each side appeared at the county courthouse in Conroe to bring charges against the other for disturbing the peace, assault, and using obscene language. Mann and King were tried and fined, but they kept the dispute alive in numerous court appearances over the next year. At one of the trials, the judge asked Archie Vick where the incident took place. "I suppose you would call it the place where they had a *cutting and shooting* scrape," he said.

Cash, Texas

Tellers of this version of the story credit Vick with giving the town its name. But they also tell how, during the heat of the confrontation at the community hall, little Jack King, George's eight-year-old son, was heard to say: "I'm scared. I'm going to *cut* around the corner *and shoot* through the bushes. . . ."

Both remarks sound to me like they came from the imagination of a storyteller who was trying just a little too hard to make his case.

Dime Box

On Ranch Road 141 ten miles north of Lincoln and 50 miles east of Austin

before there was a post office here, the residents had a community mail *box*. When they wanted to send a letter, they put the envelope in the *box* with a *dime* on top of it. A passing teamster would then carry it to a post office on his route. The teamster was also paid a *dime* for delivering a letter or parcel.

When the community had grown large enough to warrant a post office, the residents wanted to call it Brown's Mill, but the Post Office Department rejected the name, saying it would be confused with Brownsville. So a local doctor suggested *Dime Box*, and the name was accepted.

Dime Box made national headlines in 1943 when it was the first town in the U.S. to have 100 percent of its residents contribute to the March of *Dimes*.

Uncertain

East of State Route 43 on the southern shore of Caddo Lake and about 35 miles northwest of Shreveport, Louisiana

no one is certain how *Uncertain* got its name, and I am certainly not the first writer to have some rhetorical fun with this *uncertainty*. Here is a handful of explanations that are certain to leave you as *uncertain* about *Uncertain* as I am.

Some say that during steamboat days, side-wheelers moving up Caddo Lake and Cypress Bayou on their way to Jefferson had a difficult time finding the channel when the water was low. Boat captains called this narrow bend in the lake *Uncertain* Landing because they were *uncertain* whether they could continue upstream.

Others say that the name comes from the fact that fishermen and loggers were *uncertain* whether they could get a horse and wagon in and out of here during flood season. That was back when they had "corduroy" roads—logs laid side by side across the road.

Mrs. Jack B. Baldwin of nearby Marshall, Texas, told a reporter from the

Marshall *News Messenger* in 1971 that her father, S. P. Jones, and two other men who resurveyed Harrison County in the early 1890s named this spot *Uncertain* because the old boundary markers were so confusing.

Another source says the *uncertainty* was over whether the town would be a "wet" or "dry" town when it was incorporated in 1961.

Stretching your legs in Uncertain: Like Rip Van Winkle, Uncertain is waking up from a long sleep that began in another era—but slowly. It's still a quiet place to fish, spy on alligators, bird watch, reflect. The moss-covered cypress trees rising up out of the mists on Caddo Lake—Texas's largest natural lake—and Big Cypress Bayou give *Uncertain* a remote, cloistered ambience. At last count there were seven bed-and-breakfast inns in town, all new since the late 1980s. Two popular annual events are the Turtle Festival in June—turtle races and a turtle calling contest are the highlights—and the Floating Christmas Parade in December.

Other Unusual Place-Names in Texas

Altoga

On a county road a few miles northeast of McKinney and about 35 miles north-northeast of Dallas

dock Owensby, a late-19th-century champion of cooperative values, wanted to name this place *All Together*, but the Post Office Department said nothing doing. The name was too imaginative, too long, and two words. So Dock coined this name.

Ambia

On a local road seven miles southwest of Paris in the northeastern part of the state

this is the only place in the world named for spit. The word was derived from the *amber* jets of tobacco juice expectorated by the men who congregated at the local store every afternoon to swap lies.

Blanket

On U.S. Route 67 seventy-five miles southeast of Abilene in the center of the state

In 1852, a surveying party came upon a band of Tonkawa Indians drying their *blankets* on the banks of a creek near the present town.

Along with this explanation, relief postmaster and *Blanket* native Oneale Tabor told me a local joke using the name. *Question:* Why are Brownwood and Comanche such warm towns? *Answer:* Because they have a *Blanket* between them.

Blanket Hill, Pennsylvania, takes its name from a 1756 incident in which a Colonial militia group came under attack by Indians and had to retreat so suddenly they left their *blankets* behind.

Cash

On State Route 34 about 20 miles east of downtown Dallas

E. H. R. Green, the president of the Texas Midland Railroad, wanted to name the town for J. A. *Money*, a store owner who had politicked for the extension of the railroad through the town. *Money*, a modest man, declined the honor but agreed to this synonym for the green stuff, according to Fred Tarpley in *1001 Texas Place Names*, the best source of information on this subject.

Direct

On Ranch Road 1499 near the Oklahoma border in the northeastern part of the state

A revivalist preacher warned his followers that they were on the *"direct"* route to hell by allowing Indians to cross the Red River *"direct"* for whiskey, Fred Tarpley explains. Tradition has it that the church was built with money donated by a converted saloonkeeper.

Grayback

On Ranch Road 1811 thirty-five miles west of Wichita Falls in the northern part of the state

This is not a place-name to be proud of; the *grayback* is a variety of lice that infested a cowboy camp sometime around the turn of the century.

Grayburg

On State Route 326 about 20 miles west of Beaumont and 65 miles east-northeast of Houston

This was literally a *gray burg* when the name was chosen in 1909, because the Thompson-Ford Lumber Company had painted all the company houses gray. *Ecru*, Mississippi, was named for the color of its railroad station.

Grit

On State Route 29 in Mason County in the central part of the state

The name was adopted at a time (1901) when the Post Office Department was asking for short names for new towns. The other proposed names on the town's list were Hey, Rock, and Baze. Both the soil and the toughness of the early settlers may have had something to do with the nomination of the name *Grit*.

Lolita

At the intersection of Ranch Roads 1593 and 616 in central Jackson County 100 miles southwest of Houston

The citizens were so embarrassed that their town had the same name as the teenage nymphomaniac in Vladimir Nabokov's 1955 novel that they seriously considered changing the name. Instead, they waited uncomfortably until the moral storm over the book, and the film based on it, blew over.

The *Lolita* that the townspeople wanted outsiders to remember was *Lolita* Reese, one of the early pioneers.

Pluck

On a local road just north of U.S. 287 and just east of U.S. 59 ninety miles north-northwest of Houston

George H. Deason showed his respect for the first settlers when he suggested the name in 1918. It took a lot of *pluck* to put down roots here in the 1880s, he said.

An alternative story is that the name was *plucked* out of thin air when the post office was reinstated shortly after World War I.

Telephone

At the "T" intersection of Ranch Roads 273 and 2029 near the Oklahoma border in the northeastern part of the state

The first postmaster suggested the name in 1886 because he had the only *telephone* in town. Postal authorities had already rejected a number of other names. There used to be a place called *Dial* in this neck of the woods; there still is a *Direct* (see page 227).

Telegraph, in west-central Texas, was so named because the first *telegraph* poles in the county were cut from a canyon close to town.

Tell

On Ranch Road 94 in the eastern part of the base of the Texas Panhandle

This place was nicknamed *Tell*tale Flats around the turn of the 20th century because of the eagerness of some of its residents to tattle on their neighbors to the grand jury without even being asked to do so. The name was shortened when the community applied for a post office in 1888.

Trickham

Seventy-five miles southeast of Abilene in the central part of the state

After the Civil War, there was a general store and saloon here on the Jinglebob cattle trail that was known widely for the *tricks* its owner played on the cowboys who patronized the store. A favorite prank of the owner's was to fill a whiskey bottle with water colored with coffee, stopper it, put it on the shelf behind the bar with the rest of the bottles, and then see if he could sell it to a cowboy before he noticed it was fake.

The cowboys dubbed the place *Trick'em*. The Post Office Department demanded a proper spelling in 1879.

Valentine

On U.S. Route 90 twenty-five miles from the Mexican border in southwestern Jeff Davis County

Track for the Texas and New Orleans Railway reached here on *Valentine's* Day, 1882.

Low, Utah

utah

Helper

On U.S. Route 6 five miles north of Price in the east-central part of the state

This town of 2,000 in the Wasatch Mountains has had two names in its century-and-a-quarter history, both connected with railroads. It was first called *Pratt's Siding*. Teancum Pratt came to the area in 1870 to search for coal and soon established a siding on a narrow-gauge railroad used by miners. He and his two wives, Annie and Sarah, lived in a dugout, as did most early miners and trappers.

Wells had also been considered as a name, in honor of the superintendent of the Denver and Rio Grande Railroad.

The track was converted to standard gauge in 1890, and the place began to grow as a railroad town. By 1892 it was officially known as *Helper*, named after the *helper* engine that was parked at the siding and used to help pull the rail cars over the steep mountains that peaked at Soldier Summit (7,477 feet), about twenty miles north. *Helper* is at 5,830 feet elevation.

Helper was notorious for its prostitution and gambling, and it once had nineteen saloons for a population of 2,500. Gunfights were common, and members of the notorious Robbers Roost gang were frequently seen in town. One of them, Butch Cassidy, grabbed more than $8,000 in coal mine payroll money in nearby Castlegate on April 21, 1897.

A 1920s source described *Helper* as "an unsafe place to live."

Tropic

On State Route 12 on the eastern edge of Bryce Canyon National Park in the southern part of the state

This town was named by the first settlers, who found the climate mild—even *tropical*—compared to chilly Panguitch (25 miles to the northwest), from which they had migrated. *Tropic*, at 6,062 feet above sea level, is only about 600 feet lower in elevation than Panguitch, but there is often a 15 to 20 degree difference in temperature.

South and west of *Tropic* near the Arizona border is a region of Utah known as Dixie, both for its mild climate and the fact that it was settled by Mormons who were originally from the Deep South—Alabama, Mississippi, and Georgia mostly. Brigham Young sent them to the St. George Basin in 1856 to grow cotton, so the religious group could make its own clothing, according to Marian Jacklin, an official with the Dixie National Forest. The Mormon settlers also grew mulberry trees for silk production and gardenias and magnolias to remind them of back home. The small city of St. George even has some palm trees.

Other Unusual Place-Names in Utah

Angle

Just east of State Route 62 and just north of Otter Creek Reservoir in Piute County in the south-central part of the state

the ranchers here in the Otter Creek Valley named their community for the sharp *angle* at which the local access road meets the main highway. It's one of those "you-can't-miss-it" landmarks that make it easy to give directions.

Dividend

Fifteen miles west of where U.S. Route 6 crosses I-15 and 30 miles southwest of Provo

the veins of silver in the rocks here paid *dividends* to many a miner before the ore played out shortly after World War II. A grateful miner, E. J. Raddatz, gave the community its name.

Gunlock

On a secondary road off State Route 18 in the southwestern corner of the state

gunlock Bill Hamblin was the colorful brother of an even more colorful Mormon missionary to the Indian tribes of southern Utah, Jacob Hamblin. Bill was known far and wide for his hunting and *gun*smithing prowess and for his friendliness toward pioneers traveling on the Old California Trail (also known as the Spanish Trail). He settled here in the Santa Clara River Valley in 1857.

Hurricane

At the intersection of State Routes 9 and 59 in the southwestern corner of the state

mormon church official Erastus Snow was returning to St. George from visiting the Mormon colonies along the upper Virgin River when a whirlwind blew the top off his buggy as he was crossing a lava ridge. Telling the story later, he suggested the name *Hurricane* Ridge. The town, as well as three other geographical features in the area, take their name from this incident.

Locals pronounce it "*Hurikin*," skipping past the first "i" so fast the name rhymes with nearby La Verkin.

Hailstone, located 35 miles southeast of Salt Lake City, was another Utah town with a stormy name. It was named in 1864 for its founders, William Paret and Ann Davis *Hailstone.* What is left of the town is now at the bottom of the Jordanelle Reservoir.

Low

On I-80 about halfway between Salt Lake City and the Nevada border

This *low* pass between two mountain ranges is a good example of the utilitarian streak in American place naming. A Western Pacific Railroad construction and maintenance camp for many years starting in the 1880s, *Low* has pretty much vanished.

Mutual

On a back road about 12 miles northwest of Price in the central part of the state

This place was named for the *Mutual* Coal Company, which built the town and operated the mine from 1921 to 1938. Boxer Jack Dempsey trained in the Price area in the 1920s and 1930s, and some say *Mutual* toyed with changing its name to *Dempseyville.* Other locals say that is dead wrong, that the great heavyweight had no connection to *Mutual.*

Orderville

On U.S. Route 89 about 60 miles southeast of Cedar City and 25 miles north of the Arizona border

This was one of the most successful settlements of the United *Order* of the Mormon Church, a communal living experiment with strict social and economic rules designed to help its members get their moral houses in *order.* The commune flourished for about 11 years in the 1870s and 1880s.

Bread Loaf, Vermont

vermont

Morses Line

On State Route 235 fifty miles north-northeast of Burlington in the northwestern part of the state

m*orses Line* is a port of entry on the Quebec border, and was named for J. *Morse*, who was appointed postmaster in 1892. The post office was housed in *Morse's* store.

Many states have border towns whose names are dead giveaways; *Border*, Idaho, is probably the most obvious one. Iowa has *Lineville*. Its counterpart, *South Lineville*, is just across the Missouri border. Missouri also has a *West Line* on its border with Oklahoma (which has a town named *County Line*). Maryland has *Lineboro, State Line*, and *Maryland Line*, all within 60 miles of each other. North Dakota has *Northgate* and *Portal* on its border with Canada, both ports of entry. Saskatchewan obliges with *North Portal* on its side of the border. (See page 149 for border towns of another type.)

North Hero, South Hero

On North Hero Island and Grand Isle, respectively, in Lake Champlain

Originally known as the *Two Heroes*, and now, simply, the *Heroes*, the villages were part of a 1779 land grant to Ethan Allen and 364 other Revolutionary War *heroes* (the list reads like a roster of the legendary Green Mountain Boys). Most people think the two *heroes* were Ethan and his brother Ira, but the "two" in the name refers to the fact that the grant—known as "the town of Two Heroes"—was spread across two islands. The Colonial legislature's probable intent was that the two islands belonged to all 365 of the *heroes* (war veterans).

Almost from the beginning there was talk among the settlers of dividing the town, according to Esther Munroe Swift in *Vermont Place Names*, and on November 7, 1798, the northern island became *North Hero* (a separate town) and the southern one Middle Hero and *South Hero* (two precincts of the same town). Twelve years later, Middle Hero was renamed Grande Isle, so it could have its own representative in the state legislature. The first settler of *South Hero* was Ebenezer Allen, a cousin of Ethan and Ira Allen.

Victory

On a gravel road 15 miles northeast of St. Johnsbury in the northeastern part of the state

One legend has it that the name was chosen to honor John Paul Jones and the *Bonhomme Richard's victory* over the British ship *Serapis* just six weeks before a charter for the town was granted to a group of Continental Army veterans on November 6, 1780.

More likely, the mountain village was named for the general feeling in the fall of 1780 that *victory* over the British was finally possible. "As it turned out," Swift writes, "history proved the complete suitability of the name. On 6 September 1781, the very day that *Victory's* charter was issued, the French Admiral de Grasse was engaging the British fleet off Yorktown in the naval engagement that set the stage for Cornwallis's total defeat ten days later."

(See *Conquest*, New York, page 170.)

Other Unusual Place-Names in Vermont

Adamant

On a gravel road seven miles north of Montpelier

This town was named in 1905 for the hardness of the granite that was quarried there. But it might have just as accurately been named for the flintiness of its inhabitants.

Stretching your legs in Adamant: Adamant is just up the road from Montpelier, home of one of the best Sixties-style vegetarian restaurants in the U.S., the Horn of the Moon Cafe. Unlike the cooks in a lot of other natural foods eateries, Ginny Callan's cooks pay loving attention to color, texture, and flavor. Address: 8 Langdon Street, Montpelier. Telephone: (802) 223-2895.

Bread Loaf

On State Route 125 ten miles southeast of Middlebury

The town is named after a nearby mountain that looks like a *loaf* of home-baked *bread* when viewed from the north or south. (Compare with *sugarloaf*, a common name for a small, conical-shaped mountain.)

Bread Loaf is just down the road (Robert Frost Memorial Drive, aka State Route 125) from Ripton, where every August since 1926 unknown writers have rubbed shoulders with famous ones—hoping something magical will rub off—at the *Breadloaf* Writers' Conference. Current best-selling novelist Richard Ford is a *Breadloaf* alumnus.

Chiselville

On a town road 18 miles north of Bennington in the southwestern part of the state

This was the home of the Arlington Edge Tool Company, famous in the 1800s for its *chisels*.

Stretching your legs in Chiselville: Just up historic State Route 7A in Manchester Village is the American Museum of Fly Fishing. The museum has a growing collection of rods, reels, flies, and other tackle, as well as photographs, art, books, and manuscripts. Included are memorabilia of famous anglers like Cornelia "Fly Rod" Crosby and innovative fly tier Carrie Stevens. Location: Seminary Avenue and State Route 7A, Manchester Village. Telephone: (802) 362-3300. Admission charged.

Modest Town, Virginia

virginia

Central Garage
On U.S. Route 360 sixteen miles northeast of Richmond

This little crossroads tells you something about the relationship between the church and the automobile—at least here in eastern Virginia. This place was called *Sharon Church* (the oldest Baptist church in King William County, built in 1845) for some 50 years—until people started driving cars. Then it was changed to *Central Garage* to signal motorists that there was a gas pump and a mechanic on duty at this strategic spot halfway between King William and Mangohick for anyone traveling north-south and halfway between Mechanicsville (more than one mechanic?) and Millers Tavern for anyone nursing a Tin Lizzie along an east-west course across King William County.

Strategic positioning of automobile garages was very important at a time when a motorist could count on something going wrong with a car every 30 miles or so.

Maidens
On State Route 6 twenty miles west-northwest of Richmond

Originally called *Maiden's Adventure,* this James River town was named for a beautiful young *maiden* who swam across the river to warn her sweetheart of an Indian attack. (For a similarly romantic place-name legend see *Whitehorse Beach*, Massachusetts, page 114.)

Maidens once was a popular and picturesque landing for packet boats plying the James River Canal, and later was a station on the Chesapeake and Ohio Railroad. A well-known local character of that time was Isaac Smith, a black man who had lost both arms in an accident when he was sixteen years old but made his living carrying the mail from the train to the village of Shako and back each day. This was a fifteen-mile walk, and Smith held the job well into his seventies. He was said to have never missed a mail train.

Short Pump

On U.S. Route 250 thirteen miles northwest of Richmond

I n the early years of the republic, Robert H. Saunders ran a tavern at the intersection of Three Chopt Road and Pouncy Tract Road here. The well was in the front yard, close to the building. Sometime before 1815, he built a porch across the front of the tavern that covered the well and hand pump, making it impossible to complete the stroke of the pump handle without hitting the underside of the porch floor. So the architecturally challenged Saunders solved the problem by *shortening* the *pump* handle. When neighbors stopped laughing at the barkeep's folly, they gave his tavern a new name that stuck when a town grew up around it.

Today's *Short Pumpians* (and tall ones, too!) call the road to Richmond (U.S. Route 250 or Broad Street Road) the *Short Pump* Expressway, and the local newspaper refers to its market as the "Greater *Short Pump* Metropolitan Area." The Downtown *Short Pump* General Store sells T-shirts emblazoned with this message: "Born on a mountain, raised in a cave, Downtown *Short Pump* is the place I crave."

Temperanceville

On U.S. Route 13 on Virginia's eastern shore about seven miles south of the Maryland border

n o one knows for certain how this village got its name, but a number of sources mention a Mr. *Temperance,* a Quaker who settled here in the mid-1600s. The sect's meetinghouse was on his farm. Robert I. Alotta, author of *Signposts and Settlers: The History of Place Names in the Middle Atlantic States,* stands alone in claiming the community was called *Crossroads* until it became a dry town in 1824.

(See *Temperance,* Michigan, page 120.)

Other Unusual Place-Names in Virginia

Ark

On U.S. Route 17 forty-five miles north-northwest of Norfolk in central Gloucester County

I n 1888, the U.S. Post Office Department was approving short names for new post offices, and this village had a ready one in the venerable Old *Ark* Farm.

Bumpass

On State Secondary Route 618 forty-five miles north-northwest of Richmond in the northeastern corner of Louisa County

no, this is not the name of a Seventies dance. It's the last name of the village's second postmaster, John T. *Bumpass*. The name is the result of the transmogrification of *Boumpasse* from French to English.

If I were *Bumpass*, I would have stuck with the village's first name, *Second Turnout,* where a post office was established in 1847. *Bumpass* came along in 1860.

Another unusual place-name here in eastern Louisa County is *Cuckoo*. The village takes its name from the *Cuckoo* Tavern, which most likely had a picture of the bird on its sign.

Disputanta

On U.S. Route 460 six miles southeast of Petersburg

the naming of this community caused a *dispute* between two factions that was settled when a wag came up with this classical-sounding moniker. This was in 1853, when new towns were popping up along the path of the Norfolk and Petersburg Railroad, which was still under construction at its southern end.

Dot

On U.S. Route 58 thirty miles northwest of Kingsport, Tennessee, in the southwestern corner of Virginia

it's just a *dot* on the map—one of those places that has 'Welcome to . . .' and 'Come Back' on the same sign," quips local historian Alex Slagle. When he was growing up in the area, there was a house and a store here; now it's just a crossroads.

Independent Hill

On State Route 234 on the north side of Quantico Marine Corps base and 35 miles southwest of Washington, D.C.

locals like to tell the story of a turn-of-the-century storekeeper named *Hill* who liked to hunt and fish. An *independent*-minded man, he would close up shop and take to the woods whenever the urge came over him. A housewife would see him heading off with a rifle or a fishing pole over his shoulder, and, shaking her head, say, "There goes *Independent Hill.*"

Lively
On State Route 201 in Lancaster County near to where the Rappahannock River flows into Chesapeake Bay

One source says it's a family name, another says it's a shortening of *Lively* Oaks, an estate named for its tall, stately trees. "One thing it's not named for is the night life, I'll tell you that," says Susanna Collins, a librarian in the nearby village of Lancaster.

Modest Town
At the intersection of State Road 187 and Secondary State Road 679 on Virginia's eastern shore about 20 miles south of the Maryland border

Local legend says that in the early 1880s two prim and proper ladies ran a boarding house here that was also a stagecoach stop. They had strict rules designed to encourage *modest* and decent behavior, and let it be known that if that wasn't exactly what you were looking for in accommodations, you might want to continue on to *Helltown*, about a mile west.

Ordinary
Five miles north of Gloucester Point (at the mouth of the York River) and 40 miles north of Norfolk

In Colonial times, *ordinary* was another word for tavern. The word has a legal connotation that most likely comes from the licensing of public eating and drinking establishments: An *ordinary* served regular meals at a fixed price. The *ordinary* at this location was called Seawell's *Ordinary*, and during the Siege of Yorktown in 1781 it did a brisk business with French and American officers, including Generals Washington and Lafayette.
   (See *Ordinary*, Kentucky, page 91.)

Rescue
On State Secondary Route 665 across the James River from Newport News in Isle of Wight County

This is a waterman's town, so you'd think the name commemorated some dramatic *rescue* on the James River. But the legend persists that sometime around 1889 a man carrying a mail pouch rode into town on a mud-stained mule, and was greeted by a jubilant bystander, who yelled: "Hurrah, we've been *rescued*."

This was the same year that the post office opened, so perhaps the excitement was over the fact that the mail was being brought to town for the first time, instead of a local rider having to fetch it in another town. Finally, the town had been *rescued* from isolation.

(See *Rescue*, Missouri, page 136.)

Tightsqueeze

On State Route 47 fifty-five miles northeast of Danville in Mecklenburg County

The story goes that before the Civil War there lived a man here who sold whiskey to area farmers in one-gallon jugs but charged them for two gallons. His explanation: "I make a right *tight squeeze* to get it all in."

Oh! I almost forgot. If you're looking for *Tightsqueeze* on the map, you won't find it. They changed it to *Fairview* some years back.

Triangle

On U.S. Route 1 twenty miles north of Fredericksburg in southeastern Prince William County

Some people say this place was named for the angle at which Old U.S. Route 1 converged with Fuller Heights Road at the entrance to Quantico Marine Corps base. Others say it was named for the shape of Jay Amidon's automobile garage, the area's first commercial structure, built during World War I. It was probably a little bit of each.

Dusty, Washington

washington

Concrete

On State Route 20 fifty miles east-southeast of Bellingham in central Skagit County

This small town was named *Cement City* in 1905 by the promoters of a portland *cement* plant. The name was changed to *Concrete* in 1909, the year the town was incorporated. Portland *cement* mixed with sand or gravel, which makes it stronger, is called *concrete*.

Robin Wood, *Concrete's* librarian, says the plant closed about 1970. In its heyday, there were three giant smokestacks and an overhead conveyor system that brought limestone to the plant from a quarry a mile west of town. The conveyor looked like a ski lift with buckets instead of chairs and was very noisy, says Wood. The stacks spewed cement dust that settled on houses, trees, and shrubbery for miles around. "This was just a very gray city," she recalls.

Colorado and North Dakota also have towns named *Concrete* (page 182), and Oklahoma has a *Cement* and Michigan a *Cement City*.

Medical Lake

On State Route 902 thirteen miles southwest of Spokane

First the Indians and then the white men and women who started coming here in the late 1800s, were convinced of the healing powers of the silica-rich waters of the lake the Indians called *Skookum Limechin Chuch*, meaning "strong *medicine* water." First white settler Andrew Lefevre said that bathing in the lake cured his rheumatism—and the scabies of his sheep. Another early settler told of a pleasant feeling of "lightness," but he also noticed that the water took the paint off the spokes of his wagon's wheels.

Early on, salt works went up on the shore, and the extracts, tablets, soaps, plasters, ointments, and other products made from the salt were recommended for a slew of ailments, including rheumatism, kidney troubles, diphtheria, sunburn, indigestion, and enlargement of the uterus. At the sanatorium that opened in town before the turn of the century, patients took baths in red mud that was dredged from the bottom of the lake.

Children who swam in the lake all summer saw their hair turn red. This confused a new teacher who looked out on her first class and saw that all of her pupils had hair the same red color.

Pullman

On State Route 270 between U.S. 195 and Moscow, Idaho, 72 miles south of Spokane

This town in the gorgeous wheat-growing region called the Palouse had a perfectly serviceable and indigenous name—*Three Forks*—until someone hatched a plot to give the sagging local economy a jolt by renaming the town for a wealthy man. The idea was that if the mayor wrote a letter to the man notifying him of the honor and telling him of the town's plight, he'd send a big check.

So the town fathers studied a list of U.S. millionaires and picked George M. *Pullman*, inventor of the railroad sleeping car, as their target. The town was rechristened, the letter was sent, and after a while a check arrived in the mail at city hall—for $50.

Some farmers in western Maine had the wool pulled over their eyes when they agreed to name their town after Dr. Elijah *Dix* in return for his donation of a library. When the "library" arrived from Boston, it consisted of a single crate of books from the sly doctor's medical school days. *Dixfield* lives on.

(Both of these stories are told in *Ink, Ark., and All That: How American Places Got Their Names* by Vernon Pizer.)

Walla Walla

On U.S. Route 12 near the Oregon border in the southeastern part of the state

Walla *Walla* is on the *Walla Walla* River in *Walla Walla* County, home turf of the *Walla Walla* Indians. Try saying that fast three times! One source says the name is a Nez Perce word meaning "running water," and that if the name were in *Walla Walla*, it would be Wallula, which, as it turns out, is a town 30 miles west of *Walla Walla*.

Another translation of the word is "many waters" or "many rivers," and *Walla Walla* County, if not the city, certainly is that, with two major Western rivers, the Columbia and the Snake, forming its western border. It is also said that the word *Walla* is repeated in the name because the Indians didn't have a plural. But I prefer Garrison Keillor's explanation of this: "*Walla Walla*—a place so nice, they named it twice."

Other Unusual Place-Names in Washington

Beaux Arts

Just north of I-90 about three miles south of Bellevue on the east shore of Lake Washington

This was the site of a 50-acre art colony founded in 1908 by visual artists, architects, and writers influenced by the aesthetic theories of the École des *Beaux-Arts* in Paris.

BZ Corner

On State Route 141 sixty miles east-northeast of Portland, Oregon, in western Klickitat County

This town was named for William *"BZ"* Biesanz, a gregarious and witty strawberry grower here in the 1920s. He is also credited with the name *Pucker Huddle,* a locally known area and road between *BZ Corner* and White Salmon. According to a local author Keith McCoy, *BZ* once observed that the teenagers who picked his strawberries would *pucker* and *huddle* in the barns and sheds when the work day was done.

Dusty

Where State Route 127 joins State Route 26 seventy-five miles south of Spokane

This was a windy, dusty crossroads when it was named in 1898. The story is told that Homer Allen, the first postmaster, wanted the town named after him, but his wife and a schoolteacher named Anna Stenson made him cross out "Allen" and write in *Dusty* on the application for a post office. The women didn't want anybody to think for a minute that their life on the frontier wasn't gritty.

Electric City

On State Route 155 just downstream of the Grand Coulee Dam and 85 miles west of Spokane

The town was named in the 1930s for the hydro*electric* dam that generated the cheap *electric* power that helped the Northwest's economy grow.

Electron, Washington, located between Mt. Rainier and Tacoma, is also named for a power plant.

(See *Atomic City,* Idaho, page 65.)

Eltopia

On U.S. 395 about 20 miles north of Kennewick

this name is said to be a cleaned-up version of *Hell-to-Pay*, which was the name of the Northern Pacific Railroad camp located here in 1889. The traditional story is that when heavy rains washed out a just-completed track bed, a Cockney construction worker grumbled that there would be "*'el' to pay.*"

Gold Bar

On U.S. Route 2 forty-five miles northeast of Seattle

prospectors named this little economic hub in 1889 for the *gold* discovered on a *bar* in the Skykomish River. Later, when *Gold Bar* was a construction camp for the Great Northern Railroad and anti-Chinese sentiment was raging, the construction supervisor saved the lives of his Chinese workers by hiding them in crude, hastily built coffins.

Humptulips

On U.S. Route 101 south of Olympic National Park and about 75 miles northwest of Olympia

this is a humorous example of what can happen when Native American words are translated into English. The original Quinault word, *Ho-to-la-bixh*, has nothing to do with *humps* or *tulips*. It means "hard to pole"—the *Humptulips* River, that is.

Other sources say *Humptulips* means "chilly region."

Index

On U.S. Route 2 fifty-two miles northeast of Seattle

this hamlet of 140 souls is in the shadow of Mt. *Index*, which resembles an *index* finger pointing skyward.

west virginia

Letter Gap

On U.S. Route 33 about 30 miles southwest of Weston and 90 miles northeast of Charleston

You'd guess the name had something to do with the first post office—maybe it filled a *gap* in the mail service between two locations. And that may be true. But 86-year-old Glenna Queen, president of the Gilmer County Historical Society, swears by the story she's heard since she was a little girl:

Back when a lady kept her legs covered up all the way down to her shoe tops, a pretty young woman was mounting her horse (sidesaddle, of course) from an uppen block (a kind of step stool) when her skirt parted nearly to her knees. "Your skirt's a gappin'," the man holding the horse warned discreetly.

"Well, *let'er gap!*" the brash lass hooted and took off down Main Street.

Needmore

On State Route 55 fifty miles west-southwest of Winchester, Virginia, in eastern Hardy County

One of two communities in West Virginia with this name; the other, in Braxton County, no longer appears on maps. Georgia, Indiana, Kentucky, Illinois, and Tennessee each have a *Needmore*, Alabama has two, and Texas has five, as well as a *Needville*. There are probably others.

"*Needmore* embraces all that its name implies, and *needs more* of all it now possesses," a local historian wrote of the Braxton County village.

The *Needmore* in Hardy County, an unincorporated village near the Virginia state line, is just another wiggle in a very wiggly road through the mountains. Baker Run races over rocks on one side of the road. The village's commercial hub—Hillbilly Heating & Cooling, the frequently closed Past & Present Shop (second-hand merchandise), and the Creekside Cafe—is on the other.

I asked the owner of the Cafe how the village got its name. "Just look around," he said. "We *need more* of everything." And that's probably the answer you'd get in any *Needmore* in the country, none of which ever got much of what it wanted.

(See *Uneeda*, West Virginia, page 253.)

Sistersville, West Virginia

Other Unusual Place-Names in West Virginia

Exchange

A few miles west of Interstate 79 and about 75 miles northeast of Charleston in northern Braxton County

first postmistress Samantha Duffield chose the name in 1906 because the general store and other businesses in town *exchanged* owners so often.

Four States

On a county road ten miles west of Fairmont

Life here revolved around John H. Jones's coal mine, and he owned mines in *four states*—West Virginia, Virginia, Pennsylvania, and Ohio.

Hundred

On U.S. Route 250 a few miles south of the Pennsylvania border and 38 miles west of Morgantown

formerly Old *Hundred*, this place was named for two centenarians, Henry Church, who died in 1860 at age 109, and his wife, who lived to age 106. Henry had fought in the Revolutionary War—for the other side. There must have been something in the water!

Mountain

On State Route 74 forty miles east of Parkersburg in extreme northeastern Ritchie County

this place proves that anyone—even a whole community—can make a *Mountain* out of a *Mole Hill*, which was the hamlet's original name. Why was it changed? What do you think the economic and cultural prospects are for a place called *Mole Hill*?

Odd

A few miles west of Interstate 77 and about 18 miles south of Beckley in the southern part of the state

When the post office was established, the townspeople held a meeting to decide on a name. Someone suggested that the name be a very *odd* one. Mrs. M. J. Brown thought that was such a good idea she asked for a show of hands, and the name was adopted.

(See *Oddville*, Kentucky, page 90.)

Pickle Street

On U.S. Route 33 twelve miles west of Weston and 32 miles southwest of Clarksburg

here was a place so poor the only thing a schoolgirl could expect to find in her lunch pail was a jar of *pickle* beans. That's the explanation from Glenna Queen (*Letter Gap*, West Virginia), and it sounds pretty good to me.

Pie

On U.S. Route 52 near where West Virginia, Virginia, and Kentucky meet

Pie was included in the list of names sent to the U.S. Post Office Department for the delightfully simple reason that residing in the community at that time was one Leander Blankenship who loved *pies* of any kind.

(See *Pie Town*, New Mexico, page 166.)

Sistersville

On State Route 2 thirty-nine miles up the Ohio River from Parkersburg

this town was platted on land owned by two of the Wells *sisters,* Sarah and Deliah. Their father was Charles Wells, a prominent early settler in the area who sired 22 children. One genealogical account says he and his second wife christened their 20th child Twenty and nicknamed the 21st Plenty.

The Wellses and two other early families are said to have had 72 children between them. The Wells brood arrived here in 1802 after floating down the Ohio River in a flatboat they had loaded in *Wellsburg,* a town in the West Virginia panhandle that is also named for the family.

Thursday

On State Route 47 in southern Ritchie County in the northwestern part of the state

One *Thursday* in 1922, a boy armed with a fountain pen found himself alone with the community's application for a post office. He looked down the form to the place where you were supposed to write in suggested names and saw that one line was blank.

True

On State Route 20 in Summers County in the southern part of the state

according to the May 30, 1937, issue of the *Clarksburg Exponent*, the citizens of the town added a postscript to the bottom of their application for a post office: "All these facts are *true*." The word *true* was written in large capital letters—and that's the name the U.S. Post Office Department told the community to use as its postmark.

Uneeda

On State Route 85 forty-five miles south of Charleston in central Boone County

Someone had the *Uneeda* Biscuit company in mind when this hamlet was named in 1898. But a pun may also be intended: This place *needed* a lot of things in the early days, like all the towns named *Needmore* in the U.S. (see page 249).

Cream, Wisconsin

wisconsin

Embarrass

On State Route 22 about 50 miles west of Green Bay

When you're *embarrassed* by something—forgetting a person's name, saying the wrong thing at the wrong time—you experience a momentary emotional "tangle"—or *embarras* in French.

A hundred years ago, French was the first language in what was called the Pinery, the vast pine forests of northeastern Wisconsin. Lumberjacks from Quebec cut the trees and hauled them to the river banks on sleds so they could be floated to sawmills downstream. They named the stream that flows through this town the Rivière *Embarras*—Tangled River—because it had so many turns and driftwood tangles that caused the logs to jam.

In 1996, a *Toronto Star* reporter asked a waitress in an *Embarrass* cafe about the name and got this gem of a quote: "It's because the river that runs through town is so shallow we can see 'er bottom."

There is a town in northern Minnesota by the same name that is also named after a river. It was probably named before the Revolutionary War by French fur traders or missionaries traveling by canoe.

Hustler

At the intersection of County Routes A and H fifty-five miles east of La Crosse in western Juneau County

Unable to agree on a name for their up-and-coming village, the citizens sent a list of names to the Post Office Department in 1891 that included this one as a kind of a joke. It would alert the world that energetic and ambitious people lived here.

Certainly this could be said of J. H. Morrill, the freight broker, who pestered a West Wisconsin Railroad superintendent so long and so hard about building a spur to his new warehouse that the man complained that all he heard morning, noon, and night was "*Hustler.*" The farmers who paid Morrill a commission to ship their produce and livestock to market considered themselves *hustlers* when it came to work, and they offered to grade the new siding if the railroad would lay the ties and the track. The railroad superintendent finally gave in, and by the turn of the century *Hustler* was one of the leading freight stations on what was then the Omaha Railroad.

The town had a second heyday in the late 1920s when U.S. Route 12 was built. The good years lasted until the highway was rerouted to bypass the town. This, combined with a sharp decline in the agricultural freight business and the closing of the public school in the mid-1950s, ultimately made the name *Hustler* seem out of place and time, like a tottering old man nicknamed Lightning or Crusher.

Siren

On State Route 35 seventy miles northeast of Minnesota's Twin Cities in the northwestern part of the state

Charles F. Segerstrom, who wanted to be postmaster, was given the task of filling out the village's application for a post office. It was a beautiful late spring day in 1890, and when he got to the section where he had to write down the name of the post office, he looked out the window for inspiration. *Syren!* A riot of purple and white *syren* nearly surrounded his home. He could smell their lovely perfume.

Syren? Segerstrom, like many of his neighbors, was Swedish, and *syren* is the Swedish word for lilac. (He probably didn't know the English word.)

Back in Washington, where evidently there were no Swedes in the Post Office Department, the "spelling error" was corrected, and the village was stuck with a noisy name that would always need explaining.

Other Unusual Place-Names in Wisconsin

Avalanche

At the intersection of County Routes S and Y about 35 miles southeast of La Crosse in central Vernon County

an old county history explains that this hamlet was named for a geological formation on its east side that "resembles a gigantic landslide or *avalanche* suddenly stopped in its destructive course."

Beetown

On State Route 81 twenty-five miles north-northwest of Dubuque, Iowa, in western Grant County in the southern part of the state

One fine spring day in 1827, some ore hunters overturned a large tree that had been hollowed out by bees—a "*bee* tree"—and found a 425-pound nugget of lead. This discovery, during the Lead Rush (see *New Diggings*, Wisconsin), was known as the *Bee* Lead.

Blue Mounds

On County Route F just off I-18 twenty-five miles west of Madison

the town was named for two or three hills—the highest in southern Wisconsin—that take on a *bluish* cast at twilight, due to copper in the soil. But it was lead that drew Ebenezer Brigham here in 1828 to try his luck at mining. Equipped with only a windlass and a barrel, he extracted four million tons of lead from these hills. A town grew up around the smelter he built to process the ore.

Stretching your legs in Blue Mounds: Main Street (U.S. Route 151) in Mt. Horeb, the next town east, is decorated with wooden trolls carved out of old tree trunks by Mount Horeb sculptor Mike Feeney. There are about 20 of them, all from six to ten feet high. You can even take a "troll stroll."

Cream

On State Route 88 forty-five miles south-southwest of Eau Claire in central Buffalo County

towns here in the rolling pastures of "Dairyland" are like the *cream* near the top of the milk bottle. This one once had a *creamery.*

Liberty Pole

On State Route 27 forty miles south-southeast of La Crosse in south-central Vernon County

this was the first village in Vernon County to have a *liberty pole.* It was erected on July 3, 1848, in time for the Fourth of July celebration the next day.

New Diggings

On County Route W near the Illinois border in the southwestern corner of Lafayette County

before gold was discovered in California, there was a Lead Rush in northern Illinois that was centered around Galena (another word for lead ore). As the boom moved north, nobody bothered to tell the mostly Cornish miners that a treaty with the Indians prohibited them from prospecting beyond the Illinois border. "You know how white men are," says Marion Howard, director of the public library in Darlington, the county seat of Lafayette County.

This village was the site of the miners' *new diggings* in Indian territory.

Victory

On State Route 35 along the Mississippi River at the point where Wisconsin, Minnesota, and Iowa converge

This reduced speed zone on State Route 35 was named to commemorate the U.S. Army's *victory* over Chief Black Hawk in the Black Hawk War of 1832. In the final battle, which took place about a mile from the village center, army regulars, assisted by militiamen, drove about a thousand Sac and Fox Indians back across the Mississippi River. The soldiers were carrying out President Andrew Jackson's brutal Indian Removal policy, which required that all Indian tribes be removed to the lands west of the Mississippi.

Another Vernon County village, *Retreat*, takes its name from the same historical event.

(See *Conquest*, New York, page 170, and *Victory*, Vermont, page 236.)

wyoming

Jay Em

On U.S. Route 85 sixteen miles west of the Nebraska border and 34 miles north-northwest of Torrington

J*M* was the cattle brand of *Jim Moore,* a pony express rider who settled down to do some ranching in 1859. He was killed a few years later when he was thrown from a runaway hay wagon. The *JM* brand passed through several hands until it reached the Harris brothers, who in 1909 opened a store and post office on their *Jay Em* Ranch.

According to Mae Urbanek in *Wyoming Place Names,* the Harrises and other area ranchers had petitioned for the post office after another Goshen County post office closed abruptly when a postal inspector asked one too many questions. The postmaster told the inspector to pack all the post office supplies and equipment in a wooden box, and "Get out!"

The post office and store were moved to the present site of *Jay Em* in 1915. Harris is still the predominant family name here.

Stretching your legs in Jay Em: The town, all nine buildings of it, is on the National Register of Historic Places. It's a nice glimpse of the Old West in its dying days.

About ten miles north of town, a red granite monument marks the grave of Mother Featherlegs Shepherd, a colorful roadhouse madam whose place of business was a dugout on the Cheyenne-Black Hills Stage Line (you can still see the ruts). Local cowboys called her Featherlegs for the long red pantalettes she wore tied around her ankles. They said she looked like a feather-legged chicken when the pantalettes ruffled in the breeze. She was the mother of Tom and Bill Shepherd, Louisiana outlaws after the Civil War. One member of their gang, Dangerous Dick (David) the Terrapin, used Mother's place as a hideout.

In addition to serving rotgut whiskey and providing her customers with intimate entertainment, Mother was a go-between for road agents and desperadoes, for whom she stashed stolen money and jewelry. In 1879, a neighbor found the old woman dead by the spring near her dugout. She had a bullet hole in her back and $1,500 missing from her cache. It looked like the work of Dangerous Dick, who escaped but was later hanged in Louisiana for other crimes. Location: On a dirt road halfway between Jay Em and Lusk. Inquire locally for directions.

Bill, Wyoming

Ten Sleep

On U.S. Route 16 between Worland and Buffalo in the north-central part of the state

The Crow Indians measured time and distance in *sleeps,* or overnight encampments, while traveling from one place to another. Pictographs found in a small cave five miles east of the town—depicting a fish, deer, moon, tepee, and two hands (*ten* fingers)—told fellow travelers that it was a *ten*-day walk between the cave and the big Indian camp on the Platte River near what is now Casper, Wyoming (south on the "Big Trail"), and *ten* days in the opposite direction to the big camp on the Clarks Fork River, near the present site of Bridger, Montana. The fish and deer were meant to assure first-time visitors to the cave there was plenty of game along the way.

Another interpretation of the cave drawings holds that it was *ten sleeps* between the cave and Fort Laramie. Since Fort Laramie is a good hundred miles beyond Casper, the missing fact must be how many miles a Crow Indian could walk in a day in that country.

A third interpretation is that a band of Crows spotted so much game in the area that the women and children stayed in the cave while the men went on a *ten*-day hunting spree.

Take your pick.

Stretching your legs in Ten Sleep: The cave is no longer accessible; it was buried during construction of U.S. Route 16 in the 1940s. But photographs of the pictographs and petroglyphs (incised drawings), as well as other local artifacts, are on display at the Pioneer Museum. Director Louise Williams visited the cave as a young woman and is well-versed in its lore, including the strengths and weaknesses of the three *Ten Sleep* legends. Location: Main Street, Ten Sleep. No phone. Admission free.

Other Unusual Place-Names in Wyoming

Bar Nunn

On I-25 just north of Casper

Easily one of the best puns among American place-names, *Bar Nunn* got its name in the early 1970s when developer Romie *Nunn* subdivided the former Wardwell airfield into the egalitarian-sounding *Bar Nunn* Ranch Subdivision and started selling lots. The town was incorporated in 1982 and now has a population of 835.

Bill

On State Route 59 thirty-five miles north of Douglas and 85 miles northeast of Casper

b*ill* was the most common male name among local ranchers when this community needed a name for its post office.

(See *Joes*, Colorado, page 38.)

Chugwater

On I-25 between Cheyenne and Wheatland in the southeastern part of the state

t he Mandan Indians hunted buffalo by driving them over the high chalk cliffs at the edge of Slater Flats, a tableland thick with native grasses that attracted thousands of bison. The half-ton beasts hit the creek below the cliffs with a deadly *"chug."* The Mandans called the creek "the *water* where the buffalo *chug.*"

According to Mandan legend, the tribe hunted buffalo with bow and arrow until an unbrave brave named Ahwiprie—*The Dreamer*—was put in command of the autumn hunt after his father was gored and trampled by a buffalo bull. Ahwiprie thought it was too hard and dangerous to kill the bison singly, so he devised a method of funneling them toward the edge of the cliff.

Little America

On I-80 thirty-three miles west of Rock Springs in the southwestern part of the state

t his town was named for Admiral Byrd's base camp on Antarctica by S. M. Covey, who, beginning in 1932, built a sprawling complex of restaurants, motels, shops, and gas pumps beside old U.S. Route 30. Covey apparently saw his outpost in the wide open spaces west of the Green River as resembling Byrd's headquarters on the Ross Ice Shelf in that it was well-supplied for a remote location.

Covey was delivering on a promise he had made to himself 40 years earlier when, as a young sheepherder, he got lost in a blizzard with 40 degree below zero nights. If he ever got back to a comfortable house and a warm fire, he pledged, he'd build a shelter for travelers in the wide open spaces west of the Green River.

Pitchfork

On a secondary extension of State Route 290 about a 45-mile drive south of Cody

this was the brand of the giant cattle ranch on the Greybull River that Otto Franc started up in 1879 with 1,500 Herefords bought with money from his German royal family. The brand, a three-pronged *pitchfork*, looks like a capital E lying on its back on top of a short post (the handle).

Before starting the *Pitchfork* Ranch, Count Otto Franc Von Lichtenstein and his two older brothers were in the banana-importing business in New York City.

Recluse

Just a few miles north of U.S. Route 14 in the wide open rangeland 30 miles north of Gillette and 20 miles from the Montana border

a post office was established here in 1918. The name, locals say, referred to its remoteness from the ranchers who were its patrons. If that doesn't convince you that *recluse* was the best choice of words, it's better than what a young woman who lives there told me: "Pioneers on the western plains chose town names for remarkable natural features. In this case there were none, so they called it *Recluse.*"

Tie Siding

On U.S. Route 287 forty miles west of Cheyenne near the Colorado border in the southeastern corner of the state

established in 1868, the town was named for the railroad *siding* at a lumber mill that turned out *ties*, bridge props, fence posts, poles, and building lumber for the Union Pacific Railroad.

Tie Canyon in California's Death Valley National Monument got its name in 1925 when 120,000 *ties* from the abandoned Tonopah and Tidewater Railroad were stacked in a gorge.

bibliography

ninety percent of the place names in this book were found on official state transportation maps. Which means that I—yellow highlighter at the ready—had to search each map index from A to Z to make my first cut. If the index only listed the big towns, I had to do it the hard way: scan every quarter inch of the map—all those words in eye-straining four-point type. In all, I focused my eyes on some 75,000 village, town, and city names, and I paid for it; about halfway through my research, just a few weeks after my 48th birthday, I was prescribed my first pair of glasses.

After I had a good list of unusual names for a state, I went searching for their stories. And, as I said in my acknowledgments, I could not have written this book without the help of hundreds of local librarians. They sent me photocopies of newspaper clippings and of pages from town and county histories and state place-name books—anything they could find in their libraries that might help me.

I've cited many of the published sources in the text and many more here. Regrettably, I've probably missed a few; and I apologize to those authors. Like all the authors in this bibliography, your research and your insight into the sometimes murky origins of the place-names I've written about have been invaluable.

I particularly want to acknowledge my debt to the following authors of state place-name books listed in the bibliography: Helen S. Carlson (Nevada), Ernie Deane (Arkansas), Lewis L. McArthur (Oregon), Donald J. Orth (Alaska), T. M Pearce (New Mexico), Robert M. Rennick (Kentucky), Fred Tarpley (Texas), and Douglas A. Wick (North Dakota). I could not have done justice to these states without the benefit of their toponymical scholarship. I recommend their books and the other state place-name books I cite to anyone looking for other unusual names. (Another good source for individual states is the American Guide Series produced in the 1930s by the WPA Writer's Project.)

Finally, I want to mention four authors whose books I consulted frequently in my research and to whom I owe a great debt: Myron J. Quimby (*Scratch Ankle, U.S.A.*), Allan Wolk (*The Naming of America*), Vernon Pizer (*Ink, Ark., and All That*), and the dean of American place-name scholarship, George R. Stewart (*American Place-Names*).

Agee, Helene Barret. *Facets of Goochland (Virginia) County's History*. Richmond, Va.: Dietz Press, 1962.

Alotta, Robert I. *Signposts and Settlers: The History of Place Names in the Middle Atlantic States*. Chicago: Bonus Books, 1992.

Backman, Lisa. "Boardwalk, Baseball goes out of business." *The* (Lakeland, Fla.) *Ledger*, 18 Jan. 1990.

Baker, Ronald L. *From Needmore to Prosperity: Hoosier Place Names in Folklore & History*. Bloomington: Indiana University Press, 1995.

Barnes, Will C. *Arizona Place Names*. Tucson: University of Arizona Press, 1988.

Beck, Henry. *Forgotten Towns of Southern New Jersey*. New Brunswick, N.J.: Rutgers

University Press, 1961.

Birchfield, Rodger. "Town of Aroma Would Smell Sweet With Any Name." *The Indianapolis* (Ind.) *News,* 13 Feb. 1973.

Boone, Lalia. *Idaho Place Names.* Moscow, Idaho: University of Idaho Press, 1988.

Brieger, James F. *Hometown Mississippi.* Mississippi: James F. Brieger, 1980.

Bryson, Bill. *Made in America: An Informal History of the English Language in the United States.* New York: William Morrow, 1994.

Carlson, Helen S. *Nevada Place Names.* Reno: University of Nevada Press, 1974.

Chadbourne, Ava Harriet. *Maine Place Names and the Peopling of its Towns.* Portland, Maine: Bond Wheelwright, 1955.

Cheney, Roberta Carkeek. *Names on the Face of Montana.* Missoula, Mont.: Mountain Press, 1983.

Conley, Patrick T. *An Album of Rhode Island History 1636-1986.* Norfolk, Va.: Donning, 1986.

Dawson, J. Frank. *Place Names in Colorado.* Denver: Golden Bell Press, 1954.

Dawson, James T. *History of Whynot.* Meridian, Miss.:

Lauderdale County Department of Archives and History, 1992.

Deane, Ernie. *Arkansas Place Names.* Branson, Mo.: Ozarks Mountaineer, 1986.

Dickson, Paul. *What's in a Name? Reflections of an Irrepressible Name Collector.* Springfield, Mass.: Merriam-Webster, 1996.

"Difficult—On Old Fort Blount Trail." *Carthage* (Tenn.) *Courier,* 27 May 1971.

Dimitroff, Thomas P., and Lois S. Janes. *History of the Corning, Painted Post Area: 200 Years in Painted Post Country.* Corning, N.Y.: Bookmarks, 1991.

Eckstorm, Fannie Hardy. *Indian Place-Names of the Penobscot Valley and the Maine Coast.* Orono: University of Maine Press, 1978.

Eichler, George R. *Colorado Place Names.* Boulder, Colo.: Johnson, 1977.

Encyclopedia of the South. Ed. Robert O'Brien. New York: Facts on File, 1985.

Encyclopedia of Washington. New York: Somerset, 1971.

Eno, Clara B. *History of Crawford County, Arkansas.* Van Buren, Ark.: Press-Argus, 1945.

Espenshade, A. Howrey. *Pennsylvania Place Names.* State College: Pennsylvania State College, 1925.

Fitzpatrick, Lilian L. *Nebraska Place-Names.* Lincoln: Nebraska State Historical Society, 1982.

Fletcher, Christine. *Names Across the Land.* Nashville and New York: Abingdon Press, 1973.

Foscue, Virginia O. *Place Names in Alabama.* Tuscaloosa: The University of Alabama Press, 1989.

Gard, Robert E., and L. G. Sorden. *The Romance of Wisconsin Place Names.* New York: October House, 1968.

Giles, Rosena A. *Shasta County, California: A History.* Oakland, Cal.: Biobooks, 1949.

Granger, Byrd Howell. *Arizona's Names (X Marks the Place).* Tucson, Ariz.: Falconer, 1983.

Gudde, Erwin G. *California Place Names.* Berkeley: University of California Press, 1969.

Hagemann, James. *The Heritage of Virginia: The Story of Place Names in the Old Dominion.* Norfolk, Va.: Donning, 1986.

Hitchman, Robert. *Place Names*

of Washington. Tacoma: Washington State Historical Society, 1985.

Hughes, Arthur H., and Morse S. Allen. *Connecticut Place Names*. Hartford: Connecticut Historical Society, 1976.

Johnson, Dirk. "Ghost Town for Sale: Elves Included." *The New York Times*, 31 May 1995.

Jones, Margaret Jean. *Cullman County Across the Years*. Cullman, Ala.: Modernistic Printers, 1995.

Jones, Spencer. "Without Churches, Town Remains 'Uncertain'." *Marshall* (Tex.) *News Messenger*, 18 July 1971.

Julyan, Robert, and Mary Julyan. *Place Names of the White Mountains*. Hanover, N.H.: University Press of New England, 1993.

Kaysing, Bill. *Great Hot Springs of the West*. Santa Barbara, Cal.: Capras Press, 1984.

Keatley, J. K. *Place Names of the Eastern Shore of Maryland*. Queenstown, Md.: Queen Anne Press, 1987.

Kenny, Hamill. *The Place Names of Maryland, Their Origin and Meaning*. Baltimore: Maryland Historical Society, 1984.

Kenny, Hamill. *West Virginia Place Names*. Piedmont, W.Va.: Place Name Press, 1945.

Krakow, Kenneth K. *Georgia Place-Names*. Macon, Ga.: Winship Press, 1975.

Lackmann, Ronald W. *Same Time . . . Same Station: An A-*

Z Guide to Radio from Jack Benny to Howard Stern. New York: Facts on File, 1996.

Larson, Helen Kay Brander. *Valley of the Fountain*. Fountain, Colo.: Shopper Press, 1969.

Latham, Delia. "Weedpatch residents are proud of name." *The Bakersfield Californian*, 2 Sept. 1988.

Leeper, Clare D'Artois. *Louisiana Places*. Baton Rouge, La.: Legacy, 1976.

Mariner, Kirk. *Off 13: The Eastern Shore of Virginia Guidebook*. Olney, Va.: Book Bin, 1987.

Marlin, Lloyd G. *The History of Cherokee County*. Atlanta: Walter W. Brown, 1932.

McArthur, Lewis A. *Oregon Geographic Names*. Portland, Ore.: Oregon Historical Society Press, 1992.

McCoy, Keith. *The Mount Adams Country: Forgotten Corner of the Columbia River Gorge*. White Salmon, Wash.: Pahto Publications, 1987.

McCoy, Sondra Van Meter, and Jan Hults. *1001 Kansas Place Names*. Lawrence: University Press of Kansas, 1989.

McMillen, Margot Ford. *Paris, Tightwad, and Peculiar*. Columbia: University of Missouri Press, 1994.

Meany, Edmond S. *Origin of Washington Geographic Names*. Seattle: University of Washington Press, 1923.

Merriam-Webster's Collegiate Dictionary, 10th Edition. Ed. Frederick C. Mish. Springfield, Mass.: Merriam-Webster, 1996.

Morris, Allen. *Florida Place Names*. Sarasota, Fla.: Pineapple Press, 1995.

Mullinax, Gary. "Mermaid Sightings." *The* (Wilmington, Del.) *News Journal*, 23 March 1995.

Names in South Carolina, Volumes I-XII, 1954-1965. Ed. Claude Henry Neuffer. Spartanburg, S.C.: Reprint Co., 1983.

New Mexico Place Names. Ed. T. M. Pearce. Albuquerque: University of New Mexico Press, 1965.

Nilsson, Dex. *Discover Why It's Called . . .* Rockville, Md.: Twinbrook Communications, 1990.

Orth, Donald J. *Dictionary of Alaska Place Names*. Washington, D.C.: U. S. Government Printing Office, 1967.

Overman, William Daniel. *Ohio Place Names*. Akron, Ohio: Atlantic Press, 1958.

Pizer, Vernon. *Ink, Ark., and All That: How American Places Got Their Names*. New York: G.P. Putnam's Sons, 1976.

Powell, William S. *North Carolina Gazetteer*. Chapel Hill: University of North Carolina Chapel Hill Press, 1968.

Quimby, Myron J. *Scratch Ankle, U.S.A.: American Place Names and Their Derivation*. South Brunswick, N.J.: A.S. Barnes and Co., 1969.

Rennick, Robert M. *Kentucky Place Names*. Lexington: University Press of Kentucky, 1984.

Romig, Walter. *Michigan Place*

Names. Grosse Point, Mich.: Walter Romig, 1978.

Rouell, Russell. *Sandwich: A Cape Cod Town.* Taunton, Mass.: William S. Sullwold, 1996.

Rutherford, Phillip R. *The Dictionary of Maine Place Names.* Freeport, Maine: Bond, Wheelright, 1971.

Sams, Anita. *Wayfarers in Walton.* Monroe, Ga.: Walton Press, 1980.

Shaffer, Ray. *A Guide to Places on the Colorado Prairie 1540-1975.* Boulder, Colo.: Pruett, 1978.

Sherman, Steve. *Country Roads of Connecticut and Rhode Island.* Oaks, Pa.: Country Roads Press, 1994.

Shirk, George H. *Oklahoma Place Names.* Norman: University of Oklahoma Press, 1965.

Siler, Tom. *Tennessee Towns: From Adams to Yorkville.* Knoxville: East Tennessee Historical Society, 1985.

Sneve, Virginia Driving Hawk. *South Dakota Geographic Names.* Sioux Falls, S.D.: Brevet Press, 1973.

Spacek, Ella S. *Early Dime Box.* Giddings, Tex.: ColorCraft Press, 1991.

Stephenson, Clarence D. *Indiana County: 175th Anniversary History, Volume V.* Indiana, Pa.: A. G. Halldin, 1995.

Stevens, William Oliver. *Annapolis, Anne Arundel's Town.* New York: Dodd, Mead, 1951.

Stewart, George R. *American Place-Names: A Concise and Selective Dictionary for the Continental United States of America.* New York: Oxford University Press, 1970.

Swift, Esther Munroe. *Vermont Place-Names.* Brattleboro, Vt.: Stephen Greene Press, 1977.

Tarpley, Fred. *1001 Texas Place Names.* Austin: University of Texas Press, 1980.

Thomas, Bob. "Legend says Two Guns was shot down by curse." *The* (Phoenix) *Arizona Republic,* 3 May 1992.

Upham, Warren. *Minnesota Geographic Names.* St. Paul: Minnesota Historical Society, 1969.

Urbanek, Mae. *Wyoming Place Names.* Boulder, Colo.: Johnson, 1967.

Van Cott, John W. *Utah Place Names.* Salt Lake City: University of Utah Press, 1990.

Wick, Douglas A. *North Dakota Place Names.* Bismarck, N.D.: Hedemarken Collectibles, 1988.

Williams, Mark. *Off the Beaten Path.* Old Saybrook, Ct.: Globe Pequot Press, 1996.

Wolk, Allan. *The Naming of America.* New York: Simon and Schuster, 1981.

Wolle, Muriel Sibell. *Stampede to Timberline: The Ghost Towns and Mining Camps of Colorado.* Denver: Sage Books, 1949.

Wright, Kenneth Edward. "Correctionville Was Born in Dangerous Age." *Sioux City* (Iowa) *Journal,* 10 July 1955.

index of place-names

Hangtown, Calif. 54
Happy Camp, Calif. 27-28
Happy Corner, N.H. 156
Happy Jack, Ariz. 17
Hard Cash, Miss. 98
Hardmoney, Ky. 98
Hardscrabble, Del. 48
Harmony 147
Harts Location, N.H. 156
Hasty, Colo. 152
Hattertown, Conn. 45
Hazard, Ky. 92
Hazard, Nebr. 145
Headquarters, Idaho viii, 63, 65
Headquarters, N.M. 65
Head Tide, Maine 102
Helix, Ore. 193
Hell, Mich. 117
Hell-out-for-Noon, Calif. 28
Hell's Half Acre, R.I. 207
Hell-to-Pay, Wash. 198, 248
Helltown, Calif. 28
Helltown, Va. 242
Helper, Utah 231
Henpeck, N.M. 54
Highway, N.M. viii, 165
Hill 57, Mont. 54
Hog'em, Idaho 63
Hogeye, Ark. 38, 44
Ho-Ho-Kus, N.J. 161
Holland Patent, N.Y. 170
Home, Kans. viii, 83
Hominy, Okl. 191
Honea Path, S.C. 209
Honeymoon, Ariz. 18
Honor, Mich. 152
Hookers, N.C. 33
Horace, Kans. 87
Horse Corner, N.H. vii, 156
Horsehead, Md. 50
Horseheads, N.Y. 167, 169
Hot Coffee, Miss. 127
Hot Spot, Ky. 54
Hudspeths Cross Roads, Ala. 2
Humbug City, Calif. 28
Humptulips, Wash. 248
Hundred, W.Va. 251

Hurricane, Utah 232-33
Hustler, Wis. 255-56
Hygiene, Colo. 38
Idavada, Idaho 149
Ideal, Minn. 147
Ideal, S.D. 147
Igloo, S.D. 215
Igo, Calif. 28-29
Illmo, Mo. 149
Independence 147
Independent Hill, Va. 241
Index, Wash. 248
Ink, Ark. 21
Ink, Mo. 131
Inky, Ark. 21
Intake, Mont. 141
Integrity, Nebr. 54
Intercession City, Fla. 56
Intercourse, Ala. 33
Intercourse, Pa. vi, 33, 199
Interocean, Fla. 56
Ione, Colo. 38
Iota, La. 97
Irish Ripple, Pa. 204
Irrigon, Ore. 193
Ismay, Mont. 163
Issue, Md. 108
It, Miss. 130
Jack Ass Town, La. 54
Jackassville, Calif. 28
Jackpot, Nev. 150
Jay Em, Wyo. 259
Jigger, La. 97
Jiggs, Nev. 151
Jim Thorpe, Pa. 163
Joe, Mont. 163
Joes, Colo. 38
Johnnycake, Md. 54
Johnson's Crossroads, Md. 107
Jot 'Em Down, Tex. 62
Jot 'Em Down Store, Ga. 62
Joy, Nebr. 54
Jugtown, N.C. 174
Jumbo, Ohio 186
Jump, Ohio 186
Justice, N.C. 176
Kanorado, Kans. 149

Kelat, Ky. 90
Kelp, Ind. 77-78
Kenova, W.Va. 149
Kill Devil Hills, N.C. 176
Killpecker Creek, Wyo. 33
King of Prussia, Pa. 50
Kiss Me Quick Hills, S.D. 33
Kitchen, Ohio 152
Kite, Ga. 152
Klej Grange, Md. 106
Klondike, Ill. 89
Know-nothing, Calif. 28
Kokadjo, Maine 99
Ladiesburg, Md. 109
Lakemont, Fla. 53
Large, Pa. 54
Last Chance, Calif. 28
Last Chance, Colo. 38-39
Last Dollar Mountin, Colo. 98
Lebam, Wash. 76
Lemmon, S.D. 216
Letter Gap, W.Va. 249
Lewes, Del. 33
Liberal, Kans. 85
Liberty Pole, Wis. 257
Lickskillet, Ga. 44
Lickskillet, Ky. 44
Likely, Calif. 32
Lineboro, Md. 235
Lineville, Iowa 235
Lingo, N.M. 165
Little America, Wyo. 262
Lively, Va. 242
Loafer Flat, Calif. 28
Lofty, Pa. 54
Lolita, Tex. 33, 228
Lonesome Dove, Tex. 11
Lone Star, S.C. 212
Lone Star, Tex. 33
Long Society, Conn. 41-42
Los Cuernos, N.M. 164
Lost Nation, N.H. 156
Lotteryville, R.I. 198, 205
Loudville, Mass. 111
Love, Ariz. 152
Low, Utah 233
Lower Merryall, Conn. 45

About the Author

Frank K. Gallant is a long-time observer of small-town American Life—its people, lore, and traditions. In 16 years as editor of *Rural Electrification Magazine,* he has looked at small towns from just about every angle. His travels as a writer have taken him down the backroads of most of the states, from which he has brought back stories on rural doctoring, one-room schools, family farms, and Main Street economics for his and other magazines. Frank grew up on Cape Cod, Massachusetts and began his journalistic career at newspapers there and on the Maine coast, working both as a reporter and an editor. He and his wife, Karen, reside in Takoma Park, Maryland, a suburb of Washington, D.C. They have two college-age sons.

About the Illustrator

Victoria Roberts was born in New York City and grew up in Mexico and Australia. She has written and illustrated over twenty books, the most recent of which, *Cattitudes,* was published by Villard. Victoria also contributes regularly to the *New Yorker,* the *New York Times,* and the *Boston Globe.* She is presently working on a graphic novella entitled *After the Fall.* Victoria resides in New York City and Mexico.